AF521848

COOKING WHEN NO ONE IS LOOKING

Cooking When No One Is Looking

Cuisine at the Cutting Edge

Written and Illustrated
by Ruth Mellinkoff

UCLA FOWLER MUSEUM OF CULTURAL HISTORY
LOS ANGELES

Funding by private donation

The Fowler Museum is part
of UCLA's School of the Arts and Architecture

UCLA Fowler Museum of Cultural History
Box 951549, Los Angeles, California 90095-1549

Printed and bound in Hong Kong
by South Sea International Press, Ltd.

Lynne Kostman, Editor
Daniel R. Brauer, Designer and Production Manager

Library of Congress Cataloging-in-Publication Data

Mellinkoff, Ruth.
Cooking when no one is looking : cuisine at the cutting edge /
Ruth Mellinkoff.
p. cm.
ISBN 0-930741-84-6
1. Make-ahead cookery. 2. Cookery (Frozen foods) I. University of
California, Los Angeles. Fowler Museum of Cultural History. II. Title.

TX652 .M445 2000
641.5'55—dc21 00-060744

To the memory
of David Mellinkoff

CONTENTS

FOREWORD

This volume represents a savory and engaging change of pace for the publication program of the Fowler Museum. Although many museums have produced cookbooks, this is our first—albeit the sixth for Dr. Ruth Mellinkoff. Its long-sold-out predecessors are highly sought after by those who have even the slightest knowledge of Ruth's cooking. While this is the Fowler Museum's first cookbook, many of our previous publications and exhibitions have dealt with foodways as an integral component of festivals around the world. Indeed, *feasting* and *festivity* share related Latin roots suggesting their inseparability. It is perhaps in the recipes of cookbooks such as this one—which includes examples drawn from cuisines as seemingly disparate as Chinese, Moroccan, Indonesian, and Mexican—that the intersecting diasporas of the world are best exemplified. Regional cuisines are often appreciated more and meld better with those of their neighbors than ideas about dress or religion, for example.

Cooking When No One is Looking is only available as a benefit of Fowler Museum membership. This in itself is a measure of Ruth's enthusiastic support of the Museum—she is a long-time member of Manus, the highest level of museum membership participation. *Manus*, another Latin word, resonates wonderfully with the collective activity of feasting and festivals. At its most basic it means "hand," or the work of the hand, including the hand of the artist and the cook. More broadly *manus* refers to a group organized around collective interests and vocations. As chef, writer, scholar, philanthropist, and good friend, Ruth embodies an ideal Manus member.

Ruth's scholarly background reflects her eclectic embrace of the humanities. With a bachelor's degree in mathematics and philosophy from the University of Minnesota and a master's degree and doctorate in medieval art history from the Universities of California at Berkeley and Los Angeles, respectively, Ruth has published five scholarly books and numerous articles.

This cookbook is unique in its approach. It has been structured so that busy people can prepare interesting and elaborate meals with minimal stress. For nearly every recipe there is a section headed "When No One Is Looking" with special tips on advance preparation. There is also a section headed "Frozen Power," suggesting how the freezer can play a role. Speaking as the director of a busy museum and a person seriously concerned with time management and quality cuisine, I know that Ruth's book will be indispensable in my house.

I would like to join Ruth in thanking Danny Brauer and Lynne Kostman for their work on this volume. Danny has been the museum's director of publications for twelve years and has designed many of our most important books. His rapport with writers, curators, and visionaries has been instrumental in making these books happen. Lynne has edited numerous museum publications on a wide variety of topics. She has handled each with equal attention to the visual and written intentions of the author(s). I join those authors in their tremendous respect for Lynne's work.

Finally, our gratitude goes to Ruth Mellinkoff who has served many roles within the Museum. Most importantly she has provided direct and honest feedback about our activities—culinary, scholarly, or otherwise. At the same time she has promoted the Museum's mission with an energy that I both admire and appreciate. I want to thank Ruth for her many critiques, courtesies, and congratulations over the years. It is minds like Ruth's that make institutions like ours work.

Doran H. Ross
DIRECTOR

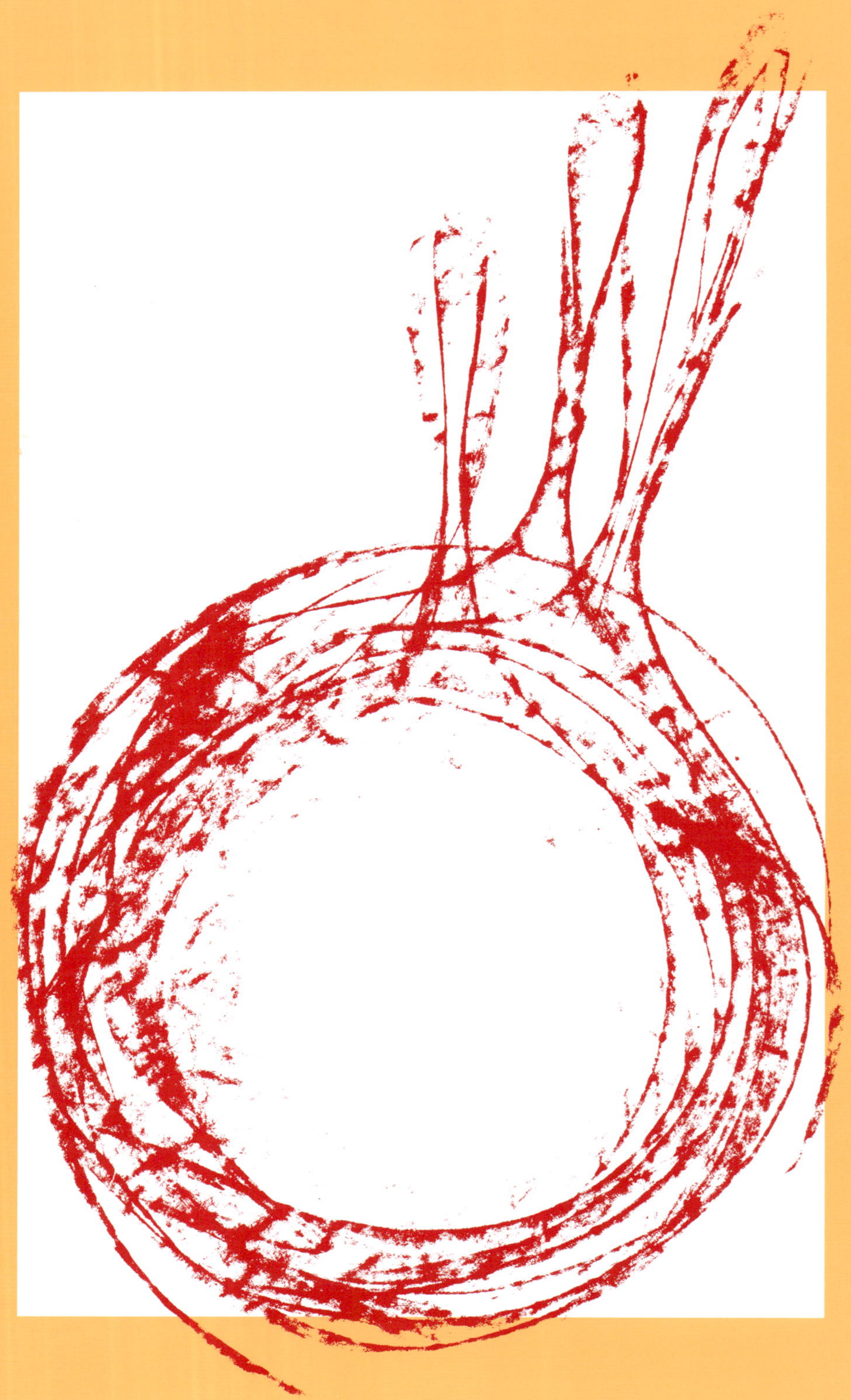

INTRODUCTION

Plot, Plan, and Prepare

STORAGE

IN THE FREEZER

Keep your culinary masterpieces hidden from view in the freezer, the ideal place to store your frozen assets! A few freezing basics follow, but be sure to check the blue, boxed items labeled "Frozen Power" in the individual recipes for additional instructions.

TEMPERATURE

The consistent coldness of your freezer and the number of times that you open it can make an enormous difference in how long your frozen cuisine will retain its quality and flavor. Homemade puff pastry that I stored in an infrequently opened basement freezer proved excellent when I used it two years later!

WRAP AND CONTAINERS

You must carefully wrap your prepared food. If you plan to store it in the freezer a long time, double-wrap—first with plastic, then with foil, or with double foil—or wrap and seal it in a plastic bag.

Use airtight containers with tight-fitting tops or plastic bags with zippers. And acquaint yourself with the new, inexpensive plastic storage containers. You may also use foil pans: fill them, then completely enclose them with foil wrap.

FREEZER-FRIENDLY INGREDIENTS

1. *Nuts:* When shelled nuts—almonds, walnuts, pecans, filberts (same as hazelnuts), macadamias, etc.—first become seasonably available, buy them in quantity and freeze them. They will keep in perfect condition for at least one year.
2. *Poppy seeds and sesame seeds:* Buy the freshest poppy seeds and sesame seeds and keep them fresh and handy in your freezer.
3. *Ripe pomegranate seeds:* These freeze magnificently; use them straight out of the freezer.
4. *Egg whites:* Egg whites are a great frozen treasure. Place them in small plastic containers with tight-fitting covers or in covered Dixie cups. Label each container with the number of egg whites it contains.

5. *Dried fruit:* Dates, apricots, raisins, prunes, etc., freeze extremely well.
6. *Candied fruit:* Buy the finest-quality candied ginger, candied pineapple, etc., when and where you can find them, and keep them beautifully in your freezer.
7. *Butter:* Buy butter when it is on sale—unsalted or salted—and freeze it happily for three to six months.
8. *Miscellaneous:* Other freezer-friendly ingredients are mentioned in the individual recipes. Check for details in the blue, boxed items labeled "Frozen Power"
9. *No! No! No!* Never freeze hard-cooked eggs, mayonnaise, or preparations that contain either. Eggs become rubbery; mayonnaise curdles.

IN THE REFRIGERATOR

PRESERVED LEMONS, MOROCCAN STYLE (RECIPE, P. 105)
These, as well as homemade jams, candied citrus peels, and similar delicious concoctions, store well in the refrigerator. Some will keep up to one year.

POMEGRANATES
Buy ripe, perfect pomegranates in the autumn and use them in the spring. They will keep well for several months if stored in a cold, well-ventilated refrigerator.

OLIVE OIL
Keep olive oil in the refrigerator to avoid its turning rancid. The cold environment will make it cloudy, but the oil will clear at room temperature.

IN THE PANTRY

Pantry shelves are a fine and adequate place to store some cuisine that has been prepared in advance.

COOKIES
If kept in containers with tight-fitting lids, many types of baked cookies keep very well on your pantry shelves for several days or longer.

DRY INGREDIENTS
Store flour, cornmeal, rice, lentils, dry pasta, and similar ingredients in glass containers with air-tight tops or in transparent plastic containers where light can reach them. Light discourages the arrival of unwelcome little beasties.

HOMEMADE JAMS AND CHUTNEYS
These may be stored in sterilized jars on your pantry shelves for one week—perhaps more. *But* for longer periods, store them in the refrigerator or freezer.

INGREDIENTS: SOME CONVENTIONAL AND A FEW IDIOSYNCRATIC

BUTTER

Although many chefs and bakers choose unsalted butter, I prefer salted, except for preparations such as buttercreams. Why? I am not sure, but I find most American unsalted butters lacking in flavor, unlike high-quality European varieties.

OILS

Use extra-virgin olive oil for most salad dressings, or a mixture of part olive oil and part corn or canola oil. Also, try nut oils such as walnut and filbert for special vinaigrettes.

Do not use olive oil for deep frying; it burns easily at too low a temperature. For deep frying use a seed or vegetable oil such as canola, corn, or peanut.

VINEGARS

I use a wide range of vinegars, including moderately priced balsamic, sherry, red and white wine, rice, cider, etc. Some of the recipes that follow specify a type; if not, use what you like.

CHOCOLATE

Most recipes in this book assume high-quality semisweet or bittersweet chocolate, such as French Valrhona or Belgian Callebault. If unsweetened chocolate is designated, use Baker's.

EGGS

I use extra-large eggs for almost everything, so assume extra-large eggs are intended in the recipes, unless otherwise specified.

HERBS

Herbs in these recipes are usually dried unless fresh are indicated. When fresh herbs are called for, you can substitute dried in most cases by using approximately ¼ the amount specified.

PARMESAN CHEESE

Always use the best, imported Parmigiano-Reggiano. Check the rind; it should be labeled as such.

TECHNIQUES

CLEANING AND STORING FRESH MUSHROOMS

STORING
Store fresh mushrooms—uncleaned and uncovered—in the refrigerator. Do not keep them in plastic bags and do not put them in the vegetable bin, or they will get moldy and slimy. They will last a long time if kept very dry.

CLEANING
Clean mushrooms just before you are going to use them. I take exception to those who tell you never to wash fresh mushrooms. I always wash them quickly under tepid running water and immediately drain them in a colander or sieve, then I wrap them in several layers of paper towels and let them stand at room temperature for ten to twenty minutes.

CLEANING AND STORING FRESH HERBS

Rinse the herbs under cold water, or fill a large basin with cold water and wash them carefully to remove dirt and grit. If necessary, wash twice. Drain thoroughly, then shake off excess moisture or spin dry. Wrap cleaned herbs in two layers of paper towels and place them inside plastic bags. Place the filled bags in the vegetable bin of the refrigerator. If you are using plastic bags with zippers, you can store them anywhere in the refrigerator.

ROASTING PEPPERS

Use the large, mature red, yellow, and orange peppers usually imported from Holland. They are the sweetest. Cut them into halves (or quarters) lengthwise and place them cut side down in a broiler pan. Place the pan as close as possible to the broiling unit in your oven, and broil until skins have blackened and blistered. Remove the peppers from the oven, place them in a plastic bag, and close it tightly. Let them stand at room temperature for fifteen or twenty minutes, then cut away stems and remove scarred skins, seeds, and membranes.

MEASURING FLOUR

One cup of all-purpose flour weighs about 4 ½ ounces. Although the best way to measure flour is by weight, few households have a kitchen scale, so measure by first sifting the flour onto parchment paper or a paper plate, then lightly scoop the flour into a measuring cup (do not pack it or shake it) and level it off with a straight-edged knife or spatula.

HIGH-TECH TOYS

FOOD PROCESSOR

Formerly available only in huge sizes intended for restaurant use, modern food processors have revolutionized home cooking. Every kitchen needs one. This high-tech machine quickly and wonderfully chops, grinds, mixes, and slices. The pulsing technique (turning the processor on and off quickly), for example, will provide finely chopped onions in a few seconds. Experimentation will help you discover many other practical tasks for the processor to tackle.

MICROWAVE OVEN

Although I rarely use the microwave oven for "cooking," I find it a miracle tool for speeding up preparation, for example, heating milk, melting butter, or melting chocolate. It is wonderful too for reheating vegetables without overcooking them or changing their color. And now that we have plastic containers that can go from the freezer straight into the microwave, it can speed up the defrosting of cooked foods as well.

FOOD MILL

A high-quality food mill is a necessity in my kitchen. I use it in the summer to make quantities of tomato sauce and tomato soup from home-grown tomatoes. The food mill allows me to cook the tomatoes without peeling them. After they are cooked, I put them through the food mill, which removes the seeds and peels for me. You can do the same with apples when preparing fresh applesauce.

The food mill is wonderful too for making perfect mashed potatoes. First put the cooked or baked potatoes through the food mill, then whip them with butter and cream.

STAND-UP MIXER

If you are a serious cook, and particularly if you like to bake, a good-quality stand-up is virtually essential. Buy the best, the one with the greatest amount of power.

ELECTRIC ICE CREAM MAKER

Electric ice cream makers are no longer a luxury item as several inexpensive kinds are now available. The less expensive ones work well, but they do require freezing a core overnight. If you frequently prepare your own ice creams and sorbets, consider investing in one of the more expensive types, which contain their own refrigeration mechanism.

FEEMSTER SLICER

Although the "Feemster" is not comparable to the fancy, pricey mandolines, it is very efficient and very inexpensive. It can be used for slicing such things as cucumbers, potatoes, and apples. The "Feemster" is not only inexpensive, it is easy to use and easy to clean.

A FEW HIP TIPS

GARLIC OIL PRESERVED IN THE FREEZER

1 whole head of garlic (or several heads)
corn or canola oil, but not olive oil
small plastic containers with lids or Dixie cups with lids

Peel garlic cloves, then put them through a garlic press or chop them very finely in a food processor. Spoon the mashed or chopped garlic into the small plastic containers or Dixie cups, but fill them only about ⅔ full. Then spoon oil to cover the garlic leaving a little room at the top of the container for the expansion that takes place when the mixture freezes. Cover each container tightly. Label the containers, then freeze until ready to use.

The garlic oil will defrost rapidly if kept in small containers. To hurry the process you can defrost for 10 seconds or so (depending on the size of container) in a microwave oven.

For recipes requiring a mere sniff of garlic, use only a bit of the oil. For a stronger flavor, use some of the pressed or finely chopped garlic at the bottom of the container.

SHALLOTS PRESERVED IN THE FREEZER

fresh shallots
canola or corn oil, but *not* olive oil
small plastic containers with lids or Dixie cups with lids

Peel shallots and chop finely in a food processor. Divide the chopped shallots in the small containers, but only fill each container about ½ full. Spoon oil over the shallots, but allow room at the top of the container for the expansion that takes place when the ingredients freeze. Cover tightly and label the containers, then freeze until needed.

Like the frozen garlic oil, the frozen shallots defrost quickly. And they too can be hurried along by a 10-second run in a microwave oven.

Whenever a recipe calls for chopped shallots, dig down and take out the needed amount. The little oil that clings to the shallots may be drained off. However, if the shallots are to be sautéed, the oil will be useful.

WHIPPED CREAM IMMOBILIZED

Keep your whipped cream from separating into a whipped top and a watery mess on the bottom. No need to face that unhappy combination if you know the simple secret: *stabilize it!* And, do so without anyone knowing—no change in taste and no change of texture. Achieve this miracle by using a tiny amount of unflavored, dissolved gelatin.

Here are the proportions:

for 1 cup whipping cream:
½ teaspoon gelatin soaked in 1 tablespoon cold water

for 2 cups whipping cream:
1 teaspoon gelatin soaked in 2 tablespoons cold water

for 6 cups whipping cream:
1 tablespoon gelatin soaked in ¼ cup plus 6 tablespoons cold water

Here is how: Place the gelatin in a Pyrex cup or bowl, add the cold water and soak for 5 minutes. Then dissolve the soaked gelatin by placing the Pyrex cup or bowl containing it in a small pot of simmering water. Whip the cream until barely stiff, being careful not to overwhip, then add desired amount of sugar and flavorings. Add the dissolved gelatin all at once, beating simultaneously, but only long enough to incorporate the gelatin. Then, use the whipped cream as desired—in a bowl with your dessert or for decorating a cake, pie, or torte.

A MAGIC TORCH FOR THE MAGIC TOUCH

Have you ever noticed an unlabeled bottle that a restaurant maître d' or waiter has on his "cooking" cart when he is flaming bananas or crêpes suzette? That unlabeled bottle is his "magic torch." If you have agonized about whether to flame or not flame because your attempts to flame cognac or other alcohols have failed, use the "magic torch," namely 151 proof rum. It is so powerful it will flame on ice!

No need to heat cognac, Grand Marnier, or other liqueur. No matter what you are preparing—main course or dessert—place 1 or 2 ounces of the 151 proof rum in a tiny glass, cover it tightly with plastic wrap, and put it in an inconspicuous place on your tray. At the very last, add this high-proof magic and flame away! But be careful! Don't use too much—at least not until you are well acquainted with its burning qualities. Don't set yourself or your house on fire.

POACHED EGGS AHEAD OF TIME

very fresh eggs
2 quarts of water
¼ cup white wine vinegar
½ teaspoon salt
bowl of ice water

for later:
salted water, kept
below simmering

WHEN NO ONE IS LOOKING
Any number of eggs can be poached a day ahead. Store them covered with plastic wrap on towel-lined trays, and keep refrigerated.

The freshest of eggs should be used because the whites will adhere better to the yolks. Combine the 2 quarts of water, vinegar, and salt, and bring to a gentle simmer. Break eggs one at a time into a saucer and slide each into the water. Poach to desired state of doneness, then remove each to the bowl of ice water to stop the cooking. Remove eggs, trim, and place them on a towel-lined tray. Cover and keep refrigerated. When ready to serve, place the egg or eggs in heated salted water, and heat the eggs but *do not* cook them. Drain with a slotted spoon, then use as desired.

FAIL-SAFE RICE

The secret to perfect rice is to cook it like Italians cook pasta: *al dente*—that is, barely tender, slightly resistant to the bite. It should never be overcooked. If unsure, keep tasting and when it reaches the tender but still firm stage, stop the cooking.

WHEN NO ONE IS LOOKING
Cook the rice ahead of time—several hours or even a day ahead. The best way to reheat it is in the microwave oven. It works beautifully!

FROZEN POWER
You will have great success freezing cooked rice. Cool the rice and package it in plastic containers. To use the rice, defrost, add additional desired ingredients such as sautéed chopped onions or peppers, then heat in a microwave oven.

APPETIZERS AND FIRST COURSES

BOURSIN—A HOMEMADE VERSION

Makes about 2 cups

16 ounces cream cheese, room temperature
3 tablespoons cream or milk
¾ teaspoon salt (or to taste)
1 teaspoon black pepper (medium grind)
1 garlic clove, mashed (or from garlic oil, p. 18)
1 teaspoon dried sweet basil
1 teaspoon dried oregano
½ teaspoon dried thyme
1 or 2 teaspoons chopped fresh parsley

WHEN NO ONE IS LOOKING
Prepare this up to 1 week ahead; keep covered and refrigerated.

FROZEN POWER
Yes, freeze. Wrap each filled crock in plastic, then wrap again in foil.

Beat cream cheese with an electric beater until smooth, gradually beating in the cream or milk. Mix in the remaining ingredients. Spoon into crocks, cover, and refrigerate. Serve with water crackers or melba toast.

MUSHROOMS WITH SOUR CREAM AND RED CAVIAR

Makes 12 servings

12 large fresh mushrooms
3 tablespoons butter
salt and black pepper
¼ cup sour cream
3 tablespoons red caviar (salmon roe)

WHEN NO ONE IS LOOKING
Prepare these in the morning. Cover and refrigerate. Serve cold or at room temperature.

Clean mushrooms, then remove stems (use for another purpose). Sauté the mushrooms in the butter for 1 minute on each side, then remove from heat and season lightly with salt and pepper. Cool to room temperature, then arrange cooked mushrooms on a serving dish with smooth sides down. Fill each cap with some sour cream, then top with red caviar.

OLD-FASHIONED CHOPPED CHICKEN LIVER, JEWISH STYLE

Makes about 2 cups

- 1 pound fresh chicken livers
- 2 large onions, coarsely chopped
- 6 hard-cooked eggs
- 4 to 8 ounces butter (or rendered chicken or duck fat)
- salt and black pepper to taste

WHEN NO ONE IS LOOKING
Prepare this 1 day ahead; keep covered and refrigerated.

Sauté the chopped onion in half the butter or other fat over moderate heat until very tender and lightly browned. Remove onions from skillet and set them aside. Add more butter or fat to the skillet and sauté chicken livers over moderate heat, covered part of the time, until they are cooked through. Combine livers, cooked onions, and hard-cooked eggs in a food processor and pulse (turn on and off) until mixture is chopped, but neither mushy nor puréed. Remove to a bowl and season with salt and pepper. Serve chilled or at room temperature with water crackers, matzos, or melba toast.

TOMATO CONFIT-PESTO TARTS

Makes 8 servings

You will need individual tart pans with bottoms about 3 inches in diameter

- 2 to 3 cups "Tomato Confit" (p. 27)
- ½ cup "Pesto" (p. 28)
- 1 pound puff pastry (p. 356) or the 17-ounce frozen puff pastry available in supermarkets
- softened butter (optional)

WHEN NO ONE IS LOOKING
Prepare the tomato confit and the pesto in advance as directed in those recipes. Bake the pastry disks one day ahead; wrap each in plastic, and refrigerate. To finish, proceed with reheating as directed in the recipe.

FROZEN POWER
Tomato confit and pesto freeze well, as mentioned in those recipes. Freeze the pastry disks too, before or after baking them.

Divide homemade puff pastry into two portions and roll each one out into a rectangle ⅛" thick. Or, if using Pepperidge Farm or other purchased frozen puff pastry—which contains 2 folded sheets—defrost the pastry according to package instructions, then roll out one sheet at a time (keep the other one chilled) to a rectangle ⅛" thick. In either case cut 4 disks larger than the tops of your tartlet pans from each portion because they will shrink in the baking. You can use anything as a cutter or as a model to cut around—an empty coffee can, a small saucer, etc. Prick the pastry disks thoroughly with a fork, then chill at least 30 minutes (or, even better, freeze for 15 minutes).

Preheat oven to 400°. I like to lightly coat pastry disks with a thin layer of softened butter to improve the flavor of the commercial pastry, then bake for 10 minutes. If pastries bubble up, prick them again with a fork. Reduce oven to 350° and bake 10 to 20 minutes longer, or until brown and crisp. Remove from oven and set aside.

Assemble: Cut small nonstick parchment circles to fit the inside bottoms of tart pans and insert them in the pans. Fill each pan ½ to ⅔ full of tomato confit, with the cut sides of the tomatoes facing up. Spoon 1 tablespoon of pesto over the confit, then set aside.

Finish: Preheat oven to 375°. Place filled tart pans and pastry disks on separate baking pans and heat in the oven, but do not overbake. Remove from oven and put each pastry disk on an individual serving plate, then turn filled tart pans upside down on the pastries. In other words, now the pastry will be on the bottom, the pesto in the middle, and the smooth sides of the tomatoes will be on top. Serve hot, warm, or at room temperature.

TOMATO CONFIT

- fresh, ripe tomatoes, peeled, each cut in half
- salt, ⅛ teaspoon for each tomato half
- sugar, ⅛ teaspoon for each tomato half
- dried thyme, a pinch for each tomato half
- garlic oil (p. 18), 1 teaspoon for each tomato half

WHEN NO ONE IS LOOKING
Prepare these 2 to 3 days ahead; cover and keep them refrigerated.

FROZEN POWER
Tomato confit freezes very well. To use, merely defrost and if the tomatoes look watery, bake them in a shallow large pan in a preheated 300° oven for about 30 minutes, or until the moisture has mostly disappeared.

Preheat oven to 275°. Arrange tomato halves cut sides down in a large shallow pan. Sprinkle them with the salt, sugar, thyme, and garlic oil. Bake uncovered for 3 to 4 hours. Tomatoes will have reduced to about ½ their original size. Remove, set aside until ready to use.

PESTO

Makes 4 to 6 servings

You must use fresh sweet basil for this dazzlingly delicious sauce; if you grow your own, double or triple the recipe

- ⅓ cup pine nuts
- 1 cup sweet basil leaves (remove stems)
- 2 garlic cloves, mashed (or from garlic oil, p. 18)
- 1 teaspoon salt
- ½ teaspoon black pepper
- 1 tablespoon hot water
- ½ cup olive oil
- ¾ cup grated Parmesan cheese

WHEN NO ONE IS LOOKING
Prepare the pesto up to 1 week ahead; keep tightly covered and refrigerated. Bring to room temperature and stir before using.

FROZEN POWER
By all means, freeze pesto. To use, defrost completely and bring to room temperature, then stir, and use as desired.

Whirl pine nuts in a food processor, then remove them to a bowl. Place basil, water, and olive oil in the processor, and process to a purée. Add to the bowl of nuts, then beat in the garlic, salt, pepper, and Parmesan.

SUN-DRIED TOMATOES AND GOAT CHEESE APPETIZERS

Makes 2 to 4 dozen

- 1 loaf of white bread, sliced medium thick with crusts removed
- melted butter
- sun-dried tomatoes preserved in oil, drained
- 5 ounces California mild goat cheese
- 1 egg
- salt and black pepper to taste

WHEN NO ONE IS LOOKING
Prepare the goat cheese mixture 1 day ahead; keep covered and refrigerated. Also prepare the toast bases 1 day ahead, and keep those tightly sealed in plastic bags; store them in the refrigerator or at room temperature. Or, completely assemble these appetizers 1 or 2 hours before baking. Cover lightly and leave at room temperature.

FROZEN POWER
Freeze the goat cheese mixture. To use, defrost and stir. Freeze the toast bases too; store them in plastic bags and seal tightly. Refresh toasts in a moderate oven before using.

Cut bread into squares or circles, then brush these with melted butter on both sides. Preheat oven to 350°, and bake bread pieces until lightly browned, turning them to brown both sides. These are the appetizer bases.

Combine goat cheese and egg, and whip by hand or in a food processor. Season with salt and pepper. Cover each toast base with a small piece of sun-dried tomato and place the toasts on a nonstick baking pan (or a pan lined with nonstick paper). Top each with ½ teaspoon of the goat cheese mixture. Preheat oven to 400°, then bake for 7 to 8 minutes, until very hot.

SUMMERTIME EGGS

Makes 8 servings

8 hard-cooked eggs
½ cup mayonnaise
¼ cup Durkee's salad dressing (or substitute Dijon-style mustard and 1 teaspoon sugar)
salt and black pepper to taste
chopped sweet pepper, red or green

WHEN NO ONE IS LOOKING
Prepare the egg mixture 1 day ahead; cover and refrigerate. Cover and refrigerate the empty shells separately.

Never freeze hard-cooked eggs; they become rubbery!!!

Prepare the hard-cooked eggs one at a time by placing them in an egg cup. Hold the egg firmly with one hand, then use a special egg cutter or a small but very sharp knife to cut through the shell and remove a little of the top of each egg. Use a small spoon to carefully remove the cooked eggs from their shells so that the shells remain intact. Reserve the empty shells.

Chop the hard-cooked eggs with a fork, as for egg salad, or use a food processor, but pulse only a few seconds. Eggs should be chopped, not puréed. Add mayonnaise, Durkee's salad dressing, salt, and pepper, and mix well. Place in a bowl, cover, and refrigerate. Keep empty shells refrigerated too.

When ready to serve, place egg shells in egg cups and fill each with prepared mixture. Garnish the tops with chopped sweet pepper. Serve cold on individual plates and with demitasse spoons. Accompany with water crackers or melba toasts.

FIVE QUESADILLA "SANDWICHES"

Makes 10 or more servings

- 10 (8-inch diameter) flour tortillas
- 9 ounces Monterey Jack cheese (in France, try Pyrénées)
- 1 (7-ounce) can diced mild green chiles (or substitute sweet green peppers, roasted, peeled, and chopped)
- 1 (7-ounce) can sliced or chopped ripe, black olives, well-drained
- chopped green onions, 1 teaspoon for each sandwich (optional)
- salt
- melted butter

WHEN NO ONE IS LOOKING
Assemble the quesadillas 1 day ahead; keep them wrapped and refrigerated.

FROZEN POWER
These freeze beautifully. Double-wrap them in foil and they will keep for many months. They do not need to be defrosted before baking, but if frozen, allow more baking time—approximately 10 minutes more.

Prepare five of the flour tortillas by brushing on both sides with melted butter. Line them up on your work surface. Sprinkle each with grated cheese, then with olives, diced chiles, and, if desired, a little chopped green onion. Salt lightly—amount will depend on the saltiness of the cheese. Brush remaining five tortillas with melted butter on both sides, then place each over the filled tortillas, thus making sandwiches. Press down. Double-wrap each sandwich in foil, then refrigerate or freeze.

To serve: Unwrap one or more quesadillas and place on a nonstick baking pan or in a pan lined with nonstick parchment paper. Preheat oven to 400°, and bake for 10 minutes in the lower part of the oven; move to the upper part of the oven and bake an additional 10 to 15 minutes, or longer if frozen. The quesadillas should be well browned—the tops and bottoms crisp. Remove from oven. If serving as appetizers, cut into 8 wedges; if serving for luncheon, cut into halves or quarters.

CORN CRÊPES

Makes 12 to 16 servings

Makes about 100 small crêpes, using the Scandinavian platt pan with seven shallow indentations, now available with a nonstick surface

- 9 extra large eggs, room temperature
- 1 ½ cups flour (11 ounces)
- ¾ cup yellow cornmeal
- 2 cups warm milk
- 1 cup heavy cream, room temperature
- ½ pound butter (2 sticks), melted
- 1 ¼ teaspoons salt
- 2 (12-ounce) cans whole kernel corn, drained (should measure 3 cups after draining)
- additional melted butter to use after the crêpes are cooked

WHEN NO ONE IS LOOKING
Prepare the crêpe batter 1 day ahead; cover and refrigerate. Bring to room temperature before cooking the crêpes. Or, cook them and stack with melted butter in between; then wrap in foil packages, 14 to a package. Keep refrigerated. Before using, warm them in their foil packages in a very low oven—only long enough to allow you to separate the crêpes easily. Then proceed as directed.

FROZEN POWER
These freeze perfectly. Cook and wrap as directed above in "When No One is Looking," then place the foil packages in sealable plastic freezer bags. To use, defrost completely, then proceed as directed.

Combine eggs in a large bowl and beat until well mixed. Gradually beat in the flour and cornmeal alternately with the milk and cream. Add the 1 cup of melted butter, the salt, and the whole kernel corn. Set aside to stand for at least 1 hour. Check consistency. Mixture should have the thickness of cream; if too thick, add more milk.

If possible cook the crêpes in the Scandinavian-style platt pan with seven shallow indentations, now available with a nonstick surface. I use ½ cup of batter at a time, dividing it among the seven indentations. Brown the crêpes, then turn and brown the other sides. Turn them with a small spatula, or place a bowl of ice water near the stove, dip your hands into it, and turn the crêpes by hand.

When almost ready to serve, preheat oven to 350°, and arrange the crêpes in an ovenproof shallow casserole. Spoon on more melted butter. Cover with foil, then place in the oven until very hot, but do not overcook. Serve hot with smoked salmon or red caviar and sour cream.

SPICY HOT WALNUTS

Makes about 4 cups

4 cups raw walnut halves
6 tablespoons melted butter
4 teaspoons dried rosemary
2 teaspoons salt
1 teaspoon cayenne

WHEN NO ONE IS LOOKING
Prepare these up to 1 week ahead; keep covered and refrigerated. Reheat briefly before serving.

FROZEN POWER
By all means, do freeze these spicy walnuts. To serve, defrost, then reheat them briefly before serving.

Combine butter, rosemary, salt, and cayenne in a bowl. Add the walnuts and stir until well covered with the mixture. Spread out the walnuts in a large baking pan in a single layer. Preheat oven to 350°. Bake the walnuts for 10 minutes, then remove and stir the them so the coating is evenly distributed. Return to the oven and bake 5 to 10 minutes longer. Serve at room temperature.

CRABMEAT PÂTÉ WITH SWEET PEPPER AND DILL

Makes about 1½ cups

6 to 7 ounces crabmeat (fresh or canned)
½ sweet red or green pepper, finely chopped
3 green onions, finely chopped
2 teaspoons finely chopped fresh dill
salt and black pepper to taste
2 or 3 teaspoons lemon juice
½ cup mayonnaise, or to taste

WHEN NO ONE IS LOOKING
Prepare this 1 or 2 days ahead; keep covered and refrigerated.

Combine all ingredients; cover and chill. The flavor improves with several hours of chilling.

SMOKED SALMON WITH PUMPERNICKEL AND DILL SAUCE

sliced smoked salmon
Danish-style pumpernickel sliced bread
soft butter
"Dill Sauce" (p. 240)
fresh dill (for garnishing)

WHEN NO ONE IS LOOKING
Prepare the dill sauce up to 1 week ahead; keep tightly sealed in a glass jar and refrigerated. The appetizers can be prepared in the morning, arranged on plates or platters, covered with plastic and kept refrigerated.

Generously butter sliced bread. Cover with slices of smoked salmon and top with some of the dill sauce. Cut into quarters and garnish each with a tiny sprig of fresh dill. Cover with plastic and refrigerate until time to serve.

TOBEY'S MAHOGANY CHICKEN WINGETTES

Makes 10 to 12 servings

3 dozen chicken wingettes (or remove tips of wings and divide the wings into two pieces)

for the marinade:
1 cup Hoisin sauce
¾ cup plum sauce
½ cup soy sauce
⅓ cup cider vinegar
¼ cup dry sherry
¼ cup honey
1 large garlic clove mashed (or from garlic oil, p. 18)

WHEN NO ONE IS LOOKING
Prepare these 1 day ahead; keep covered and refrigerated. Bring to room temperature, then reheat in a moderate oven.

FROZEN POWER
Freeze these wingettes either by double-wrapping them in foil or by placing them in airtight containers. To serve: defrost, bring to room temperature, then reheat in a moderate oven.

Combine marinade ingredients in a large bowl and mix well. Place wingettes in the marinade, cover and refrigerate for 24 hours, stirring once or twice during that period.

Preheat oven to 375°. Drain wingettes, reserving the marinade. Place wingettes in a nonstick heavy-duty baking pan and bake for 20 minutes, basting once. Remove pan from oven, turn the wingettes, then baste with some of the reserved marinade. Return to oven and bake another 20 to 30 minutes, or until tender

TOBEY COTSEN VICTOR'S FABULOUS ASIAN RAVIOLI

Makes 3 to 4 dozen

for the sauce:
½ cup chopped fresh basil
2 teaspoons grated orange peel
½ cup olive oil
4 cloves garlic, minced (or from garlic oil, p. 18)
½ cup lime juice
6 to 7 tablespoons soy sauce
¼ cup honey
2 teaspoons Chinese chili sauce
2 teaspoons grated nutmeg

for the filling:
9 or 10 ounces fresh baby spinach leaves (available prewashed and packaged)
½ cup jicama chunks
¾ cup carrot chunks (or peeled baby carrots)
1 green onion, finely chopped
1 tablespoon finely minced ginger
½ pound bay scallops
¼ pound ground raw chicken
2 tablespoons soy sauce
2 teaspoons dry sherry
¼ teaspoon white pepper
2 (10-ounce) packages of potsticker wrappers (or wontons trimmed into circles)

WHEN NO ONE IS LOOKING
Prepare both the ravioli and the sauce 1 day ahead. Keep each refrigerated—the ravioli uncovered, the sauce covered.

FROZEN POWER
Freeze the ravioli on trays, and when completely frozen, store them in plastic containers that have a tight seal. Freeze the sauce too in a separate container.

Prepare the filling: Place half the spinach in a food processor and process until somewhat chopped. Add all remaining ingredients, except the wrappers, and process for a few seconds, then add remaining spinach and process until almost, but not quite, puréed. Remove to a bowl, stir well and set aside. Place about 2 teaspoons of this filling in the center of each wrapper. Moisten edges with water and fold in half over the filling, being careful not to flatten the filling. Press the edges together and be sure that they are firmly sealed. Moisten the ends of these half-moon-shaped raviolis and fold them back so that the moistened ends overlap. Place ravioli on a baking sheet and refrigerate, uncovered.

Prepare the sauce: Combine all filling ingredients in a food processor and process until everything is blended and smooth. Set aside. Bring at least 5 quarts of water to a fast boil. Add the ravioli and stir gently. When they float to the surface—about 3 minutes—remove with a slotted spoon to drain, then transfer to serving plates and spoon some of the sauce over each.

ROQUEFORT (OR BLUE CHEESE) APPETIZER MIX

Makes about 2 cups

- 8 ounces Roquefort or blue cheese
- 8 ounces cream cheese
- 8 ounces butter

WHEN NO ONE IS LOOKING
Prepare this 5 or 6 days ahead, but be sure to keep the filled containers covered tightly and refrigerated.

FROZEN POWER
A perfect appetizer for freezing. Double-wrap the filled containers and they will keep well for many months.

Bring ingredients to room temperature, then whip them together with an electric beater. Spoon into crocks or small bowls, cover, and refrigerate. Serve slightly cool or at room temperature with unsalted crackers or melba toast.

QUAIL EGGS IN PASTRY BARQUETTES

It takes practice and careful timing to soft-boil quail eggs so that the yolks remain soft while the eggs are cooked enough to peel. But do not despair—this dish is also excellent prepared with hard-cooked quail eggs!

- fresh quail eggs, soft-boiled or hard-cooked
- inexpensive salmon or lumpfish caviar
- sour cream
- finely chopped green onions or chives
- small pastry barquettes (homemade or purchased)

WHEN NO ONE IS LOOKING
Cook the eggs 1 day ahead. Peel the eggs, then place them in a single layer on a dish or dishes. Cover tightly with plastic and refrigerate. Fill the barquettes 1 or 2 hours before serving; keep covered and refrigerated until time to serve.

FROZEN POWER
If you have baked your own pastry barquettes, freeze them in firm containers that have tight-fitting lids; they should keep well for several months.

Do not substitute canned quail eggs for fresh. They are dreadful! If you cannot find fresh quail eggs, substitute quartered small hard-cooked eggs. Although fresh quail eggs are rarely found in ordinary supermarkets, they are almost always available in Japanese markets because they are used for certain kinds of sushi.

Place a thin layer of caviar inside the barquettes. Fill each with two or three cooked quail eggs. Top each egg with a tiny dab of sour cream and garnish with the chopped green onion or chives.

WARM CRABMEAT DIP

Makes about 10 servings

8 ounces cream cheese, room temperature
7 or 8 ounces crabmeat (fresh or canned)
1 cup mayonnaise
2 teaspoons soy sauce
1 teaspoon Worcestershire sauce
¼ to ½ teaspoon Tabasco sauce
dash of cayenne
2 cloves garlic, mashed (or from garlic oil, p. 18)
salt to taste

WHEN NO ONE IS LOOKING
Prepare this up to 2 days ahead; keep covered and refrigerated.

FROZEN POWER
Spoon mixture into containers that can be sealed and freeze. To serve, defrost completely and proceed as directed

Soften the cream cheese and mix until smooth. Stir in the remaining ingredients. Taste for seasoning. Cover and set aside for several hours so the flavors have time to blend, or store overnight in the refrigerator. To serve, cover with plastic and heat in a microwave oven only until hot. Serve as canapés with water crackers or crisp toast.

CRABMEAT AND CHEESE HOT APPETIZERS

Makes 5 dozen or more

The cheese mixture is delicious used alone for toasted cheese canapés or toasted cheese sandwiches. It can be made in quantity, divided in portions, and frozen.

sliced white bread (homemade quality), crusts removed, then cut into rounds
melted butter or olive oil

for the crabmeat mixture:
4 tablespoons flour
4 tablespoons butter (2 ounces)
1 ½ cups milk, heated
2 cups crabmeat (fresh is best, but good-quality canned will do)
salt and black pepper to taste
1 teaspoon dry mustard
1 teaspoon Worcestershire sauce

for the cheese mixture:
1 ½ cups grated Cheddar cheese (room temperature)
2 tablespoons soft butter
¼ cup milk (room temperature)
¼ teaspoon salt (or to taste)
pinch of paprika
1 teaspoon Worcestershire sauce
1 egg

WHEN NO ONE IS LOOKING
Prepare the crabmeat mixture 1 day ahead; keep covered and refrigerated. Prepare the cheese mixture 4 or 5 days ahead; keep it covered and refrigerated. Assemble the canapés the morning of the party; cover them with plastic and keep refrigerated. Bring to room temperature 1 hour before time to broil.

FROZEN POWER
Freeze these appetizers after they are assembled but before they are broiled. Place them in a single layer on a pan and freeze. Once they are solidly frozen, layer them between sheets of waxed paper or plastic in tins or cartons that can be sealed. To serve, defrost for about 30 minutes, then proceed as directed.

Prepare canapé bases: Brush cut bread rounds on both sides with butter or oil, then toast in a 350° oven until lightly browned. Remove from heat, cool, then cover and chill.

Prepare crabmeat mixture: Melt butter and stir in the flour, then whisk in the milk. Cook, stirring constantly, until mixture comes to a boil. Reduce heat, add remaining ingredients, and stir until mixed. Simmer 2 minutes.

Prepare cheese mixture: Cream grated cheese with the butter. Beat in the milk, salt, dry mustard, paprika, and Worcestershire sauce, then add the egg and continue to beat until mixture is fluffy. Chill.

Assemble and finish: Spread about 1 teaspoon of crabmeat mixture on each toasted bread canapé base. Top with a tiny spoonful of the cheese mixture. Continue with the remaining toasts. When ready to serve, place under a broiling unit, and broil until the cheese is puffy and well browned. Watch so they do not burn! Serve hot.

VERY EASY DUXELLES TURNOVERS

Makes 24 servings

24 very thin slices of white bread; or use an unsliced bread and slice it yourself
melted butter
1 egg or 2 egg whites, slightly beaten

for the duxelles:
1 ½ pounds fresh mushrooms
3 to 4 tablespoons finely chopped shallots (or use frozen shallots, p. 18)
¼ pound butter (1 stick)
salt and black pepper to taste
6 tablespoons dry sherry

WHEN NO ONE IS LOOKING
Prepare the duxelles 1 day ahead; keep covered and refrigerated. Or, assemble the turnovers 1 day ahead; cover, refrigerate, and bake them the next day.

FROZEN POWER
Freeze the duxelles. Defrost, then reheat and stir to remove some of the moisture, and proceed as directed.

Make the duxelles: Finely chop the mushrooms in a food processor. Heat butter in a large skillet or large pot and sauté the chopped mushrooms and shallots in the butter, stirring over moderate to high heat until all moisture has evaporated and mushrooms have started to brown. Add salt and pepper, and cook, stirring, for another minute. Add the sherry and turn off heat. Stir for 1 or 2 minutes. Remove and cool, then place in a bowl, cover, and refrigerate.

Assemble the turnovers: Remove crusts from the bread slices and flatten them with a rolling pin. Place 1 tablespoon of duxelles into the center of the bread slices. Moisten bread edges with egg, then fold over filling into triangle shapes. Press down firmly on the edges. Brush tops and bottoms with melted butter.

Bake: Preheat oven to 450°. Place turnovers on a nonstick pan and bake for 5 to 10 minutes—until crisp and brown.

CHICKEN LIVER PÂTÉ BRANDIED AND HERBED

Makes 4 to 6 small crocks

My long-time favorite!

1 pound fresh chicken livers
2 medium-size onions, coarsely chopped
6 ounces butter (1 ½ sticks)
2 teaspoons garlic, mashed (or from garlic oil, p. 18)
1 tablespoon flour
1 teaspoon salt
½ teaspoon black pepper
1 bay leaf
⅛ teaspoon thyme
⅛ teaspoon oregano
⅛ teaspoon tarragon
3 tablespoons cognac or California brandy

WHEN NO ONE IS LOOKING
Prepare this pâté 1 or 2 days ahead; keep it covered and refrigerated.

FROZEN POWER
This freezes beautifully—an ideal appetizer to keep on hand for culinary emergencies.

Sauté onions with the garlic in ½ of the butter until onions are very tender. Remove onions from skillet and set aside. Add remaining butter to skillet and sauté livers until almost cooked, then sprinkle with flour, add salt, pepper, bay leaf, thyme, oregano, and tarragon. Cover and simmer over low heat until livers are cooked through—2 to 3 minutes. Discard bay leaf. Combine cooked livers and onions, then stir in the cognac.

Whirl the mixture in a food processor until smooth, stirring and scraping down the sides once or twice. Place in a bowl, then stir and let cool briefly. Divide into crocks. Cover tightly with plastic wrap, then wrap in foil. Refrigerate.

PÂTÉ PANGLOSS

Makes 8 to 10 servings

Foolproof and delectable—reminiscent of fine French foie gras

- ½ pound fresh chicken livers
- 1 small clove garlic, mashed (or from garlic oil, p. 18)
- 1 small onion, chopped
- 4 tablespoons butter (2 ounces)
- ¾ teaspoon salt
- ¼ teaspoon black pepper
- ⅛ teaspoon thyme
- ⅛ teaspoon oregano
- ⅛ teaspoon tarragon
- 2 slices firm white bread, crusts removed, then torn into pieces
- ½ cup light cream
- 2 eggs
- 1 teaspoon soy sauce
- 1 tablespoon cognac or California brandy

WHEN NO ONE IS LOOKING
Wrap this pâté very well and keep it refrigerated up to 5 days ahead. Once unwrapped, the pâté should be eaten promptly.

FROZEN POWER
Since this pâté loses its delicate texture after freezing, do not freeze it except for use as leftovers.

Preheat oven to 300°. Put cream and eggs in a large bowl, then beat together. Add bread and set aside. Sauté chopped onions in the butter until tender but not browned. Add garlic and cook half a minute. Add chicken livers and cook 1 minute. Remove from heat and add salt, pepper, herbs, soy sauce, and cognac, then combine with the bread mixture. Place in a food processor and process until mixture is puréed. Turn into a bowl and mix well. Spoon into a greased pan (about 3 ¾ x 7 ½ x 2 inches). Cover tightly with greased heavy foil (or double foil) and place in a large baking pan. Pour hot water into larger pan until it reaches half way up the side of the pâté pan. Bake for 1 ½ hours. Cool on a rack without removing foil. When room temperature, unmold and wrap first in plastic, then in foil. Chill thoroughly.

PÂTÉ EN BRIOCHE

Makes 2 loaves; serves 16 to 20 as a first course

A superb beginning for an elegant dinner

for the pâté:
1 pound fresh chicken livers
1 garlic clove, mashed
(or from garlic oil, p. 18)
1 onion, chopped
6 ounces butter (1 ½ sticks)
1 ¾ teaspoons salt
½ teaspoon black pepper
¼ teaspoon thyme
¼ teaspoon oregano
¼ teaspoon tarragon
4 slices of firm white bread, crusts removed, then cut or torn into pieces
1 cup light cream
3 extra large eggs
1 teaspoon soy sauce
2 tablespoons cognac or California brandy

WHEN NO ONE IS LOOKING
Start preparation 2 days before you plan to serve.
First day: bake pâtés and refrigerate; also, make brioche dough and refrigerate.
Second day: Assemble and bake loaves; cool; wrap; and chill.
Party day: Serve! If these loaves are kept tightly wrapped, refrigerated, and left unopened, you can prepare them up to 5 days ahead. Once unwrapped, they must be eaten promptly.

FROZEN POWER
Freeze the brioche dough up to a month; defrost overnight in the refrigerator, then proceed as directed. However, since the pâté loses its fine texture in the freezing process, only freeze for use as leftovers.

Combine eggs and cream in a large bowl and beat slightly. Add bread and stir, then set aside. Sauté onions in the butter until tender but not browned. Add garlic and cook half a minute. Add chicken livers and cook one minute. Remove from heat, then add salt, pepper, herbs, soy sauce, and cognac, and combine with the bread mixture. Whirl in a food processor until puréed, stopping once or twice to scrape down the sides. Pour into a bowl and stir well.

Preheat oven to 300°. Grease two pans—each about 3 ¾ x 7 ½ x 2 inches—heavily with butter or vegetable shortening. Pour or spoon prepared mixture into the greased pans, then cover them tightly with greased double foil. Place the pans in a larger baking pan and pour hot water into the larger pan half way up the sides of the pâté pans. Bake for 1 ½ to 2 hours. Remove from oven and cool on racks without removing foil. When cooled, unmold and wrap each loaf in plastic, then in foil. Chill thoroughly, if possible, overnight.

for the brioche:
1 package dry yeast
⅓ cup warm water
⅓ cup milk, room temperature or warm
½ pound butter (2 sticks), melted
¼ cup sugar
2 teaspoons salt
4 whole eggs
4 egg yolks
5 cups sifted flour (22 ounces)
1 egg, slightly beaten (for egg wash)

Sprinkle yeast on the warm water and stir until dissolved. Combine milk, butter, sugar, and salt in a large bowl and stir thoroughly. Beat eggs and egg yolks together and add to milk mixture. Test to see that it is lukewarm, then add dissolved yeast. Gradually beat in the flour with an electric dough hook, or beat it with a wooden spoon until dough begins to pull away from sides of the bowl. Place dough in an oiled bowl, cover and let rise 45 minutes or until doubled in bulk (depending on room temperature). Knock down the dough, cover and refrigerate at least 3 hours, or better, overnight. If dough begins to rise in the refrigerator, press it down.

Assemble and finish: Remove pâtés from the refrigerator a few hours before assembling. Grease two loaf pans approximately 5 x 8 x 2 ½ inches. Divide brioche dough into two equal portions. Then take each portion and divide again into two pieces, but this time in the ratio of ⅓ to ⅔. Roll out the two larger portions and place each in the bottom of the loaf pans. Press them in so that the dough reaches about half way up the sides of the pans. Egg wash dough but gently so as not to drip on the pans themselves. Place a pâté loaf on top of the brioche and egg wash each. Roll out or pat out the smaller portions of dough and egg wash one side of each. Place these—egg-washed sides down—on top of the pâtés and press all around so that the top pieces join the bottom ones on all sides. Let rise 30 minutes to 1 hour or a little longer. The brioche dough should have puffed almost to double. Preheat oven to 400°. Bake the loaves for 10 minutes. Reduce heat to 350° and bake an additional 35 to 40 minutes. If tops brown too quickly, cover tops loosely with foil. When well browned and firm to the touch, remove from oven. Loosen breads from pan sides with a small knife, then remove from pans and cool them right sides up on racks. When cooled to room temperature, double-wrap them in foil and refrigerate. Serve chilled or at room temperature.

ALSATIAN ONION PIE MY WAY

Serves 8 to 10 as a first course; 4 to 6 as a luncheon entrée

¾ of a recipe of "Pâte Brisée" (p. 355)

for the filling:
8 cups sliced onions
¼ pound butter (1 stick)
2 teaspoons salt
¼ teaspoon black pepper
1 tablespoon flour
4 extra-large eggs
1 cup heavy cream
¼ cup grated Parmesan cheese

WHEN NO ONE IS LOOKING
Prebake the pastry up to 2 days ahead; keep it wrapped and refrigerated. Sauté the onions 1 or 2 days ahead; keep them covered and refrigerated, but do not add the eggs and cream. Bring pastry and onions to room temperature several hours before the final baking, then proceed as directed in the recipe.

FROZEN POWER
Pastry freezes beautifully. Freeze the shell baked or unbaked.

Prepare the pastry: Preheat oven to 425°. Roll pastry to fit a 10-inch quiche dish that is 2 inches deep or an 11-inch or 12-inch one 1½ inches deep. Line with greased foil and fill with rice or beans to weigh down the foil. Bake for 15 minutes, remove foil and beans, then reduce heat to 375° and bake 10 more minutes. Remove from oven and cool.

Make the filling: Sauté the onions slowly in the butter, stirring frequently, until tender and golden but not brown. This takes 15 to 20 minutes. Sprinkle with salt, pepper, and flour, then simmer, stirring occasionally, for 2 minutes. Remove from heat and set aside until ready to bake. Preheat oven to 450°. Beat eggs and cream together, stir in cheese, and pour over onions; combine thoroughly. Pour filling into prepared pastry shell and place in the oven, then *immediately* reduce heat to 350°. Bake approximately 55 minutes; top should be well browned. Serve hot or warm.

QUAIL EGGS IN SALAMI NESTS WITH RUSSIAN SALAD

Makes 8 servings

24 to 32 thin slices Italian salami
8 fresh quail eggs (look for fresh ones in Japanese markets; do *not* use tinned ones; if necessary substitute quartered regular-size eggs)
Boston lettuce
thin slivers of sweet or sour pickles
2 tablespoons mayonnaise, thinned with cream

for the Russian salad:
1 cup finely chopped celery
1 cup chopped cooked carrots
1 cup diced cooked green beans
1 cup tiny cooked peas
1 cup diced cooked potatoes
3 green onions, finely chopped
1 tablespoon lemon juice
1 cup mayonnaise
1 tablespoon anchovy paste
salt and black pepper to taste

WHEN NO ONE IS LOOKING
Prepare the Russian salad and hard-cooked quail eggs 1 day ahead. Place salad and eggs in separate containers; cover and refrigerate.

Hard-cook the quail eggs, then drain them, peel, and chill. Combine ingredients for the Russian salad and mix together. Taste for seasoning, then chill for several hours or overnight.

Cut salami slices into thin matchstick-size pieces. Place lettuce on individual plates. Arrange a generous tablespoon of Russian salad on each plate and flatten with a spoon. Arrange slivered salami to resemble mock bird nests on top of the salads, then insert a quail egg into each. Coat eggs lightly with the thinned mayonnaise and garnish with one or two pickle slivers.

RED CAVIAR AND SMOKED SALMON ROULADE

Serves about 8

9 ounces cream cheese
1 ½ cups sour cream
6 ounces smoked salmon, diced
4 ounces red caviar (salmon roe)
salt, only if needed
1 or 2 tablespoons chopped chives (or green onions)
2 ounces butter (½ stick)
¼ cup flour
¼ teaspoon salt
2 cups milk
4 egg yolks
4 egg whites

WHEN NO ONE IS LOOKING
Bake and fill the roulade 1 day ahead. Cover with plastic wrap and refrigerate. The extra filling should also be kept covered and refrigerated.

Prepare the pan: Grease a jelly roll pan (11 x 17 inches) with vegetable shortening. Line with baking parchment paper, and grease the paper.

Prepare the filling: Beat cream cheese until smooth, then gradually beat in sour cream. Fold in the diced salmon and caviar. Add half the chives. Taste for salt, then chill.

Make the roulade: Preheat oven to 325°. Melt butter in a large saucepan, stir in flour and salt. Add milk and stir constantly until mixture begins to boil. Remove from heat, then beat in egg yolks one at a time. In a separate bowl beat egg whites until stiff but not dry, then fold into yolk mixture. Spread this batter in prepared pan. Bake for 40 to 50 minutes or until browned on top. Remove from oven and turn out upside down onto a slightly damp towel. Remove paper and cut off the hard edges of the roulade. Roll up from the long side to obtain the longest possible roll. When cool, unroll and spread with about ⅓ of the filling, then roll up again. Place on a serving platter and cover with plastic wrap. Chill.

To serve: Frost top of roulade with a thin coating of prepared filling and sprinkle with remaining chives. Cut in slices about ½ to ¾ inch thick and serve on individual plates with a spoonful of filling at the side.

SMOKED SALMON WITH CAPERS AND PICKLES

Makes 4 to 6 servings

Adapted from Roy Pitkin's recipe

- 1 tablespoon Dijon-style mustard
- 2 teaspoons white wine vinegar
- 3 tablespoons olive oil
- 1 tablespoon chopped shallots
- 1 tablespoon chopped capers
- 2 tablespoons chopped cornichon pickles
- 1 tablespoon finely chopped green onions
- ½ pound smoked salmon, cut into ½ inch pieces

WHEN NO ONE IS LOOKING
Prepare this 1 day ahead; keep it covered and refrigerated.

Whisk together the mustard, vinegar, and olive oil. Stir in the shallots, capers, pickles, and green onions. Add the smoked salmon and stir gently. Serve with water crackers or with small squares of rye bread

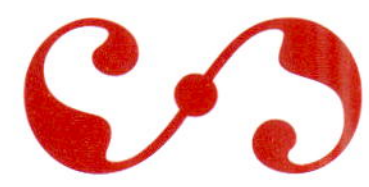

FINNAN HADDIE MOUSSE

Makes 10 to 12 servings

for the mousse:
1 3/4 pounds finnan haddie (smoked haddock)
milk and water for poaching
1 1/2 cups mayonnaise
4 hard-cooked eggs
1/2 cup heavy whipping cream
1 tablespoon unflavored gelatin
1/2 cup cold water
juice of half a lemon, or to taste
salt and black pepper to taste

for the aspic:
1 (10 1/2 ounce) can condensed consommé
1 tablespoon unflavored gelatin
1/2 cup cold water
2 teaspoons lemon juice
3 tablespoons dry sherry

for the garnish:
lemon slices
sliced stuffed olives
sliced radishes
chopped parsley

WHEN NO ONE IS LOOKING
Prepare the mousse 1 day ahead, but add the aspic topping the morning of the party.

Prepare the mousse: Cover finnan haddie with a mixture of half water and half milk, then poach gently for 10 to 15 minutes, or until cooked. Drain, bone, and flake the fish, then combine with the mayonnaise and eggs. Place in a food processor and process until puréed. Soak gelatin in cold water (in a Pyrex cup or small bowl) for 5 minutes, then dissolve it by placing the Pyrex cup or bowl in simmering water. Add cream to fish mixture, stir, then add dissolved gelatin all at once, stirring it in quickly. Add lemon juice and season with salt and pepper to taste. Pour into an oiled 9-inch round metal cake pan and refrigerate until firm.

Prepare the aspic: Soak gelatin in cold water for 5 minutes. Bring consommé to a boil, reduce heat to low and simmer for ½ minute. Stir in soaked gelatin. Remove from heat and add lemon juice and sherry. Chill only until syrupy.

Assemble: Unmold the mousse. Cover top with a thin layer of aspic and chill until aspic is firm. Decorate with garnishes, then spoon a thin layer of aspic over the garnishes to hold them in place. Chill again. Serve in wedges with melba toast.

PAPAYAS FILLED WITH SEAFOOD

Makes 6 servings

- 1 pound cooked tiny bay shrimp or crabmeat
- 3 ripe papayas (or substitute cantaloupes)
- ¼ cup toasted pine nuts or toasted slivered almonds
- 1 lemon and 1 lime (or 2 lemons)
- 1 cup mayonnaise
- 2 teaspoons curry powder
- ¾ teaspoon ground cumin

WHEN NO ONE IS LOOKING
Combine the mayonnaise mixture 1 day ahead; cover and refrigerate. Fill the papaya halves several hours before serving; cover each with plastic and refrigerate.

Cut papayas in half and remove seeds. Place seafood in a bowl and cover with the juice of half the lime and half the lemon (or the juice of one lemon). Combine mayonnaise with the juice of the other halves of lime and lemon (or the other lemon), curry powder, and cumin. Keep seafood and dressing separate. Cover each and refrigerate. Shortly before serving, fill papaya halves with the seafood and top with the mayonnaise mixture. Sprinkle with the toasted nuts.

CAPONATA WITH RAISINS

Makes about 1½ quarts

1 medium-size eggplant (do not peel)
2 cups sliced celery
¾ cup olive oil
1 large onion, coarsely chopped
1 sweet red pepper, chopped
1 clove garlic mashed (or from garlic oil, p. 18)
3 to 4 tablespoons tomato paste
½ cup balsamic vinegar
2 tablespoons sugar
¾ cup dark raisins, soaked in hot water, then drained
⅓ to ½ cup capers
1 cup pitted and halved Kalamata olives (or other ripe dark olives)
salt and black pepper to taste
freshly chopped parsley

WHEN NO ONE IS LOOKING
Prepare this 2 to 3 days ahead; keep covered and refrigerated.

FROZEN POWER
Perfect for freezing—freeze either the entire amount in a single airtight container, or divide into smaller portions and place in small containers.

Dice eggplant into ½-inch cubes. Heat ½ cup of the olive oil in a large, heavy pot and sauté the eggplant cubes for 5 to 8 minutes. Stir frequently. Remove eggplant and set aside. Add remaining olive oil to the pot and sauté the chopped onion with the garlic for several minutes. Add celery and sweet peppers and sauté a few more minutes. Return eggplant to the pot and add remaining ingredients. Stir, then cover and simmer over very low heat for 8 to 10 minutes. Taste for seasoning and if needed, add more salt, pepper, vinegar, and sugar. Garnish with chopped parsley. Serve chilled or at room temperature.

SMALL RED POTATOES FILLED WITH SMOKED SALMON

Makes 24 small servings

12 very small red potatoes
salt and black pepper
4 to 6 ounces smoked salmon, cut in ½-inch pieces
1 cup crème fraîche or sour cream
3 or 4 ounces salmon caviar (roe) or 12 to 24 tiny bay shrimp

WHEN NO ONE IS LOOKING
Bake the potatoes several hours ahead, then reheat them briefly in a moderate oven. Scoop and fill them with the salmon 1 hour ahead; cover with plastic and leave at room temperature. Shortly before serving, cover them loosely with foil and reheat in a preheated moderate oven for about 5 minutes; then add the crème fraîche (or sour cream) and the caviar or shrimp.

Preheat oven to 400°. Bake potatoes for 40 to 50 minutes—until cooked through. Cut them into halves and scoop out the insides, leaving ¼-inch shells. Season the shells with salt and pepper, then fill each with some salmon. Top with the crème fraîche or sour cream and garnish with salmon caviar or bay shrimp. Serve warm.

HUMMUS TAHINI

Makes about 4 cups

- 3 ½ cups cooked garbanzo beans (two 15 ½-ounce cans)
- 1 ½ cups tahini paste (15 ounces)
- 1 garlic clove, mashed (or from garlic oil, p. 18)
- juice of 2 to 3 lemons
- 1 ½ teaspoons salt, or to taste
- ½ teaspoon black pepper, or to taste
- ¼ cup olive oil
- ¼ cup hot water (or more if needed)

WHEN NO ONE IS LOOKING
Prepare this several days to a week ahead; keep covered and refrigerated.

FROZEN POWER
This freezes beautifully. Divide it into portions and store in plastic cartons that can be tightly sealed.

Place tahini paste in a food processor and process until it is puréed and has a smooth consistency. Place the tahini in a large bowl, then purée the garbanzo beans in the food processor with the garlic, lemon juice, salt, pepper, olive oil, and hot water. Add this mixture to the puréed tahini. Mix by hand until well combined. Taste for seasoning, and if mixture is too stiff, add a little more water or oil. Serve at room temperature with sesame crackers or pita bread.

ENDIVE WITH BLUE CHEESE, PINE NUTS, AND GRAPES

Belgian endive
"Blue Cheese Mix" (p. 37)
pine nuts, lightly toasted
seedless grapes

WHEN NO ONE IS LOOKING
Prepare the blue cheese mix 1 week ahead; cover and keep refrigerated. Toast the pine nuts several days ahead. Arrange the appetizers several hours ahead, cover and refrigerate until time to serve.

FROZEN POWER
Freeze the blue cheese mix as directed. Defrost overnight in the refrigerator or for several hours at room temperature. Toast and freeze pine nuts.

Separate endive into leaves. Place a small spoonful of the "Blue Cheese Mix" in the center portion and spread. Top with a few grapes and a few of the pine nuts. Cover loosely with plastic and refrigerate until time to serve.

SOUPS

TORTILLA SOUP

Makes about 4 servings

for the soup:
4 ripe tomatoes, peeled and chopped (or use canned)
1 (8-ounce) can tomato sauce
4 ounces diced green chiles (canned)
2 teaspoons garlic oil (p. 18)
½ teaspoon dried oregano
1 teaspoon chili powder (or more)
1 teaspoon ground cumin (or to taste)
1 quart rich, strong chicken broth
salt to taste

for the garnishes:
fried tortilla strips
avocado cubes
shredded Jack cheese
strips of cooked chicken

WHEN NO ONE IS LOOKING
Prepare the soup and garnishes 1 day ahead. Cover and refrigerate them separately. Reheat soup and serve as directed.

FROZEN POWER
This soup freezes perfectly. Defrost, reheat, and taste for seasoning (might need a trifle more); then serve as directed.

Combine soup ingredients in a large pot and bring to a boil. Turn heat down and simmer uncovered for 20 to 30 minutes. Taste for seasoning. Serve hot and pass the garnishes separately.

FRESH TOMATO SOUP, COLD OR HOT

Makes 2 to 4 servings

for the soup:
2 pounds fresh, ripe tomatoes
1 or 2 tablespoons chopped shallots (or use frozen shallots, p. 18)
2 tablespoons olive oil
2 tablespoons brown sugar
¼ cup chopped fresh basil
salt and pepper to taste
1 or 2 tablespoons mayonnaise

for the garnishes:
1 tomato, peeled, seeded, and chopped
2 tablespoons chopped fresh basil
4 tablespoons finely chopped celery
4 tablespoons finely chopped sweet pepper (red, green, or yellow)
⅓ cup sliced almonds, toasted

WHEN NO ONE IS LOOKING
Prepare this up to 2 days ahead. Keep covered and refrigerated.

FROZEN POWER
This freezes beautifully.

Remove stems from the tomatoes, quarter them, and place in a large pot. Add the chopped shallots, olive oil, brown sugar, chopped basil, salt, and pepper. Bring to a boil and cook only until tomatoes are soft. Put the entire mixture through a food mill, which will remove the tomato skins and seeds. Return sieved mixture to the pot, and then whisk in the mayonnaise over low heat. Taste for seasoning. Chill until time to serve. Serve soup by placing the garnishes on top of each bowl of soup, or pass them separately. If you plan to serve the soup hot, reheat gently, then serve in warm bowls.

FRESH TOMATO SOUP, MORE AND EASIER

Makes 6 to 12 servings

- about 6 pounds of fresh, ripe tomatoes, stems removed, then quartered
- 2 very large onions, coarsely chopped
- about ¾ cup fresh basil (leaves only, no stems)
- about ½ cup fresh oregano (leaves only, no stems)
- ¼ cup brown sugar (pack to measure)
- 3 tablespoons olive oil
- salt and pepper to taste
- ¼ cup mayonnaise

WHEN NO ONE IS LOOKING
Prepare this up to 2 days ahead; keep covered and refrigerated. If you serve the soup hot, reheat it gently.

FROZEN POWER
This soup freezes magnificently.

Place all ingredients, *except* mayonnaise in a large pot—stainless steel if possible. Bring to a boil and cook over medium heat until tomatoes and onions are very soft. Put mixture through a food mill (to remove tomato skins and seeds), then return to the pot. Taste for seasoning and add more salt, pepper, and sugar if needed. Whisk in the mayonnaise and simmer for 1 or 2 minutes. Serve hot or cold.

FRESH CURRIED CARROT SOUP

Makes 4 to 6 servings

¾ pound fresh carrots (weigh after peeling)
1 large onion, coarsely chopped
2 tablespoons oil
4 to 5 cups rich chicken broth
1 teaspoon curry powder
½ teaspoon nutmeg
salt and pepper to taste

WHEN NO ONE IS LOOKING
Prepare this 1 or 2 days ahead; keep covered and refrigerated. Reheat gently before serving.

FROZEN POWER
Yes, freeze this soup.

Cook carrots in boiling water until tender, then drain. While carrots are cooking, sauté the onion in the oil until tender. Combine onion with the carrots and place in a food processor. Add some of the chicken broth and process until puréed. Place puréed mixture in a saucepan, add remaining broth, curry powder, nutmeg, salt, and pepper. Bring to a boil, reduce heat, and simmer for about 2 minutes. Serve hot.

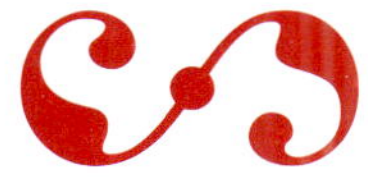

VERY EASY CHICKEN SOUP

Makes 4 to 8 servings

6 cups water
1 onion, thickly sliced
5 or 6 celery stalks, sliced
2 or 3 large boiling carrots, peeled and sliced
½ jar of Spice Islands chicken stock concentrate
salt and pepper to taste (add later)
6 to 8 chicken pieces—breasts and thighs, excess fat removed

WHEN NO ONE IS LOOKING
Prepare this soup 1 to 2 days ahead. Cool it rapidly, then cover and keep refrigerated.

FROZEN POWER
Yes, this chicken soup freezes.

Place water in a large pot with the onion, celery, carrots, and chicken concentrate. Cover and bring to a boil, then cook over moderate heat for 30 minutes. Add the chicken thighs first, cover and cook for 10 minutes; then add the chicken breasts, cover and cook about 15 minutes longer. Taste for seasoning because the chicken stock concentrate contains salt. Add salt and pepper, if needed. If possible, chill overnight, then remove all fat.

Note: Of course you can make your own delicious chicken stock base by cooking the bony parts of chicken, such as wings and backs, with vegetables, salt, and pepper for 1 or 2 hours. Chill, remove fat, reheat, and strain.

MATZO BALLS MY WAY

You will need a small or medium-size ice cream scoop!

for 12 small or 8 medium-size matzo balls:
3 tablespoons melted butter or oil
3 eggs, slightly beaten
¾ cup matzo meal
1 ¼ teaspoons salt
4 tablespoons stock

for 16 small or 12 medium-size matzo balls:
4 tablespoons melted butter or oil
4 eggs, slightly beaten
1 cup matzo meal
1 ½ teaspoons salt
5 or 6 tablespoons stock

WHEN NO ONE IS LOOKING
Prepare these 1 day ahead and place them in the chicken soup. Cover and refrigerate. Reheat gently before serving.

FROZEN POWER
These freeze well in your chicken soup. Defrost, then reheat gently.

Mix butter or oil with the eggs. Stir in the matzo meal and salt. Gradually stir in the stock. Cover and chill at least 30 minutes. Bring a large quantity of salted water to boil, then use a tiny ice cream scoop to form small balls or a medium-size scoop to form large ones (keep in mind that they expand); using the scoop will give you light, fluffly matzo balls. Drop the matzo balls into the boiling water. Turn down the heat so water simmers lightly. Cover and cook gently for 35 to 40 minutes. Remove balls to warm or hot chicken soup in a large pot and set aside. When ready to serve, simmer very gently for 4 to 5 minutes.

MANHATTAN CLAM CHOWDER

Makes 8 to 10 servings

- ¼ pound butter (1 stick)
- 4 onions, chopped
- 1 sweet green pepper, chopped
- 1 stalk celery, chopped
- 1 large can (46 ounces) tomato juice
- 1 large can (28 ounces) peeled tomatoes
- 3 small potatoes, peeled and cubed
- 2 (7-ounce) cans chopped clams
- 2 (7-ounce) cans minced clams
- 3 cups water
- 2 bay leaves
- 1 teaspoon thyme
- 1 teaspoon caraway seed (optional)
- salt and pepper to taste

WHEN NO ONE IS LOOKING
Prepare this 2 to 3 days ahead; keep covered and refrigerated. Reheat gently so as not to toughen the clams.

FROZEN POWER
This freezes well. Defrost, then reheat gently so as not to toughen the clams.

Drain the clams, retaining their liquid, and set clams and liquid aside separately. Sauté the onions, celery, and green pepper in the butter until lightly browned. Add all ingredients including the clam liquid but *not* the reserved clams. Simmer for about 2 hours, then add the clams, taste for seasoning, and simmer a few minutes.

GARBURE

Makes 6 to 10 servings

1 cup dried lima beans, soaked overnight in 3 cups water
3-pound piece of smoked ham
3 boiling potatoes, peeled and diced
4 quarts water
1 garlic clove, mashed (or from garlic oil, p. 18)
2 onions, chopped
4 large carrots, peeled and chopped
4 celery stalks, chopped
½ large cabbage, coarsely shredded
¼ teaspoon thyme
½ teaspoon each basil and oregano
salt and pepper to taste

WHEN NO ONE IS LOOKING
Prepare the soup 1 day ahead. Cover and refrigerate. Reheat soup and serve as directed.

FROZEN POWER
This soup freezes perfectly. Defrost, reheat, and taste for seasoning (might need a trifle more); then serve as directed.

Combine all ingredients and bring to a boil. Cover, turn down heat, and simmer for 2 hours. Remove cover and simmer another hour. Taste for seasoning. Remove ham, dice meat, then return it to the soup.

CABBAGE BORSCHT—SWEET AND SOUR STYLE

Makes 6 to 10 servings

4 pounds beef brisket, or a chuck blade roast
3 quarts water
3 onions, coarsely chopped
3 cups canned tomatoes
1 (8-ounce) can tomato sauce
½ cup lemon juice
½ cup brown sugar (packed to measure)
1 large firm cabbage, shredded or coarsely cut
salt and pepper to taste

WHEN NO ONE IS LOOKING
The beef is much easier to trim and dice after it has been chilled, so this is better if made 1 or 2 days ahead and kept covered and refrigerated.

FROZEN POWER
This freezes well.

Remove excess fat from the meat. Place meat in a large pot and cover with the water. Bring to a boil, add the onions, tomatoes, tomato sauce, and a little salt and pepper. Cover and cook slowly until beef begins to get tender but is not completely cooked (about 1½ hours). Add remaining ingredients and simmer uncovered for another hour or until meat is tender. Taste and adjust salt, pepper, lemon juice, and sugar. Remove the meat, trim and dice it, then return diced meat to the soup. Serve hot.

MARIANNE BIRNBAUM'S COLD DILL PICKLE SOUP

Makes 6 to 8 servings

1 (22–24 ounce) jar of halved or quartered dill pickles
4 cups water
3 tablespoons dill weed (dried)
1 (10 ½-ounce) can condensed chicken broth
juice of 1 lemon
1 ½ cups mayonnaise
salt and pepper to taste (go easy because pickles are salty)
2 hard-boiled eggs, sliced

WHEN NO ONE IS LOOKING
This is best prepared a day ahead.

FROZEN POWER
Mayonnaise separates when frozen, so this should definitely *not* be frozen.

Remove pickles from the jar and rinse them once lightly. Drain. Separate them into two stacks. Place one stack in a food processor with 2 cups of the water and process until finely chopped. Remove, then repeat with remaining pickles and water. Place in a large bowl and add the dill weed, chicken broth, lemon juice, mayonnaise, salt, and pepper. Return to the food processor and process until completely blended. Chill, overnight if possible. Serve with sliced hard-boiled eggs in each bowl—about 2 slices per serving.

RUTH MELLINKOFF'S VEGETABLE SOUP

Makes about 8 quarts

8 cups chicken or beef stock
2 large cans tomatoes
(1 pound, 12 ounce size)
total of 6 cups
3 large onions, chopped
4 large carrots, peeled and
diced
4 boiling potatoes, peeled
and diced
3 cups chopped celery
4 cloves garlic, mashed
(or from garlic oil, p. 18)
1 very large cabbage,
shredded or cut
salt and pepper to taste
2 teaspoons sugar
1 cup or more diced smoked
turkey (or cooked chicken)
1 cup diced beef salami
(optional)

WHEN NO ONE IS LOOKING
Prepare the soup up to 3 days ahead; cover and keep refrigerated.

FROZEN POWER
Divide the soup into the size portions you desire, place each portion in a plastic carton with a tight-fitting lid, and freeze.

Place the stock in a large cooking pot, then add the juice from the canned tomatoes. Mash the tomatoes either in a food processor or with a fork and add them to the pot. Bring mixture to a boil, then add the onions, carrots, potatoes, celery, garlic, and cabbage. Add salt, pepper, and sugar, then cover and bring to a boil. Reduce heat to a gentle boil and simmer for 1½ to 2 hours, tasting occasionally for seasoning, and adding more as needed. Add the diced turkey and salami, then heat gently for a few minutes.

ELAINE'S SOUP AU PISTOU

Makes about 6 quarts

1 pound small white dry beans
1 large onion, chopped
salt and pepper
1 cup chopped celery
2 leeks, white tops only, sliced
¾ pound green beans, cut in 1-inch pieces
2 boiling potatoes, peeled and diced
3 small- to medium-size zucchini
2 large carrots, peeled and diced
2 ripe tomatoes, mashed (or substitute canned)
½ pound thin spaghetti broken into 2-inch pieces
1 cup "Pesto" (p. 28)

WHEN NO ONE IS LOOKING
Prepare this soup 1 or 2 days ahead; keep covered and refrigerated.

FROZEN POWER
Yes, this soup freezes beautifully (as does the pesto).

Rinse and pick over the white beans. Soak beans in 8 cups of water overnight. Or do a quick soak: cover the beans with water, bring to a boil, turn off heat, then let them stand for 1 hour. Place soaked beans in a large pot and add about 4 to 6 more cups of water, the chopped onion, and some salt and pepper. Cover and cook for 1 to 1½ hours—until beans are tender. Add the celery, leeks, green beans, potatoes, zucchini, carrots, and tomatoes. Cook for about 30 to 45 minutes. Add the broken spaghetti pieces and cook 12 additional minutes. Taste for seasoning. Stir in the pesto over low heat and keep warm.

FISH AND SHELLFISH

POACHED SHRIMP FOR SHRIMP COCKTAIL—ONE VERSION

Makes 4 servings

1 pound large raw (green) shrimp (16 to 20 per pound), in the shell
2 teaspoons salt
2 ½ cups water
1 cup dry white wine
5 whole peppercorns
1 or 2 sprigs fresh basil
1 sprig fresh oregano
¼ teaspoon dried thyme
juice of half a lemon

WHEN NO ONE IS LOOKING
Poach the shrimp 1 day ahead; keep them covered and refrigerated.

Peel, devein, and rinse shrimp, but *save the shells.* Put shells, water, and salt in a saucepan and bring to a boil; then reduce heat to low, cover, and simmer 15 to 20 minutes. Strain shrimp through a sieve reserving the stock. Place stock in a saucepan with the white wine, peppercorns, basil, oregano, thyme, and lemon juice. Bring to a boil and continue to boil for 2 minutes. Turn off the heat, then stir in shrimp. Cover and let stand until pink and firm—about 4 minutes. Immediately drain and cool. Chill. Serve with "Red Cocktail Sauce" (see below).

RED COCKTAIL SAUCE

Makes 1 ¼ cups

1 ¼ cups ketchup
⅓ cup prepared horseradish (or to taste)
juice of half a lemon
1 teaspoon Worcestershire sauce
few drops of Tabasco sauce

WHEN NO ONE IS LOOKING
Prepare this sauce up to one week ahead; keep it covered and refrigerated.

Combine ingredients, stir, and refrigerate.

POACHED SHRIMP, ANOTHER VERSION

Makes 4 to 8 servings

1 ½ pounds of large raw (green) shrimp (16 to 20 per pound), in the shell

for the broth:
7 cups water
1 small onion, quartered
1 tablespoon salt
3 sprigs fresh basil
2 sprigs fresh oregano
2 sprigs fresh thyme
1 sprig fresh rosemary
juice of 1 lemon
2 tablespoons white wine vinegar

WHEN NO ONE IS LOOKING
Prepare the broth up to 2 days ahead; keep covered and refrigerated. You may cook the shrimp 1 day ahead; keep them covered and refrigerated.

Combine ingredients for the broth in a large cooking pot and bring to a boil. Reduce heat, cover, and simmer for 30 minutes. Put shrimp in the pot, bring to a boil, then immediately turn off the heat but keep covered. Let the shrimp stand covered until pink and firm—2 to 3 minutes. Drain thoroughly, cool briefly, then remove shells and devein. Cover and refrigerate. Serve with "Red Cocktail Sauce" (p. 74) or "Dill Sauce" (p. 240).

A THIRD VERSION—FOR PERFECTO SHRIMP

Makes 4 servings

1 pound large raw (green) shrimp (16 to 20 per pound), in the shell

for the brine:
1 ½ quarts water
¼ cup kosher or sea salt
1 large onion, coarsely sliced
3 celery stalks, coarsely chopped
1 teaspoon cayenne pepper
juice of ½ large lemon
½ cup cider vinegar
1 tablespoon balsamic vinegar
1 or 2 garlic cloves, mashed (or from garlic oil, p. 18)
½ teaspoon Worcestershire sauce
1 teaspoon dried thyme
1 teaspoon dried sweet basil
½ teaspoon dried tarragon
2 bay leaves
melted butter for serving

WHEN NO ONE IS LOOKING
Prepare the brine 2 days ahead; strain it, and keep it covered and refrigerated. Bring to a boil before adding the shrimp, then proceed as directed.

Clean the shrimp: Most large shrimp come frozen. Unless you can locate large fresh ones, first defrost the shrimp, then rinse them in cold water. Do *not* remove the shells, but cut them open on their backs using kitchen scissors and remove the veins. Drain and refrigerate until time to cook.

Prepare the brine: Combine brine ingredients in a large pot, cover, and bring to a boil, then lower heat and simmer for 30 to 40 minutes. Strain brine into another pot and discard the onions, etc. Set aside.

Cook and serve: Bring the prepared brine to a boil, then add the cleaned shrimp and cook for 1 to 3 minutes on moderate heat—only until shrimp have turned a bright pink. Remove from heat, strain, and serve the shrimp hot or at room temperature. Let the guests help themselves. Serve with melted butter for dipping and with other sauces if desired. Provide plenty of paper napkins!

BARBECUED SHRIMP TERIYAKI

Makes 4 servings as a main course, 6 to 8 as an appetizer

2 pounds extra large raw (green) shrimp in the shell
1 onion, sliced
1 piece ginger (about 2 inches), peeled and sliced
1 clove garlic, mashed (or from garlic oil, p. 18)
¼ cup soy sauce
juice of 1 lemon
⅓ cup red wine vinegar
½ teaspoon salt
¼ teaspoon black pepper
1 tablespoon sugar
1 ½ cups vegetable oil (not olive)

WHEN NO ONE IS LOOKING
Prepare marinade 2 or 3 days ahead; cover it and keep refrigerated. Add the shrimp to the marinade several hours before placing them on skewers. And to save time, skewer them a few hours before cooking and leave them at room temperature.

Shell and devein shrimp. Combine remaining ingredients to make a marinade, and marinate shrimp for 2 to 3 hours. Drain shrimp and skewer them on metal or bamboo skewers, 3 or 4 on each. If using bamboo skewers, soak the skewers in water for several hours before grilling to avoid burning. Grill skewered shrimp for 1 ½ to 2 minutes on each side.

SHRIMP THERMIDOR

Makes 4 servings

for the sauce:
2 tablespoons butter
4 teaspoons flour
½ cup rich chicken stock
1 egg yolk
2 tablespoons milk
⅛ teaspoon cayenne pepper
1 tablespoon lemon juice
salt and pepper to taste

for the shrimp:
1 pound medium-size raw (green) shrimp, peeled and deveined
2 tablespoons butter
2 tablespoons olive oil
3 tablespoons cognac or California brandy
1 tablespoon grated Parmesan cheese

WHEN NO ONE IS LOOKING
Prepare the sauce in the morning or 1 day before. Keep covered and refrigerated until an hour or so before finishing. Then, reheat sauce gently, whisking to prevent curdling or lumps forming. Then proceed as directed.

Prepare the sauce first. Melt butter, then stir in the flour and cook over moderate heat, stirring constantly for 1 to 2 minutes. Remove from heat, then stir in the chicken stock. Return to heat and bring to a boil, stirring constantly. Reduce heat and simmer for 1 to 2 minutes. Whisk the egg yolk and milk together in a bowl, then whisk in the hot mixture. Return to the saucepan and cook, stirring, for 2 minutes. Season with cayenne, lemon juice, salt, and pepper.

Dry the peeled shrimps well on paper towels. Heat butter and oil in a large skillet over high heat. Add shrimp and cook rapidly only until they are pink—1 to 2 minutes. Remove from heat, add cognac or brandy, and stir well. Remove shrimp with a slotted spoon to a casserole large enough to hold them in a single layer. Add any remaining juices to the prepared sauce, then spoon sauce over the shrimp and sprinkle with the grated Parmesan. Place in a preheated 350° oven and bake only long enough to heat.

SHRIMPS EXTRAORDINAIRE

Makes about 4 servings

- 1 pound extra large raw (green) shrimp, peeled and deveined
- 2 tablespoons butter
- salt and black pepper to taste
- 2 teaspoons Worcestershire sauce
- 2 teaspoons garlic oil (p. 18)
- 2 green onions, finely chopped

for finishing:

- 2 tablespoons dry bread crumbs
- 3 tablespoons grated Parmesan cheese
- 2 ounces butter (½ stick), melted

WHEN NO ONE IS LOOKING
Prepare Parmesan-crumb mixture in the morning; cover and leave at room temperature. Sauté shrimp several hours ahead. Cover and leave at room temperature. Finish the final baking shortly before serving.

In a large skillet heat the 2 tablespoons butter. Add shrimp and toss over high heat for 1 minute. Do *not* overcook because they will cook more later. Remove from heat and add the salt, pepper, Worcestershire sauce, garlic oil, and chopped green onions. Toss to combine, then set aside. Mix bread crumbs and grated Parmesan together. Preheat oven to 450°. Place shrimp and any juices in a nonstick baking pan in a single layer. Sprinkle each shrimp with the Parmesan-crumb mixture, then spoon melted butter over each. Place shrimp in the preheated oven for 2 to 4 minutes—then remove and serve.

SHRIMP BAKED WITH LEMON

Makes 3 to 4 servings

1 pound large raw (green) shrimp (16 to 20 per pound), peeled and deveined
4 ounces butter (1 stick)
1 teaspoon salt (about)
1 teaspoon mashed garlic (or from garlic oil, p. 18)
zest of 1 lemon
juice of half a lemon
¼ cup chopped parsley

WHEN NO ONE IS LOOKING
Prepare the garlic-butter mixture and the lemon-butter mixture 1 day ahead; keep refrigerated until time to use, then reheat gently to thin them. Peel and devein the shrimp in the morning; keep covered and refrigerated until time to bake.

Place shrimp in a single layer in an ovenproof baking dish or pan. Sprinkle with salt. Combine half the melted butter with the garlic and spoon over the shrimp. Combine remaining butter with the lemon zest, lemon juice, and parsley, then set aside. Bake shrimp in a preheated 450° oven for 4 to 5 minutes. Remove from oven and spoon lemon mixture over the shrimp. Return to oven for 2 to 4 minutes and serve hot. (If shrimp are cold when you place them in the oven, they may need more time.)

SHRIMP GREEK STYLE

Makes 4 servings

- 1 ½ pounds large raw (green) shrimp
- 1 large onion, chopped
- 2 garlic cloves, mashed (or from garlic oil, p. 18)
- ¼ cup olive oil
- 1 (16-ounce) can tomato purée
- 1 teaspoon salt (or to taste)
- ½ teaspoon pepper
- ½ teaspoon sweet basil
- ½ teaspoon oregano
- 4 ounces Feta cheese

WHEN NO ONE IS LOOKING
Prepare the sauce up to 3 days ahead; keep covered and refrigerated. Or, assemble the casserole in the morning of your party, and keep it refrigerated until 2 hours before baking.

FROZEN POWER
Freeze the sauce!

Sauté the garlic and onion in the olive oil for several minutes, then add tomato purée, salt, pepper, sweet basil, and oregano. Simmer for about 30 minutes, part of the time uncovered.

Devein the shrimp, but if desired, you may leave them in their shells. Place a large spoonful of the tomato sauce in the bottom of a casserole. Place shrimp on the sauce; cover with remaining sauce and crumble feta cheese on top. Bake uncovered in a preheated 350° oven for 25 to 35 minutes—until very hot but not overcooked. Shrimp should cook in that time unless they are very cold.

SHRIMP AS SCAMPI

Makes 4 to 6 servings as a main course, 8 to 12 as an appetizer

24 extra large raw (green) shrimp, in the shell
salt and pepper
½ cup melted butter or olive oil
2 cloves of garlic, mashed (or from garlic oil, p. 18)
¼ cup lemon juice
⅓ cup Madeira or sherry
chopped parsley

WHEN NO ONE IS LOOKING
Prepare both the sauce and shrimp in the morning, but do not combine them. Refrigerate separately until about 2 hours before time to cook, then proceed with the recipe.

Use kitchen scissors to devein shrimp by cutting through the shells on their backs, but do *not* remove the shells. Butterfly the shrimp by cutting through each downward from the deveined part and toward the shell but not through it. Flatten and place the shrimp shell sides down in a single layer in a large shallow baking pan (they can overlap slightly). Season with salt and pepper. Combine remaining ingredients except parsley and spoon over the shrimp. Bake in a preheated 500° oven for 5 to 10 minutes (depending on how cold the shrimp are when you place them in the oven). Sprinkle with parsley and spoon remaining juices over the baked shrimp.

BOUILLABAISSE

Makes 8 to 10 servings

6 cups "Fish Stock" (p. 84)
3 large onions, chopped
2 carrots, chopped
2 sweet peppers (green or red), chopped
2 celery stalks, chopped
2 cloves garlic, mashed (or from garlic oil, p. 18)
½ cup olive oil
½ teaspoon thyme
2 bay leaves
1 can (1 pound 12 ounces) tomatoes (mash the tomatoes)
1 cup dry white wine
2 teaspoons sugar
salt, black pepper, and hot pepper flakes, to taste
1 teaspoon saffron
grated rind of 1 orange
3 pounds sea bass (or comparable fish), cut into chunks
3 pounds fresh clams, washed in cold water and brushed clean
2 ½ pounds large raw (green) shrimp, peeled and deveined

WHEN NO ONE IS LOOKING
Prepare the fish stock 1 day ahead; keep covered and refrigerated. Or prepare the whole "base" 1 day ahead and keep covered and refrigerated.

FROZEN POWER
Freeze the fish stock, or complete the "base" and freeze it.

Make the "base": In a large cooking pot sauté the onions, carrots, peppers, celery, and garlic in the olive oil, stirring frequently, until lightly browned. Add the thyme, bay leaves, tomatoes, fish stock, white wine, sugar, and some salt, pepper, and hot pepper flakes. Bring to a boil, reduce heat, and simmer, uncovered, 1 ½ hours. Mix 2 tablespoons of the stock with the saffron, then add it with the orange rind to the pot. Taste for seasoning. Remove bay leaves.

Shortly before serving bring the "base" to a boil. Add the sea bass and immediately reduce the heat; cook for 2 or 3 minutes over low heat. Add clams, cover and cook over low heat until they begin to open. Add shrimp and cook over lowest heat only until shrimp turn pink.

FISH STOCK

Makes 1½ to 2 quarts

- 6 pounds of non-oily fish bones
- 1 cup dry white wine
- ⅔ cup dry vermouth
- ½ cup dry sherry
- 2 large onions, sliced
- ¼ cup lemon juice
- 2 to 3 teaspoons salt

WHEN NO ONE IS LOOKING
Prepare the stock 1 or 2 days ahead. Keep covered and refrigerated.

FROZEN POWER
Freeze this stock to use later in delicious concoctions such as bouillabaisse.

Rinse fish bones in cold water. Put all ingredients into a large cooking pot. Add only enough water to barely cover the fish bones. Bring to a boil, then reduce heat, cover and simmer for 15 minutes. Uncover, stir well, breaking up the bones. Cover again and simmer for another 15 minutes. Remove from heat, cover a sieve with a double or triple layer of cheesecloth and strain. Cool, then cover and refrigerate.

CLAM, SCALLOP, AND SHRIMP STEW

Makes 6 to 10 servings

- ¼ cup chopped shallots (or use frozen shallots, p. 18)
- 2 large onions, chopped
- ½ cup oil
- 5 pounds fresh tomatoes, peeled or substitute canned
- ½ cup fresh basil leaves
- 32 ounces clam juice (bottled)
- ¾ teaspoon thyme
- 1 ½ tablespoons sugar
- salt and pepper to taste
- 2 to 3 pounds boiling potatoes, peeled and thinly sliced
- 4 pounds small clams, soaked in cold water and scrubbed
- 1 pound large sea scallops, thickly sliced
- 1 pound medium or large shrimp, peeled and deveined

WHEN NO ONE IS LOOKING
Prepare the "base" one day ahead; keep covered and refrigerated. Shortly before serving heat the "base" and proceed as directed.

FROZEN POWER
Freeze the "base," then when needed, defrost it and proceed as directed.

Sauté the onions and shallots in the oil. Process tomatoes with the fresh basil in a food processor, then add to the onions and shallots. Add clam juice and bring to a boil. Reduce heat and simmer uncovered for 30 minutes, then add the thyme, sugar, salt, pepper and simmer again for another 30 minutes. Add potatoes and continue to simmer, mostly uncovered, or partially covered, for an hour or so. Taste for seasoning and set aside until needed. This is the "base."

Shortly before serving bring the "base" to a boil, reduce heat to simmer and add the clams. Cover and simmer gently for 4 or 5 minutes, or until a few begin to open. Add sliced scallops and shrimp, cover, and cook over lowest heat for 2 to 3 minutes. Then immediately turn off the heat and serve in heated bowls.

CRAB, SHRIMP, AND OYSTER GUMBO

Makes 6 to 8 servings

2 pounds baby okra, or 2 (10-ounce) packages frozen baby okra
¼ pound butter (1 stick)
2 large onions, chopped
2 tablespoons flour
3 cups canned tomatoes, including liquid
5 cups rich chicken broth
salt and pepper to taste
dash cayenne pepper
2 pounds raw (green) shrimp, peeled and deveined
1 ½ pints oysters
2 whole cooked crabs, each 1 ½ to 2 pounds, well cracked

WHEN NO ONE IS LOOKING
Prepare the sauce for the gumbo 2 days ahead; keep covered and refrigerated. To serve, heat sauce, then add seafood as directed in the recipe.

FROZEN POWER
The sauce for the gumbo freezes beautifully; defrost, heat, then add seafood as instructed.

Keep seafood refrigerated until needed. Chop or slice the okra, then sauté in 6 tablespoons of the butter in a heavy skillet, cooking and stirring over moderate heat until all white okra strings have completely disappeared. This will take at least 15 to 20 minutes. Remove okra from skillet. Add remaining butter to skillet and sauté the onions until well browned. Sprinkle with the flour, stir, then add tomatoes and cook, stirring constantly, until mixture comes to a boil. Add chicken broth and okra, season, cover, and simmer for 2 to 3 hours, stirring occasionally. Taste for seasoning. Gumbo should be peppery.

Before serving, bring sauce to a simmer and add the raw shrimp. Cook 1 to 2 minutes. Add oysters and cook another minute. Add cracked crab and cook only until mixture reaches a gentle simmer. Do not overcook or seafood will toughen. If it is necessary to reheat, do it on the lowest heat possible. Serve gumbo in large heated soup bowls, with or without a spoonful of cooked rice.

CRAB CAKES MY WAY

Makes 4 or 5 servings

> **WHEN NO ONE IS LOOKING**
> Prepare crab mixture in the morning; keep covered and refrigerated until time to cook.

- 7 to 8 ounces crabmeat
- 4 or 5 green onions, finely chopped
- ½ of a sweet red pepper, finely chopped
- 1 or 2 jalapeños, finely chopped
- 1 teaspoon salt (or to taste)
- ¼ teaspoon black pepper (or to taste)
- 1 teaspoon Worcestershire sauce
- 1 teaspoon ancho chile powder
- ½ teaspoon Old Bay seasoning (optional)
- 1 egg
- ¼ cup mayonnaise
- 2 ½ tablespoons dry bread crumbs
- 2 tablespoons olive oil

Combine all ingredients (except olive oil) in a bowl and mix thoroughly. Cover and chill until ready to cook. When almost ready to serve, heat olive oil in a nonstick skillet and place 4 or 5 large spoonfuls in the pan and pat them down a little. Sauté over moderately high heat for 2 to 3 minutes on each side—until well browned.

CRABMEAT EGG FOO YUNG

Makes 4 servings

½ onion, finely chopped
3 tablespoons vegetable oil
½ of a sweet green pepper, finely chopped
½ cup sliced fresh mushrooms
1 tablespoon freshly chopped ginger
1 cup fresh bean sprouts
6 to 7 ounces crabmeat
salt and pepper to taste
6 eggs
oil for sautéing

for the sauce:
1 ½ cups beef stock or canned bouillon
2 tablespoons soy sauce
1 tablespoon cornstarch dissolved in ¼ cup cold water

WHEN NO ONE IS LOOKING
Prepare vegetable-crabmeat-egg mixture in the morning; keep covered and refrigerated until ready to cook.

Make the sauce: Heat the bouillon, soy sauce, and dissolved cornstarch in a saucepan, stirring until mixture boils. Set aside and rewarm before serving.

Sauté the chopped onion in the 3 tablespoons of oil over high heat quickly, then add the chopped pepper, mushrooms, ginger, and bean sprouts. Stir-fry over high heat for 1 minute. Stir in the crabmeat, salt, and pepper, and remove from heat. Spoon into a large bowl and cool to room temperature. Beat eggs and add them to the vegetable-crabmeat mixture.

Heat additional oil in a large skillet. Add the vegetable-crabmeat-egg mixture and cook over medium heat until eggs are firm and brown underneath. Divide into desired portions and turn them over to brown the other sides. Remove to a warm platter and pour rewarmed sauce over them.

PARMESAN-CRUSTED BAKED SALMON

Makes 4 to 6 servings

- 2-pound fresh salmon filet (or two smaller ones)
- salt and pepper
- 2 tablespoons Dijon-style mustard
- 5 tablespoons olive oil
- ⅔ cup fine bread crumbs
- 1 cup grated Parmesan cheese
- 1 teaspoon salt
- ½ teaspoon black pepper (or to taste)

WHEN NO ONE IS LOOKING
Prepare the salmon with the mustard and crumb coating in the morning and refrigerate uncovered. Remove from refrigerator 2 hours before baking to bring it to room temperature so that it will cook evenly.

Preheat oven to 450°. Season the salmon with salt and pepper. Place mustard and olive oil in a bowl and whisk together until combined. In another bowl mix the bread crumbs, grated cheese, salt, and pepper together with a fork or a whisk. Place the salmon skin side down on a lightly oiled baking pan—preferably nonstick. Cover the top of the salmon (the skinless side) with the mustard mixture. Then top this with all of the crumb mixture, patting it down firmly. Bake in the preheated oven for 15 to 17 minutes.

Note: Four salmon steaks can be substituted in this recipe. Arrange them in a single layer, divide the Parmesan mixture among them, and proceed as directed.

FRESH SALMON AND POTATO CASSEROLE

Makes 4 to 6 servings

- 1 ½ pounds of fresh salmon filet
- 3 boiling potatoes (about 1 ½ pounds after peeling)
- salt and pepper
- 2 ounces butter (½ stick)
- 3 eggs
- 1 ½ cups milk.

WHEN NO ONE IS LOOKING
Assemble the casserole in the morning, refrigerate until 2 hours before baking, then proceed as directed. Or bake it 1 day ahead and reheat it, or serve it cold.

Slice salmon filet into ¼- to ½-inch thick slices. Slice potatoes thinly. Butter a casserole (I use a square one about 10 x 10 inches). Place half of the salmon slices in the bottom and season with salt and pepper. Cover with half the potato slices and season again. Top potatoes with remaining salmon slices and again season. Add the remaining potato slices, season and dot with the butter. Beat the eggs with the milk and pour over the salmon and potatoes. Place in a preheated 325° oven and bake about 1 hour.

GRILLED SALMON WITH GINGER AND SESAME

Makes 4 servings

- 4 fresh salmon steaks
- vegetable oil
- salt and pepper
- 4 tablespoons finely chopped fresh ginger
- 2 tablespoons soy sauce
- 2 tablespoons rice vinegar
- 2 green onions, chopped
- 2 teaspoons mashed garlic (or from garlic oil, p. 18)
- 2 tablespoons sesame seed oil

WHEN NO ONE IS LOOKING
Prepare the ginger-sesame mixture 1 or 2 days ahead; cover and refrigerate. Or, prepare the marinade in the morning; cover and leave at room temperature

Rub salmon steaks generously with vegetable oil, then season with salt and pepper. Combine remaining ingredients in a bowl and set aside. Grill salmon steaks on one side for about 3 minutes; turn them, then top each steak with some of the mixture and cook to desired doneness without turning. Serve hot with the remaining ginger-sesame sauce reheated to a simmer.

SALMON TERIYAKI

Makes 4 servings

4 fresh salmon steaks
grated rind and juice of
    2 oranges
1 cup soy sauce
4 tablespoons brown sugar
1 clove of garlic, mashed
    (or from garlic oil, p. 18)
1 or 2 tablespoons minced
    fresh ginger

WHEN NO ONE IS LOOKING
Prepare the marinade and strain it a day ahead; cover and refrigerate. Or, prepare the marinade in the morning; cover and leave at room temperature.

Combine the rind and juice of the oranges with the soy sauce, brown sugar, garlic, and ginger in a saucepan. Stir over moderate heat until sugar has dissolved and mixture begins to boil. Reduce heat and simmer for 5 minutes. Remove from heat, strain, and cool to room temperature.

About 1 ½ hours before cooking, marinate the salmon steaks in the strained marinade. Remove salmon from the marinade and bring the remaining sauce to a simmer. Either on a hot grill or under a very hot broiler, cook the salmon steaks for 3 to 4 minutes on each side. Pass the remaining simmered marinade.

FRESH SALMON STEAKS EN PAPILLOTE

Makes 4 servings

4 large (14 x 18-inch) pieces of nonstick parchment paper
6 ounces melted butter (1 ½ sticks)
4 large salmon steaks (¾" to 1" thick)
salt and pepper to taste
4 tablespoons chopped green onion
12 thin lemon slices
fresh dill sprigs

WHEN NO ONE IS LOOKING
A marvelous do-ahead for an elegant dinner entrée. Assemble the papillotes in the morning and refrigerate. Remove them from the refrigerator 2 hours before baking

Fold parchment papers in half, then cut them into a half-heart shapes. Open each and spoon 1 tablespoon of butter on one side of each heart. Season salmon with salt and pepper, then place salmon steaks on top of buttered sides of parchment hearts. Top each with chopped green onion, lemon slices, and dill sprigs. Spoon remaining butter—2 tablespoons each over salmon steak. Fold papers over and seal by folding edges together so that each fold covers another, ending with a tip that you can fasten with a metal paper clip. Place papillotes on baking pans (with sides) and refrigerate until 2 hours before baking. Place papillotes in a preheated 425° oven and bake for 12 minutes. Turn oven heat off and leave in the oven an additional 2 to 3 minutes. Do not overbake. Serve papillotes on large dinner plates and let guests open their own so they can savor the aroma. "Dill Sauce" (p. 240) is a fine sauce to pass separately.

SALMON IN A CHAMPAGNE SAUCE

Makes 6 servings

- 6 fresh salmon filets (each enough for 1 serving)
- salt and black pepper
- 1 cup champagne or dry white wine
- sprig of parsley
- 1 cup canned tomatoes, drained, the tomatoes chopped; freeze juice for another purpose
- ¾ pound fresh mushrooms, sliced
- 2 tablespoons butter
- 2 tablespoons flour
- ½ teaspoon freshly chopped tarragon (or ⅛ teaspoon dried)
- 1 cup heavy whipping cream

WHEN NO ONE IS LOOKING
Prepare the entire dish 1 day ahead, but do not do the final baking and be careful not to overcook the salmon. Pour sauce over the fish, cool, cover, and keep refrigerated. Finish final baking shortly before serving.

FROZEN POWER
Pour the sauce over this fish dish and freeze it; prepare to be surprised at how well it does. In principle it freezes well because the fish is covered with sauce. Defrost and finish final baking shortly before serving.

Preheat oven to 350°. Season salmon with salt and pepper, then place filets in an ovenproof pan—nonstick or glass, but *not* aluminum. Add the champagne (or white wine), parsley, chopped tomatoes, and sliced mushrooms. Cover with foil and bake for 20 minutes. Do not overcook. Remove from oven and lift salmon filets (using a spatula) into another baking dish large enough to hold them in a single layer. Scatter the mushrooms over the fish. Cook remaining juices until reduced to 1 cup, then strain.

Melt butter, stir in flour, then add the strained juices and cook, stirring constantly, until mixture comes to a boil. Add cream and simmer gently for 1 or 2 minutes, then pour over the fish. Increase oven heat to 375°. Bake fish only a few minutes—until hot and bubbly. Garnish with chopped parsley and serve hot.

SALMON STEAKS—AN EASY PARTY ENTRÉE

Makes 10 servings

10 fresh salmon steaks
salt and pepper
lemon juice
2 tablespoons butter
2 tablespoons flour
1 teaspoon salt
½ teaspoon pepper
2 cups sour cream
2 onions, sliced wafer thin
3 green peppers, sliced into thin rings

WHEN NO ONE IS LOOKING
Assemble this in the morning and refrigerate. Bring to room temperature about 2 hours before baking, then proceed as directed.

Season salmon steaks with salt, pepper, and lemon juice. Place them in a single layer in a very large ovenproof casserole or two small ones. Melt butter, stir in flour, and add salt and pepper. Add the sour cream and stir until mixture comes to a boil. Remove from heat.

Arrange the onion and green pepper rings over the salmon steaks. Spoon the prepared sauce over each. Cover with foil and bake in a preheated 425° oven for 10 minutes. Remove foil and bake 15 to 20 minutes longer.

BAKED TOMATOES STUFFED WITH FRESH SALMON

Makes 6 servings

- 1 pound fresh salmon (weight after boning)
- 4 tablespoons olive oil
- 1 teaspoon salt
- ½ teaspoon black pepper
- 2 to 3 tablespoons chopped fresh dill
- 1 teaspoon mashed garlic (or from garlic oil, p. 18)
- 2 tablespoons dry bread crumbs
- 6 medium to large fresh tomatoes
- salt and black pepper

WHEN NO ONE IS LOOKING
Prepare the salmon mixture in the morning; cover and keep refrigerated. Fill tomatoes and bake before serving. Or, prepare the whole thing several hours ahead, then either reheat briefly or serve at room temperature.

Preheat oven to 350°. Remove all skin and bones from the salmon, then cut the fish into ½-inch cubes. Place fish cubes in a bowl, add olive oil and mix gently. Add the salt, black pepper, dill, garlic, and mix again. Stir in the bread crumbs and set aside.

Cut off tops of tomatoes, then scoop out all the seeds and centers to make a hollow. Drain the hollowed tomatoes, then soak up excess juice with paper towels. Season centers lightly, then stuff with the salmon mixture. Place tomatoes on an oiled pan and bake in the preheated oven for 30 minutes. Serve hot or warm with "Dill Sauce" (p. 240) or "Russian Dressing" (p. 239).

SCALLOPS WITH TOMATOES AND GARLIC

Makes 4 to 6 servings

- 1 large onion, finely chopped
- 5 tablespoons olive oil
- 1 ½ pounds scallops
- salt and pepper
- flour
- 2 garlic cloves, mashed (or from garlic oil, p. 18)
- ⅔ cup dry white wine
- 2 cups chopped tomatoes (fresh or canned), but not too much liquid
- 4 tablespoons dry bread crumbs
- 2 tablespoons freshly chopped parsley

WHEN NO ONE IS LOOKING
Prepare the scallops up to the point of final heating 1 day before; keep covered and refrigerated. Bring to room temperature about 2 hours before serving, then proceed with the baking.

Preheat oven to 400°. Sauté onion for 2 or 3 minutes in 1 tablespoon of the olive oil. Remove from skillet. Season scallops with salt and pepper, then dust with flour, shaking off any excess. Sauté scallops in 2 tablespoons of olive oil over moderate heat until lightly browned. Do not overcook. Sprinkle with half the cooked onion, add the wine, cover, and simmer for only 30 seconds. Remove from heat and set aside.

In another skillet heat 2 more tablespoons olive oil to sizzling; add tomatoes and stir vigorously. Add remaining onions and the garlic, then reduce heat and simmer for 2 minutes. Place this tomato mixture in the bottom of a shallow ovenproof casserole. Cover with the scallops and sprinkle top with the bread crumbs and parsley. Bake uncovered in preheated oven for 7 to 10 minutes. Scallops should be very hot but not overcooked.

HERBED AND BAKED SCALLOPS

Makes 2 or 3 servings

- 1 pound small scallops, dried on paper towels
- ⅛ pound (½ stick) butter, melted
- ¼ cup oil
- ⅔ cup dry bread crumbs
- 1 teaspoon salt
- ½ teaspoon pepper
- 1 teaspoon sugar
- 1 tablespoon chopped fresh sweet basil, or 1 teaspoon dried
- 1 tablespoon chopped fresh dill

WHEN NO ONE IS LOOKING
Combine the crumb mixture several days ahead; keep tightly covered. Ready the scallops for baking in the morning. Cover and refrigerate until about 1 hour before baking, then proceed as directed.

Combine butter and oil in a bowl, then mix remaining ingredients, *except scallops,* together in another bowl to form the "crumb mixture." Dip scallops in the butter-oil mixture, then roll them in crumb mixture; finally, place them in a single layer on a foil-lined baking pan. Preheat oven to 425°, then bake for 12 to 15 minutes. Serve with lemon wedges and a sauce, such as "Remoulade" (p. 239), "Dill" (p. 240), or "Green Mayonnaise" (p. 241).

SEAFOOD SAUSAGES WITH A BUTTER SAUCE

Makes 8 to 10 servings as a first course

- ½ pound sole fillets, cut into 1-inch pieces
- ½ pound salmon fillet, cut into small dice
- ½ pound raw shrimp, shelled and cut into small dice
- 1 cup heavy cream
- 2 extra-large eggs
- 1 ½ teaspoons salt
- ¼ teaspoon white pepper

for the sauce :

- ½ cup dry white wine
- 1 tablespoons white wine vinegar
- 1 small onion, sliced
- ¼ teaspoon salt
- ½ pound butter (2 sticks), sliced

WHEN NO ONE IS LOOKING
Poach the sausages 1 day ahead. Rewrap in fresh foil, then keep covered and refrigerated. Reheat in very hot water, but do *not* cook. Sauce can be prepared a day ahead also. Reheat over low simmering water and whisk constantly; do *not* try to make it piping hot or it will separate.

Make the seafood sausages: In a food processor purée the sole. Add the cream, eggs, salt, pepper, and blend with the sole. Remove to a bowl, then stir in the diced salmon and shrimp. Test for seasoning by poaching a small spoonful in simmering water; taste and, if needed, add salt and pepper.

Divide the mixture on two 12-inch square sheets of Saran wrap (this brand works the best!), and form each into a log. Use the Saran wrap to roll the logs, then twist the ends of the wrap securely. Wrap each sausage again; this time securely in foil. Place "sausages" in a large kettle and cover with cold water. Set a lid or a plate over the sausages to weigh them down and keep them immersed. Cover the kettle with a regular lid and bring water to a barely simmering boil. *Do not fully boil; water should only shiver.* Cook for 20 minutes. Remove from heat and let sausages stay in water 10 to 20 minutes.

Remove sausages and unwrap carefully. Discard any accumulated liquid. Transfer them to an ovenproof, buttered shallow casserole; cover and keep warm in a 170° oven.

Make the sauce: Bring wine, vinegar, sliced onion, and salt to a boil and cook until only about 2 tablespoons of liquid remains. Strain, then return liquid to a saucepan. Whisk in the sliced butter.

If possible serve these seafood sausages on individual warmed plates. Place some sauce on each plate, then top with a slice of the sausage and coat with a little more sauce. If you do not want to arrange individual servings, just slice sausages in their casserole and coat with the sauce.

REX SOLE WITH TOMATOES AND GREEN CHILES

Makes 3 to 6 servings

6 small rex sole (about 2 pounds), or substitute filets of sole or red snapper
salt and pepper
3 tablespoons olive oil or melted butter
1 onion, coarsely chopped
1 (7-ounce) can green chiles, drained, then sliced
2 tomatoes, diced

WHEN NO ONE IS LOOKING
Prepare the onion, chile, tomato mixture 1 or 2 days ahead; keep covered and refrigerated. Bring to room temperature before using.

Season the fish and place in a single layer in a shallow roasting pan. Preheat oven to 400°. Sauté the chopped onions in the oil or butter until tender but not browned. Stir in the sliced chiles and diced tomatoes and season to taste, then cook for 2 or 3 minutes. Spoon this mixture over the fish, then place in the preheated oven uncovered and bake for approximately 12 minutes, or a few minutes longer if the fish is cold.

FILETS OF SOLE WITH MUSHROOMS

Makes 6 servings

12 medium-size filets of sole (about 2 pounds)
salt and black pepper
3 tablespoons melted butter
1 cup dry vermouth

for the sauce:
¼ pound fresh mushrooms, finely chopped
⅛ pound butter (½ stick)
3 tablespoons flour
2 cups liquid—use stock after poaching fish, plus milk
about ½ teaspoon salt
about ¼ teaspoon pepper
freshly chopped parsley

WHEN NO ONE IS LOOKING
Prepare this 1 day ahead; cover and refrigerate. Bring to room temperature before heating, then cover loosely with foil and reheat in a moderate oven until hot but not overcooked.

FROZEN POWER
This freezes well. Double-wrap it. To serve, defrost, then reheat in a moderate oven until hot but not overcooked.

Preheat oven to 400°. Season sole filets with salt and pepper, then fold them in half lengthwise. Place in a single layer in a large Pyrex, enamel, or stainless steel baking pan with the butter and vermouth. Bake for 15 to 20 minutes, basting once or twice. *Do not overcook.* Remove from oven and drain juice to use for the sauce.

Sauté the chopped mushrooms in the butter, stirring until lightly browned. Reduce heat, sprinkle the flour on the mushrooms and stir. Add the 2 cups of liquid and stir constantly until sauce boils. Reduce heat and simmer for 5 or 6 minutes. Taste and adjust seasoning. Place sole filets in a large heat-proof dish (or in individual casseroles), cover with the sauce, then reheat in a 375° oven until hot, but not overcooked. Sprinkle with parsley just before serving.

BAKED SEAFOOD SALAD

Makes 8 servings

½ pound baked ham or Canadian bacon, diced
2 tablespoons butter
¾ pound fresh mushrooms, sliced
1 garlic clove, mashed (or from garlic oil, p. 18)
1 pound cooked shrimp
¾ pound crab meat
1 bunch green onions, chopped
1 to 1½ cups finely chopped celery
1 sweet pepper, chopped
1 cup mayonnaise
3 tablespoons lemon juice
1 teaspoon Worcestershire sauce
few dashes of Tabasco sauce
salt and pepper to taste

for the topping:
½ cup dry bread crumbs
2 tablespoons grated Parmesan cheese
2 tablespoons butter

WHEN NO ONE IS LOOKING
Prepare the topping 1 day ahead; keep covered and refrigerated. Assemble the casserole 1 day ahead too, and refrigerate. Topping and casserole should be stored separately. Remove from refrigerator about 2 hours before serving, cover seafood with the topping, and bake as directed.

Sauté diced ham or Canadian bacon in the 2 tablespoons butter for 1 or 2 minutes. Add mushrooms and cook another 5 minutes, then remove from heat. Place in a large bowl and add all the ingredients *except* those for the topping. Mix well and set aside.

Prepare topping: Combine the bread crumbs, butter, and Parmesan cheese in a skillet and heat slowly, stirring until crumbs are lightly browned—2 or 3 minutes.

Spoon seafood mixture into a casserole and cover with the prepared topping. Bake in a preheated 350° oven for 15 to 20 minutes—only long enough to get hot.

POULTRY

MOROCCAN CHICKEN

Makes 8 to 12 servings

3 whole chicken breasts, split (6 pieces)
6 chicken thighs
salt and pepper
⅓ cup olive oil
2 onions, chopped
1-inch piece fresh ginger (or more), peeled, sliced, then chopped with the onions
2 garlic cloves, mashed (or from garlic oil, p. 18)
½ teaspoon cinnamon
½ teaspoon powdered saffron
½ cup chopped fresh cilantro
6 canned tomatoes (no juice)
4 or more "Preserved Lemons Moroccan Style" (p. 105), throw away the pulp, then cut the rinds into ¼-inch strips
1 or more cups of black olives, preferably pitted Kalamatas

WHEN NO ONE IS LOOKING
Prepare this 1 day ahead; keep covered and refrigerated. Bring to room temperature before reheating.

FROZEN POWER
By all means, freeze this. To serve, defrost, then proceed as directed.

Season chicken pieces with salt and pepper, then place them in a skillet and brown them in olive oil only long enough to make them a light golden color. Remove chicken from skillet and place in a roasting pan. Using the same skillet, sauté chopped onions and ginger together with the garlic. Brown lightly. Chop tomatoes in a food processor, then add them to the onion mixture. Add the cinnamon, cilantro, and saffron. Stir over moderate heat until it begins to boil. Cover, turn down heat, and simmer gently about 5 minutes. Spoon this sauce over the chicken. Cover roasting pan and bake in a preheated 350° oven for 30 to 40 minutes. Do not overcook; chicken will cook some when reheated. Before serving stir in olives and preserved lemon strips and baste the chicken with the sauce. Cover and place in a moderate oven until hot. If desired, uncover and bake a few minutes longer. Serve with couscous (p. 177).

PRESERVED LEMONS MOROCCAN STYLE

6 to 10 lemons
about ¾ to 1 cup salt

WHEN NO ONE IS LOOKING
Prepare these lemons up to 6 months or 1 year ahead of using them, but be sure to keep them refrigerated in sealed jars.

Soak lemons in warm water for 1 hour. Drain and dry them. Quarter each lemon. Place the quartered lemons in a large glass or ceramic bowl and cover with the salt. Cover with a plate and press down. Weight the plate and let the bowl stand until juices are exuded—about 2 or 3 days. Pack lemons in glass jars that you can seal. Pour the exuded liquid over the lemons to cover them completely. Add additional lemon juice if needed. Screw jar lids on tight and let the lemons ripen at room temperature. Turn the jars upside down each day to distribute the salt and lemon juice. Let them ripen this way for 14 to 20 days, then refrigerate the lemons in their sealed jars. The pickling juice can be strained and reused.

To use: Rinse lemons quickly under cold water (do *not* soak) and drain. Remove pulp and use only the rinds.

BISTEEYA (B'STILLA)

Makes 8 to 12 servings

for cooking the chicken:
5 pounds chicken parts (breasts and thighs)
1 extra-large onion (or 2 small ones), chopped
⅛ pound (½ stick) butter
1 tablespoon salt (or to taste)
½ teaspoon black pepper
⅛ to ¼ teaspoon saffron
¼ teaspoon turmeric
1 ¼ teaspoons powdered cinnamon
1 teaspoon powdered ginger
2 cloves garlic, mashed (or from garlic oil, p. 18)
⅓ cup chopped fresh cilantro
4 cups water

for egg mixture:
10 extra large eggs
1 teaspoon salt
1 ½ cups stock left from cooking the chicken

for almond mixture:
2 cups raw almonds, toasted in a 325° oven for about 10 minutes
¼ cup sugar
1 teaspoon powdered cinnamon

for the phyllo:
½ to ¾ pound phyllo pastry leaves
½ pound melted butter

WHEN NO ONE IS LOOKING
All of the elements for the bisteeya can be prepared 1 day ahead. Cook and bone the chicken; scramble the eggs; prepare the almond mixture. Place each element in a separate container, cover, and refrigerate. The entire bisteeya can be assembled in the morning and refrigerated until 2 to 3 hours before baking. Bring it to room temperature before baking.

FROZEN POWER
Cook the chicken, then freeze it in its broth. Bone it after defrosting when you are ready to prepare the bisteeya.

to garnish:
powdered sugar
powdered cinnamon

In a large pot combine ingredients for cooking the chicken and bring to a boil. Reduce heat, cover and simmer until tender, about 1 hour. Remove chicken and cool. Reserve broth. Bone and skin the chicken. Throw out the skin, but put the bones in the broth and boil them for a few minutes. Strain the broth and reserve. Cut boned chicken into bite-size pieces and set aside.

Place 1 ½ cups of strained broth in a saucepan and bring to a simmer. Beat eggs with the salt as for an omelet, then pour the eggs into the simmering broth. Whisk the eggs until they become soft, creamy curds. Taste for salt, drain, and set aside.

Grind the toasted almonds in a food processor, then mix them with the sugar and cinnamon. Coat the bottom of a 12- or 14-inch round cake pan or heavy skillet with melted butter. Butter 6 phyllo leaves—one at a time—and place them overlapping in the pan to cover bottom and extend about 8 inches beyond. Butter 4 more leaves and cover the center. Arrange all of the chicken pieces to cover the bottom. Distribute the egg mixture over this chicken layer, then top it with the almond mixture.

Fold the overhanging phyllo leaves up over the top and press them down firmly. Butter 4 to 6 more phyllo leaves and cover the top of the pie, tucking the ends under the pie. Brush all with more melted butter. Preheat oven to 425°. Bake the pie for 10 minutes, then reduce heat to 350° and bake about 30 minutes or longer, until well browned and completely heated through and piping hot. The amount of time will depend on the temperature of the bisteeya. If it browns too quickly, cover the top loosely with foil.

Remove from oven, then sift powdered sugar on the bisteeya and run criss-crossing lines of cinnamon over the top. Serve hot.

CHICKEN AND WHITE BEANS A FAVORITE WAY

Makes 2 to 4 servings, depending on appetites

- 1 frying chicken, cut in quarters
- salt and pepper
- ¼ cup oil
- 1 large onion, chopped
- 1 garlic clove, minced or mashed (or from garlic oil, p. 18)
- 1 cup tomato sauce, or 2 fresh tomatoes, peeled and diced
- 2 cups dry red wine, or use part dessert wine
- 2 (15-ounce) cans white beans (cannellini), well drained

WHEN NO ONE IS LOOKING
Prepare this 1 day ahead; keep covered and refrigerated. Reheat it for approximately 30 minutes in a preheated 350° oven—or until hot.

FROZEN POWER
Foolproof for the freezer. Be sure to cover the chicken and sauce and double-wrap. To serve, defrost, then reheat 30 to 40 minutes in a preheated 350° oven—until very hot.

Rub chicken pieces with oil, then season with salt and pepper and place them skin sides down in a broiler pan. Broil until lightly browned, then turn and broil the skin sides. Remove and place chicken skin sides up in a large roasting pan. Preheat oven to 350°. In a skillet sauté the onion and garlic in a little oil until lightly browned. Add the tomato sauce (or diced tomatoes) and the wine, then bring to a simmer. Cover and cook over low heat for 5 minutes. Pour this sauce over the chicken and stir in the drained beans. Bake uncovered for 1 to 1½ hours, occasionally basting and turning the chicken pieces and stirring the beans—until chicken is tender. Serve hot.

CHICKEN SESAME ASIAN

Makes 4 to 6 servings

4 chicken breasts (2 whole ones), boned and skinned
rich chicken stock

for the sauce:
½ cup soy sauce
¼ cup sesame seed oil
¼ cup dry sherry
3 generous tablespoons finely minced ginger

for the garnish:
2 to 4 tablespoons toasted sesame seeds
1 to 2 tablespoons chopped green onion

WHEN NO ONE IS LOOKING
Cook the chicken 1 day before; cover and keep refrigerated. Prepare the sauce 1 week before; keep covered and refrigerated. *Note!* After you have spooned the sauce on the chicken, eat it soon. If the sauce remains on the chicken too long, the chicken will turn mushy.

FROZEN POWER
Freeze the chicken breasts in the stock. Defrost completely before using. Do not freeze the sauce.

Poach chicken breasts in chicken stock for approximately 15 minutes. Remove from heat and cool chicken breasts in the stock, then refrigerate them in the stock for at least 4 hours. Combine sauce ingredients in a bowl, cover and refrigerate or leave at room temperature. Several hours before serving, remove chicken from refrigerator and from the stock. Cut in ¼-inch slices and arrange in a shallow casserole or in a serving dish with sides. Cover with half the prepared sauce and if not ready to eat, return to refrigerator until time to serve, but no longer than 3 hours. Just before serving, spoon on the remaining sauce, then sprinkle with toasted sesame seeds and chopped green onion.

CHINESE CHICKEN SALAD TWO WAYS (WITH RICE STICKS OR CRISPY NOODLES)

Makes 4 servings

2 to 3 cups diced or shredded cooked chicken
3 cups shredded solid head lettuce or romaine
4 green onions, finely chopped
3 cups fried rice sticks, ¼ of a package, or easier, 3 cups crisp chow mein noodles (canned)
vegetable oil if frying rice sticks
½ cup sliced almonds, lightly toasted
2 to 3 tablespoons toasted sesame seeds
1 small can sliced water chestnuts (optional)

for the dressing:
3 tablespoons sugar
1 ¼ teaspoons salt
¼ teaspoon pepper
5 tablespoons white rice vinegar
3 tablespoons vegetable oil
1 tablespoon sesame seed oil

WHEN NO ONE IS LOOKING
Fry the rice sticks 1 day ahead; place them in plastic bags, close tightly, and keep refrigerated. When ready to serve, reheat rice sticks on a baking pan in a preheated 325° oven to crisp. Also, prepare the chicken, toasted almonds, and sesame seeds 1 day ahead; cover and refrigerate separately. Bring refrigerated items (except for the lettuce) to room temperature before serving. Make the dressing several days before; store in a glass jar in the refrigerator.

FROZEN POWER
Fry and freeze the rice sticks; store them in containers or plastic bags that can be sealed. After defrosting, reheat in a moderate oven to crisp. Cooked chicken in its broth freezes well too.

Make dressing by combining ingredients. Fry rice sticks in ¾ inch of oil and drain. Place lettuce and onions in salad bowl and scatter the chicken, almonds, sesame seeds, and sliced water chestnuts over all. Just before serving add rice sticks (or noodles) and dressing; toss and serve.

IN THE MANNER OF CHICKEN FAJITAS

Makes 3 to 4 servings

"In the manner of" because these are not authentic fajitas, rather, a simplified version

4 chicken breast halves with bones and skin
2 cups chicken stock
salt and pepper to taste
2 to 3 teaspoons chili powder
½ teaspoon oregano
2 onions, sliced
1 or 2 tablespoons vegetable oil
2 tablespoons garlic oil (p. 18)
"Fresh Tomato Salsa" (p. 233)
guacamole
flour or corn tortillas

WHEN NO ONE IS LOOKING
Cook the chicken, remove skin and bones, then cut and shred it 1 day ahead; keep covered and refrigerated.

FROZEN POWER
Cook and freeze the chicken in its broth. To use, defrost completely, then skin, bone, and cut the chicken.

Cook chicken breasts in seasoned chicken stock at a gentle simmer for 20 to 30 minutes. Do not overcook. Remove from heat and cool chicken in the stock. Bone and skin chicken breasts, then cut or shred chicken into large pieces. Sauté the onions in the vegetable oil until lightly browned and almost tender, then set aside. When ready to serve, heat garlic oil in a skillet, add chicken pieces, sprinkle with chili powder and oregano, then stir over moderate heat only until hot. Add onions, toss and briefly reheat. Bring to table and let guests help themselves by filling their tortillas with the chicken/onion mixture and with salsa and guacamole.

CHICKEN BREASTS WITH COCONUT AND A SWEET RED PEPPER SAUCE

Makes 4 servings

4 chicken breast halves, split and skinned, but not boned
salt and pepper
2 teaspoons mashed garlic (or from garlic oil, p. 18)
2 tablespoons Dijon-style mustard
2 teaspoons ground (powdered) ginger
3 tablespoons olive oil
flour
egg wash made by beating 2 eggs with 2 tablespoons water
2 cups sweetened flaked coconut
2 tablespoons butter
2 tablespoons oil

for the sweet red pepper sauce:
2 (7-ounce) jars roasted sweet red peppers
juice of 1 lemon
2 teaspoons sugar
1 teaspoon salt
½ teaspoon pepper

WHEN NO ONE IS LOOKING
Prepare the sweet red pepper sauce and the garlic paste 1 day ahead; keep them separate, each covered and refrigerated. The chicken can be completely cooked several hours ahead of time; reheat in the oven before serving.

FROZEN POWER
Freeze the sweet red pepper sauce. To use, defrost completely and stir well before using.

Make the sauce by placing the sweet red peppers in a food processor with the lemon juice, sugar, salt and pepper, then process to a purée. Set aside at room temperature or cover and refrigerate. Season chicken breasts with salt and pepper. Make a paste of the mashed garlic, mustard, ginger, and olive oil. Spread this mixture on both sides of the chicken. Dredge chicken in flour and shake off excess. Place the egg wash and coconut in separate pans or shallow bowls. Dip chicken breasts in the egg wash and let excess drip off, then coat each with coconut, pressing the coconut to make it stick. Heat butter and oil in a large skillet over moderately high heat and sauté the chicken breasts about 3 minutes on each side, until coconut is golden brown. Remove from heat. Use a large spatula and place chicken breasts in an ovenproof baking dish. Bake in a preheated 350° oven for 30 to 40 minutes. Serve hot with the sweet red pepper sauce at the side.

CURRY-MUSTARD-HONEY GLAZED CHICKEN

Makes 6 servings

6 chicken thighs or 6 breast halves with skin and bones
salt and pepper
⅛ pound (½ stick) melted butter or olive oil
2 tablespoons curry powder
juice of ½ lemon
½ cup Dijon-style mustard
⅓ cup honey
1 tablespoon garlic oil (p. 18)
1 tablespoon soy sauce

WHEN NO ONE IS LOOKING
Prepare the curry-mustard-honey mixture 1 or 2 days ahead.

Season chicken with salt and pepper. Combine remaining ingredients and mix until smooth. Place chicken pieces skin sides up in a single layer in a large roasting pan. Spoon ⅔ of the prepared curry-mustard-honey mixture over the chicken and bake in a preheated 350° oven for 30 minutes, basting occasionally. Remove and spoon on remaining curry-mustard-honey mixture and bake an additional 15 to 20 minutes or until browned and tender. (If chicken seems too dry during the roasting, add a little stock or water.)

CHICKEN BREASTS ROASTED WITH A MIREPOIX

Makes 6 servings

6 chicken breast halves with skin and bones
1 onion, finely chopped
3 medium-size carrots, finely chopped
3 stalks celery, finely chopped
2 tablespoons butter
2 tablespoons oil
salt and pepper
¼ cup cognac or California brandy
½ cup Madeira or sherry

WHEN NO ONE IS LOOKING
Prepare this 1 day ahead, but do not roast the chicken the full time; the chicken will cook further in the reheating. Cool, cover, and refrigerate. Remove chicken from refrigerator several hours before serving, then place in a preheated 400° oven, basting occasionally, until very hot.

FROZEN POWER
Freeze the mirepoix, that is, the sautéed onions, carrots, and celery. Defrost completely, then proceed as directed.

Heat butter and oil in a skillet and sauté the vegetables until lightly browned and tender. Add the cognac (or brandy), salt, and pepper, and cook until cognac is absorbed. Remove from the heat. Season chicken breasts with salt and pepper and place skin sides down in a single layer in a roasting pan. Spoon cooked vegetables in the cavities of the chicken breasts and roast uncovered in a preheated 400° oven for 20 minutes. Remove from oven, turn chicken over with skin sides up and return to oven for 10 minutes. Add the Madeira or sherry and roast, basting occasionally, for 10 more minutes or longer—until well browned and tender. If chicken begins to dry out during the roasting, add a little stock and cover lightly with foil. Spoon vegetable-Madeira sauce over each chicken breast and serve hot.

NOUVEAU CHICKEN

Makes 2 to 4 servings

- 1 frying chicken split into halves
- juice of 1 lemon
- salt and pepper
- 1 head of romaine lettuce
- 4 tablespoons chopped shallots (or use frozen shallots, p. 18)
- ⅓ cup oil
- 2 cups dry white wine
- 1 cup chicken stock
- 1 cup sugar snap peas
- ¼ pound fresh mushrooms, sliced
- 2 tablespoons butter

WHEN NO ONE IS LOOKING
Ready the sugar peas and mushrooms in the morning; cover and leave them at room temperature.

Season chicken halves with lemon juice, salt, and pepper. Place them skin sides down in a shallow broiler pan. Cover with shallots and oil and broil each side until lightly browned. Add white wine, turn chicken skin sides up and roast in a 400° oven for 20 minutes, basting once or twice. Add stock and continue to roast, basting occasionally for 20 to 30 minutes, or longer if needed—until chicken is tender and well browned. While chicken is roasting, blanch sugar peas and set aside; sauté mushrooms in the butter for 1 minute and set them aside. Tear romaine into largish pieces and arrange on dinner plates. Remove chicken from roasting pan, cut into serving pieces, and reserve remaining juices. Add sugar peas and mushrooms to remaining juices and reheat briefly. Place chicken pieces on romaine and top each with some of the sauce and vegetables.

CHICKEN BREASTS WITH FETA, OLIVES, PINE NUTS, AND SUN-DRIED TOMATOES

Makes 8 servings

4 whole chicken breasts, halved and boned, but skin left on
salt and pepper
⅓ cup vegetable oil

for the stuffing:
1 onion, finely chopped
¼ cup olive oil
2 teaspoons mashed garlic (or from garlic oil, p. 18)
1 cup Kalamata olives, pitted and cut in strips
1 cup drained oil-packed sun-dried tomatoes, rinsed and patted dry on paper towels
7 or 8 ounces Feta cheese (about 2 cups)
½ cup grated Parmesan cheese
½ teaspoon salt, or to taste, depending on the Feta cheese
¼ teaspoon pepper

WHEN NO ONE IS LOOKING
Prepare the stuffing 1 day ahead; cover and refrigerate. Bring to room temperature before filling the chicken breasts. Or, assemble them completely in the morning; cover and refrigerate. Remove from refrigerator 1 or 2 hours before broiling and roasting.

Make the stuffing: Sauté the onion in the olive oil until lightly browned and tender. Add remaining ingredients and stir over low heat for 1 or 2 minutes. Taste for seasoning and cool at room temperature. Season chicken with salt and pepper. Cut a deep pocket in each breast and place some stuffing inside each, then roll each in vegetable oil. Place the breasts skin sides up in a single layer in a large nonstick broiling pan. When ready to cook, broil for 3 to 5 minutes, long enough to brown the skin. Turn oven to 350° and roast for 45 minutes, or longer if needed—until browned and cooked through.

CHICKEN BREASTS WITH A MEXICAN FLAVOR

Makes 6 servings

6 boned and skinned chicken breast halves
salt and pepper
1 (7-ounce) can green chiles
¼ pound Monterey Jack cheese
½ cup dry bread crumbs
¼ cup grated Parmesan cheese
1 teaspoon chili powder
1 teaspoon salt
¾ teaspoon ground cumin
¼ teaspoon pepper
6 tablespoons melted butter
3 tablespoons garlic oil (p. 18)

for the sauce:
1 (15-ounce) can tomato sauce
2 teaspoons minced dried onion
¾ teaspoon ground cumin

WHEN NO ONE IS LOOKING
Prepare the sauce 1 or 2 days ahead; keep covered and refrigerated. Assemble and refrigerate the chicken 1 day ahead. Remove from refrigerator 2 hours before baking. Preheat oven to 400°, then bake for 45 minutes or longer. Serve with the sauce.

FROZEN POWER
Freeze the sauce. Defrost completely before using.

Combine sauce ingredients and bring to a boil, then reduce heat and let sauce simmer 3 to 5 minutes. Set aside and reheat before serving. Pound chicken breasts between pieces of plastic wrap until about ¼ inch thick. Drain and remove seeds from chiles. Cut Monterey Jack cheese into six portions (1 x 1½-inch pieces). In one large bowl combine bread crumbs, Parmesan, chili powder, 1 teaspoon salt, cumin, and pepper. In another bowl combine melted butter and garlic oil. Season chicken breasts with salt and pepper. Roll each piece of cheese in a chile pepper (or in several), then place them on the chicken breasts. Roll breasts up to enclose the filling. Dip these rolled bundles in the butter/oil, drain off excess, then roll in the crumb mixture. Place them seam sides down, without letting sides touch, in a nonstick baking pan. Spoon remaining butter/oil on each. Cover and chill about 4 hours or as long as overnight. Remove from refrigerator several hours before baking. Preheat oven to 400°. Bake the chicken for approximately 45 minutes or longer—until browned and tender.

CHEESE AND CHILE STUFFED CHICKEN BREASTS IN PHYLLO

Makes 8 servings

8 boned and skinned chicken breast halves
salt and pepper
2 cups grated Monterey Jack cheese
2 cups grated sharp Cheddar cheese
1 cup diced green chiles (canned, but well drained)
16 large phyllo pastry sheets
½ pound melted butter (or more)

WHEN NO ONE IS LOOKING
These lend themselves to preparation a day ahead. Assemble the chicken rolls, then refrigerate overnight. Remove them from the refrigerator about 2 hours before baking, then proceed as directed.

Flatten the chicken breasts to about ¼ inch thick. (This is best done by placing them between sheets of heavy plastic wrap and pounding them with a flat mallet or the flat side of a heavy chopping knife.) Sprinkle them generously with salt and pepper. Top each breast with ¼ cup Monterey Jack cheese, ¼ cup Cheddar, and 2 tablespoons of diced chiles. Roll up the chicken breasts and place them seam sides down on a large tray. Refrigerate to firm them for an hour or longer.

Brush 1 phyllo sheet with butter, top with a second sheet and brush again with butter. Place a chicken roll in the center of the short side of the phyllo sheets. Roll up, tucking in the sides as you roll. Repeat with the remaining seven chicken rolls. Place in a single layer, not touching, in a large, oiled roasting pan (or two if necessary). Brush each phyllo package with butter, then refrigerate uncovered until ready to bake. Remove from refrigerator 2 hours before baking. Place phyllo-wrapped chicken rolls in a preheated 350° oven and bake 40 to 45 minutes—longer if they were still cold when you put them into the oven. Serve them with a tomato sauce (mild or hot).

CHICKEN BREASTS WITH PARMESAN AND MUSTARD

Makes 6 servings

- 6 chicken breast halves, skin removed but not the bones
- 1 cup dry bread crumbs
- 1 cup grated Parmesan cheese
- 1 ¼ teaspoons salt
- ½ teaspoon black pepper
- 1 teaspoon Worcestershire sauce
- 2 tablespoons Dijon-style mustard
- 1 cup olive oil

WHEN NO ONE IS LOOKING
Prepare the crumb mixture a day ahead or in the morning, and do the same with the oil-mustard mixture. Refrigerate the crumb mixture until several hours before preparing the chicken. Or, assemble the chicken ready to bake in the morning. Refrigerate uncovered until about 2 hours before baking, then remove and bring to room temperature and proceed as directed in the recipe.

Combine the crumbs, Parmesan, salt, and pepper in a shallow bowl or dish. In another shallow dish combine the oil, Worcestershire sauce, and mustard. Dip each chicken breast in the oil mixture, then roll in the crumb mixture. Place chicken in a single layer in a large baking pan, skin sides up. Spoon any remaining oil-mustard mixture over the chicken. Bake uncovered in a 350° oven for 1 hour, then baste and bake approximately 15 to 30 minutes longer.

MONTE ALBAN CHICKEN EN PAPILLOTE

Makes 8 servings

8 large chicken breast halves, skin removed but leave the bones
salt and pepper
flour
¼ pound butter (1 stick) and ¼ cup vegetable oil

for Monte Alban sauce:
2 tablespoons butter or oil
1 onion, coarsely chopped
2 garlic cloves, mashed (or from garlic oil, p. 18)
1 (1-pound) can tomatoes
1 tablespoon dried oregano
1 tablespoon ground cumin
½ teaspoon salt
1 teaspoon chili powder
¼ pound cold butter (1 stick), sliced

WHEN NO ONE IS LOOKING
Prepare the Monte Alban sauce two days ahead; keep covered and refrigerated. Sauté the chicken and assemble the papillotes in the morning, but keep refrigerated until 2 hours before the final baking.

FROZEN POWER
Freeze the completely assembled papillotes first on trays. When they are firm, store them in large sealable plastic bags. Defrost completely before the final baking.

Make the sauce: Sauté the onion and garlic in the 2 tablespoons butter or oil for 3 or 4 minutes, then add the tomatoes, mashing them well. Simmer for 5 minutes, then add the oregano, cumin, salt, and chili powder. Simmer covered for 15 minutes; uncover and simmer an additional 5 minutes. Remove and cool for 3 to 5 minutes, then place sauce in a blender or food processor and add the cold butter slices. Process until smooth, then set aside and, as soon as possible, chill for at least 2 hours or overnight in the refrigerator.

Remove the flat bony part of the chicken breasts' ribs, thereby making them narrower, then season with salt and pepper. Roll in flour, shake off excess, and sauté 4 of the breasts in half of the butter and oil over moderate heat until browned and almost, but not quite, tender. Repeat with the other four chicken breasts and remaining butter and oil. Take 8 nonstick baking parchment sheets, each about 12 x 18 inches, and fold them in half. Cut folded sheets in the shape of half a heart, then open them up. Place a chicken breast in the center on one side of the heart and cover with ¼ to ⅓ cup of the chilled sauce. Fold over and seal the edges of the parchment by folding them over and over each other; fasten ends with metal paper clips. Place packages in a large baking pan with sides (or in two smaller ones) and bake in a preheated 350° oven for approximately 30 minutes (if they are cold, for about 45 minutes). Let guests open their own papillotes, but provide large bowls at the table for discarded papers.

OLD-FASHIONED FRIED CHICKEN

- chicken breasts, thighs, or drumsticks with bones and skin
- salt and black pepper
- flour
- vegetable oil or vegetable shortening

WHEN NO ONE IS LOOKING
Fry the chicken several hours ahead of serving. Cover lightly and leave at room temperature, then reheat as directed.

Season chicken generously with salt and pepper. Roll pieces in flour and shake off excess. Heat enough oil or shortening to form a ½-inch layer in a heavy skillet, then place chicken in the skillet skin sides down. Do not crowd the chicken pieces. Cover skillet and cook over moderately high heat until well browned on skin sides. Remove cover, turn chicken so skin sides are up, and continue cooking—uncovered now—until undersides of chicken are browned and chicken is completely cooked. Drain on paper towels, then place in an ovenproof dish or baking pan in a single layer. Cover lightly with waxed paper and leave at room temperature. Shortly before serving, place chicken in a preheated 400° oven for 10 to 15 minutes, until very hot.

COUNTRY CAPTAIN CHICKEN

Makes 16 to 24 servings

- 5 large onions, finely chopped
- 18 ounces butter (2 ¼ sticks) or olive oil
- 7 large sweet green peppers, finely chopped
- 2 large bunches parsley, chopped (tops only)
- 2 garlic cloves mashed (or from garlic oil, p. 18)
- salt to taste (about 2 or 3 teaspoons)
- 1 or more teaspoons pepper
- 2 teaspoons mace
- 4 teaspoons curry powder
- 6 cups canned tomatoes, well mashed
- 24 large chicken breast halves with bones and skin
- salt and pepper
- flour
- corn oil or vegetable shortening
- chicken stock (about 1 cup)
- 2 cups raisins, soaked in hot water, then drained and patted dry on paper towels
- 3 cups blanched almonds, toasted

WHEN NO ONE IS LOOKING
Prepare this dish 1 day ahead, but do not add the raisins and almonds. Keep chicken covered and refrigerated. Be careful not to overcook the chicken because it will cook more in the reheating. After reheating, top with the raisins and almonds.

FROZEN POWER
Cook and freeze but without the almonds and raisins. Do not overcook since the chicken will cook more in the reheating. Add the almonds and raisins before serving.

Sauté onions in the butter (or olive oil) until lightly browned. Add chopped green peppers and continue cooking 5 more minutes. Add chopped parsley, garlic, salt, pepper, mace, curry, and tomatoes, and simmer, stirring occasionally, until mixture thickens slightly—about 30 minutes. Taste for seasoning and set aside.

Season chicken with salt and pepper, dust with flour, then sauté in oil or shortening until browned but not cooked through. Place chicken breasts skin sides up in a large roasting pan (or two) and cover with prepared sauce. If sauce seems too thick, add a little chicken stock. Cover tightly and bake in a preheated 325° oven for 30 to 40 minutes—until tender but not overcooked. Arrange chicken breasts on a large hot serving platter and spoon sauce over them. Sprinkle prepared raisins and toasted almonds on top.

SESAME SEED FRIED CHICKEN

chicken breasts and thighs with skin and bones
salt and black pepper
flour
beaten eggs
a large quantity of sesame seeds
vegetable oil or shortening for frying

WHEN NO ONE IS LOOKING
Fry the chicken several hours ahead of serving. Cover lightly and leave at room temperature, then reheat as directed.

Arrange the flour, beaten eggs, and sesame seeds in three large shallow dishes. Season chicken generously with salt and pepper, then roll in flour and shake off excess. Dip each piece in beaten egg and roll in sesame seeds so that the chicken pieces are completely covered with the sesame seeds. Heat enough oil or shortening to form a ½-inch layer in a heavy skillet, then place chicken in skillet skin sides down. Do not crowd the chicken pieces. Cover skillet and cook over moderately high heat until well browned on skin sides. Remove cover, turn chicken so skin sides are up, and continue cooking—uncovered now—until undersides of chicken pieces are browned and chicken is completely cooked. Drain on paper towels, then place in an ovenproof dish or baking pan in a single layer. Cover lightly with waxed paper and leave at room temperature. Shortly before serving, place chicken in a preheated 400° oven for 10 to 15 minutes, until very hot.

EXOTIC INDONESIAN-STYLE CHICKEN

Makes 4 generous servings

2 chickens (about 2 pounds each), split into halves, with skin and bones
salt and black pepper

for marinade:
¼ cup vinegar
grated rind and juice of 1 lemon
1 clove garlic, mashed (or from garlic oil, p. 18)
¼ cup chopped onion (or use 1 tablespoon minced dried onion)
1 teaspoon salt
1 teaspoon celery seeds
1 teaspoon dried oregano
2 tablespoons curry powder
2 tablespoons soy sauce
1 tablespoon A-1 sauce
2 dashes Tabasco sauce
⅓ cup Dijon-style mustard
⅓ cup honey
2 tablespoons vegetable oil

WHEN NO ONE IS LOOKING
Prepare the marinade 2 to 3 days ahead; cover and leave it at room temperature. Cook the entire dish 1 day ahead, but underbake it; cover and refrigerate. Bring to room temperature, then reheat and baste in a 350° oven.

FROZEN POWER
This freezes very well. To freeze, underbake slightly. To serve, defrost, bring to room temperature, then proceed with reheating and basting.

Combine all ingredients for the marinade in a saucepan, then stir only until sauce comes to a boil Remove from heat and cool. Season chicken with salt and pepper. Place in a roasting pan skin sides down. Spoon ⅓ of the marinade on the chicken and bake in a preheated 350° oven for 40 minutes. Add a little water to pan if the marinade starts to burn. Turn chickens over with skin sides up and spoon another ⅓ of the marinade on the chicken. Bake an additional 30 to 45 minutes, or until chickens are tender. Add more marinade and water as needed during the baking. If you have leftover marinade, gently reheat it to a simmer, then serve as a sauce at table.

BONED CHICKEN BREASTS MARSALA

Makes 8 servings

- 8 chicken breast halves, boned and skinned
- salt and black pepper
- flour
- 2 ounces butter (½ stick) or oil
- ½ pound fresh mushrooms, sliced
- 2 tablespoons butter
- ¾ cup chicken stock
- ½ cup dry Marsala
- ¼ cup grated Parmesan cheese

WHEN NO ONE IS LOOKING
Assemble this 1 day ahead or in the morning up to the point of baking. Cover and refrigerate but bring to room temperature before baking, then proceed as directed.

Season the chicken breasts with salt and pepper, then dust with flour. Sauté gently in the butter (or oil) until lightly browned on both sides. Do not overcook. Reserve any butter or oil left in the skillet. Place browned chicken in an ovenproof casserole or baking pan large enough to hold the breasts in a single layer. Preheat oven to 350°. Add the 2 tablespoons of butter to the skillet and sauté the mushrooms. Add seasoning, then spoon mushrooms over the chicken. Add the stock and Marsala to the skillet and reduce a little, then spoon over the mushrooms and chicken. Sprinkle with the Parmesan. Cover tightly with foil and bake for 20 to 25 minutes. Remove foil and bake an additional 5 to 7 minutes.

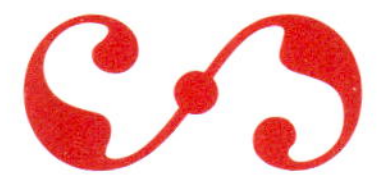

ROAST CHICKEN MARSALA

Makes 4 to 6 servings

- 1 large roasting chicken (6 to 7 pounds) with giblets
- salt and black pepper
- 1 or 2 tablespoons dried rosemary
- 2 onions, coarsely chopped or sliced
- garlic oil (p. 18)
- ⅓ cup dry Marsala

WHEN NO ONE IS LOOKING
Prepare the chicken in the morning up to roasting time, and refrigerate until 2 hours before cooking (then bring to room temperature). Or, assemble the chicken 2 to 3 hours ahead, place in the roasting pan or casserole, cover, and leave at room temperature until time to roast.

Preheat oven to 450°. Bring chicken to room temperature, then season it inside and out with salt, pepper, rosemary, and garlic oil. Put one chopped onion inside the chicken and the other on the bottom of a large, heavy casserole or roasting pan. Place chicken on top of the onion. Season giblets and arrange them around the chicken.

Cover casserole or roasting pan as tightly as possible with a heavy cover, or lacking a cover, with heavy duty foil. Seal it as tight as possible! Roast in the preheated oven without lifting the cover for 1 hour and 10 minutes. Remove from oven, uncover, add the wine, then cover again. Reduce oven to 350° and roast about 10 to 15 minutes longer. Bring the chicken to table in the roasting pan and remove the cover in front of your guests. Place the chicken on a large platter to carve. Spoon the delicious rich sauce that has been created on each serving.

AN ITALIAN-STYLE CHICKEN PARMESAN

Makes 8 servings

- 8 chicken breast halves, skins removed but not the bones
- salt and black pepper
- 2 eggs
- 1 tablespoon water
- ¾ cup dry bread crumbs
- ¾ cup grated Parmesan cheese
- 2 teaspoons salt
- ½ teaspoon black pepper
- ½ teaspoon dry oregano
- ½ teaspoon dry sweet basil
- ¼ pound butter (1 stick) or more as needed
- ½ pound grated mozzarella or imported Swiss
- 2 cups tomato sauce

WHEN NO ONE IS LOOKING
Prepare this 1 day ahead up to the point of baking. Cover and refrigerate. Bring to room temperature before baking, then proceed as directed.

Cut off the flat bony part of the ribs of each chicken breast. (Use those bones for another purpose; they can be frozen and used to make stock.) Beat eggs slightly with the water and set aside. Combine bread crumbs, Parmesan, salt, pepper, and herbs. Dip chicken breasts in the egg mixture, then coat with the crumb mixture. Sauté chicken in the butter over moderate heat—only long enough to lightly brown each side. Place chicken pieces in a single layer in a large baking pan or shallow casserole. Divide the grated mozzarella or Swiss cheese over the chicken, then spoon tomato sauce on top. Cover tightly with foil. Bake 30 to 40 minutes at 350°. Remove foil, baste, then bake about another 10 minutes.

CHICKEN BREASTS WITH AN EASY MUSHROOM SAUCE

Makes 10 servings

- 10 chicken breast halves, skinned and boned
- salt and black pepper
- flour
- ¼ pound butter (1 stick), or olive oil
- ½ pound fresh mushrooms, finely chopped
- 4 green onions, finely chopped
- 4 tablespoons flour
- 1 teaspoon freshly chopped tarragon or ¼ teaspoon dried
- 2 cups rich chicken stock
- 1 cup sour cream
- 3 tablespoons cognac (or California brandy)
- freshly chopped parsley

WHEN NO ONE IS LOOKING
This dish lends itself beautifully to preparation either 1 day ahead or the morning of the party. Keep covered and refrigerated, but bring to room temperature before reheating. Cover and reheat in the oven.

FROZEN POWER
This preparation freezes beautifully. Defrost, then cover and reheat in the oven.

Season chicken breasts with salt and pepper. Roll them in flour, shake off excess, then sauté gently in half of the butter or olive oil until lightly browned—do not overcook. Remove from skillet. Add remaining butter or oil to the skillet and sauté the mushrooms over high heat for about 2 minutes. Reduce heat to moderate, then add the green onions, sprinkle with the flour, and stir until blended. Add tarragon and chicken stock, then stir constantly until sauce comes to a boil. Remove from heat. Place chicken breasts in a large baking pan and spoon the mushroom sauce over the chicken. Cover with foil and bake in a preheated 325° oven for about 25 to 30 minutes. Remove from oven and place chicken breasts in an ovenproof serving dish. Add the sour cream and cognac to the baking pan and stir over heat until sauce is hot, but not boiling. Pour this sauce over the chicken and return to oven for 3 to 5 minutes, only long enough to become hot. Garnish with chopped parsley and serve.

HONEY, ORANGE, GINGER CHICKEN

Makes 4 servings

2 frying chickens, split in halves
salt and black pepper
¼ cup vegetable oil
¾ cup soy sauce
1 cup honey
grated rind and juice of 2 oranges
2 to 4 tablespoons finely chopped fresh ginger
1 garlic clove, mashed (or from garlic oil, p. 18)

WHEN NO ONE IS LOOKING
Prepare the marinade 3 to 5 days ahead; cover and keep refrigerated. Or, complete the entire cooking several hours ahead; cover lightly and leave at room temperature, then reheat before serving.

Season chicken halves with salt and pepper, then place them skin sides down in a baking pan. Combine the remaining ingredients and pour ¾ of this marinade mixture over the chicken. Bake about 1 hour in a preheated 350° oven, basting occasionally. If chicken begins to dry out and burn, add some water or stock to the pan. Turn chicken so skin sides are up, pour remaining marinade over the tops, then bake 15 to 30 minutes longer, basting several times.

CHICKEN WITH A MEXICAN GREEN SAUCE

Makes 8 to 10 servings

3 frying chickens, quartered
salt and black pepper
2 cups rich chicken stock
1 cup dry-roasted sunflower seeds
1 cup blanched almonds, lightly toasted
1 (7-ounce) can whole green chiles (seeds removed)
2 (12-ounce) cans tomatillos, well drained
1 onion, coarsely chopped
½ cup fresh cilantro (leaves only)
2 tablespoons vegetable oil

WHEN NO ONE IS LOOKING
Prepare this 1 day ahead, but do not overcook; cover and refrigerate. Bring to room temperature (about 2 hours before serving), then reheat, covered, in a 350° oven.

FROZEN POWER
This freezes beautifully. Again, do not overcook. Defrost, then cover and reheat in a 350° oven.

Season quartered chickens, then place them in a large roasting pan. Pour chicken stock over the chicken, cover and roast in a preheated 350° oven for about 40 minutes or until almost tender. Do not overcook. Remove from oven, drain off the juices and reserve them for making the sauce.

Pulverize the sunflower seeds and almonds in a food processor and set aside. Place green chiles, tomatillos, onion, and cilantro in the processor, purée and then combine with the pulverized mixture. Heat the oil in a skillet and add this mixture plus the juices you have reserved and simmer 3 to 5 minutes. Taste for seasoning and adjust. Put chicken back in the roasting pan (if you have removed it), pour prepared sauce over it, then cover and bake in the 350° oven for about 20 to 30 minutes—only until tender.

GAME HENS WITH RICE AND WATER CHESTNUT STUFFING

Makes 12 servings

12 Cornish game hens
salt and black pepper
¼ cup olive oil (or corn oil)
1 cup soy sauce
½ cup honey
2 tablespoons freshly grated or finely chopped ginger
¾ cup stock (make it with the necks and giblets)
1 garlic clove, mashed (or from garlic oil, p. 18)

for the rice and water chestnut stuffing:
1 ½ cups uncooked rice
⅛ pound butter (½ stick)
1 onion, finely chopped
1 sweet red or green pepper, finely chopped
salt and black pepper to taste
1 (8-ounce) can sliced water chestnuts, drained and chopped

WHEN NO ONE IS LOOKING
Prepare the rice and water chestnut stuffing 1 day ahead; keep covered and refrigerated. Bring to room temperature before using. Game hens can be roasted two hours before serving, but undercook slightly. Cool, cover lightly, and leave at room temperature. About 45 minutes before serving, reheat uncovered in a 325° oven, basting occasionally and adding a little water if needed to prevent burning.

FROZEN POWER
The rice and water chestnut stuffing freezes well. Defrost completely before using.

Make the stuffing first. Cook rice until barely tender—al dente. Drain and cool. Sauté onion in the butter until tender but not browned. Add red or green pepper and cook another minute. Add salt and pepper to taste, then stir in the water chestnuts. Combine with the rice and mix well. Season game hens, then fill cavities with the rice and water chestnut stuffing. Place hens in two large roasting pans. Rub outside of hens with oil, then roast uncovered in a preheated 400° oven for 15 minutes. Combine soy sauce, honey, ginger, stock, and garlic, then pour over the hens. Reduce oven to 350° and roast, basting occasionally, for about 1 hour or longer—until hens are tender. Watch that they do not burn; add more stock or water if necessary.

GILDED GAME HENS

Makes 4 servings

4 Cornish game hens with necks and gizzards
salt and black pepper
2 tablespoons vegetable oil
½ cup chopped carrots
½ cup chopped celery
1 cup chopped onions
2 tablespoons chopped shallots
¼ pound (1 stick) melted butter
1 (17-ounce) package of frozen puff pastry (2 sheets)
egg wash made by mixing 1 egg with 2 tablespoons cold water
2 cups rich chicken stock
½ cup semisweet sherry (or a dessert wine)
2 tablespoons cornstarch dissolved in ⅓ cup cold water

WHEN NO ONE IS LOOKING
Roast the hens, cool them, and wrap in pastry in the morning. Store them uncovered in the refrigerator until 1 ½ hours before the final baking; then proceed with the final baking. Prepare the sauce in the morning too; cover and refrigerate, then reheat before serving.

FROZEN POWER
Remember that homemade puff pastry (p. 356) freezes, or buy it already frozen.

Preheat oven to 450°. Remove giblets from the game hens. You will need the necks and gizzards, but save the livers for another purpose. Rub hens with oil, then season them inside and out with salt and pepper. Truss the legs of the hens together. Place the chopped vegetables with the necks and gizzards in a large roasting pan. Season with salt and pepper, then sprinkle with oil. Roast for 15 to 25 minutes or until vegetables and giblets are browned. Remove from oven, add the hens, and spoon the butter over them. Return to the oven (at the same temperature) and roast for 15 additional minutes. Remove, baste, and reduce oven to 350°, then roast 10 more minutes. Remove from oven again and this time remove trussing strings. Return to oven and roast for 5 to 15 minutes—until hens are cooked through, but not overcooked. Cool, cover with plastic wrap and refrigerate for 2 hours or longer.

Each sheet of puff pastry should be sufficient for two hens. Roll one sheet out on a floured board to a square about 18" x 18". Cut in half. Place a hen breast side down in the center of one of the pastry halves, brush pastry with egg wash, then wrap the pastry around the hen, sealing it with a more egg wash. Cut off excess pastry (use to make cut-out decorations). Repeat with the second hen. Start over with the second sheet of pastry and do the same for the remaining two hens. Chill wrapped hens uncovered in the refrigerator for at least 1 hour or up to 6. Preheat oven to 400°, then bake the hens for about 40 minutes.

While the hens are baking—or earlier—make the sauce. Deglaze the roasting pan containing the remaining vegetables and giblets with the chicken stock and sherry (or dessert wine). Strain and pour into a saucepan. Bring strained liquid to a boil, then thicken to your taste with the dissolved cornstarch. Taste for seasoning, reheat and serve a spoonful at the side of each hen.

ROAST DUCKLINGS WITH AN ORANGE SAUCE

Makes 4 to 8 servings

2 "Long Island" (Peking-style) ducklings
salt and black pepper
2 onions, peeled and quartered
3 celery stalks, sliced
1 ½ cups duck or chicken stock (can be made from the duck giblets)
2 tablespoons butter
2 tablespoons flour
juice and grated rind of 2 oranges
grated rind of 1 lemon
½ cup currant jelly
fresh orange segments (optional)

WHEN NO ONE IS LOOKING
Prepare the ducklings and sauce in the morning; cover and refrigerate separately. Bring to room temperature about 2 hours before serving, then reheat them separately—the ducklings in a preheated 400° oven—only long enough to heat—and the sauce on the stove top. Add orange segments just before serving.

Season ducklings with salt and pepper. Place 1 quartered onion and some celery slices in the cavity of each duckling. Place in a roasting pan and roast uncovered in a preheated 325° oven for 2 to 3 hours, removing fat as it accumulates. Increase oven to 425° and roast another 15 to 30 minutes—until skin is browned and crisp, and ducklings are tender. Remove ducklings to an ovenproof platter and keep warm in a 200° oven—only long enough to finish the sauce.

Make the sauce: Remove fat from roasting pan. Deglaze pan by adding the stock and bringing it to a boil, scraping the brown bits that are sticking on the pan into the stock. In a separate saucepan, melt the butter and stir in the flour, then strain the stock into the butter-flour mixture and stir constantly until mixture comes to a boil. Add the orange juice, orange and lemon rinds, and currant jelly. Season to taste and simmer gently for 3 to 5 minutes.

To serve: Place ducklings on a platter and surround with orange segments. Spoon a little sauce over the ducklings. Carve, serve, and pass additional sauce separately.

ONE-BASTE DUCKLINGS WITH PEACHES

Makes 6 to 8 servings

- 2 "Long Island" (Peking-style) ducklings
- salt and black pepper
- 3 onions, thickly sliced
- 3 celery stalks, sliced
- 2 cups duck or chicken stock
- 2 tablespoons cornstarch
- ¼ cup cold water
- 6 or 8 peach halves, fresh or canned

WHEN NO ONE IS LOOKING
Cook the ducklings and sauce 1 day ahead, but undercook the ducklings. Keep covered and refrigerated. Bring to room temperature about 2 hours before serving. Heat ducklings, uncovered, in a 400° oven and heat sauce separately.

Remove excess fat from the ducklings, then season them inside and out with salt and pepper. Stuff each with some of the onion and celery, then place the ducks in a roasting pan on top of the remaining onion and celery. Prick skin of the ducklings, cover pan tightly with heavy foil and roast in a preheated 350° oven for 1½ to 2 hours. Do not uncover during this time.

Remove pan from oven and discard onion, celery, and all of the accumulated fat. Increase oven heat to 425°, prick duckling skins again, baste, then return to oven—this time, uncovered—for about 30 minutes. Remove, place ducklings on an ovenproof platter and cover loosely with foil, then keep warm in a 225° oven.

Make the sauce: Heat peaches in a low oven while you make the sauce. Discard fat in roasting pan, add stock, and deglaze the pan. Dissolve cornstarch in the water, then add to the sauce and bring to a boil, stirring constantly. Reduce heat and simmer for 5 minutes.

To serve: Place ducklings on a large platter and surround with the peaches. Carve ducklings (or cut them with a poultry scissors) and serve with a peach half and some sauce.

ROAST TURKEY WITH WILD RICE STUFFING

Makes 8 or more servings

1 turkey (about 12 pounds)
salt and black pepper
¼ pound (1 stick) melted butter or corn oil
1 large onion sliced
1 cup dry sherry or white wine

for the wild rice stuffing:
2 onions, finely chopped
¼ pound butter (1 stick)
1 cup chopped celery
6 cups cooked wild rice (about 2 cups uncooked), or part white rice
salt and pepper to taste

WHEN NO ONE IS LOOKING
Prepare the stuffing 1 day ahead. Keep covered and refrigerated.

FROZEN POWER
Freeze the stuffing. Defrost completely and use it promptly.

Make the stuffing: Sauté the chopped onion in the butter until lightly browned. Add the celery and cook a few minutes longer. Combine with cooked rice and season to taste. Cool, then cover and chill.

Season turkey with salt and pepper and fill cavities with the stuffing. To avoid any bacterial growth, roast the turkey as soon as it has been stuffed. Place turkey in a large roasting pan, surround with the sliced onion, then pour butter or oil over it and cover the whole turkey loosely with foil. Roast in a preheated 325° oven for 2 hours, then add the sherry or wine. Roast another 1½ hours or longer, until turkey is browned and tender, basting 2 or 3 times during the roasting. Remove turkey from oven and place on a platter to rest for 15 or 20 minutes before carving.

ROAST TURKEY WITH A CORNBREAD STUFFING

Makes 12 or more servings

1 turkey (14 to 16 pounds)
salt and black pepper
¼ pound (1 stick) melted butter or oil
1 onion, sliced
1 cup dry Marsala wine

for cornbread stuffing:
4 onions, finely chopped
¼ pound (1 stick) butter or oil
2 cups finely chopped celery
1 pound fresh pork sausage
4 cups crumbled cornbread
2 cups fresh bread crumbs
2 or 3 teaspoons poultry seasoning
salt and pepper to taste

WHEN NO ONE IS LOOKING
Prepare the stuffing 1 day ahead. Keep covered and refrigerated.

FROZEN POWER
Freeze the stuffing; use it promptly after defrosting.

Make the stuffing: Sauté the chopped onions in the butter or oil until lightly browned. Add celery and cook a few minutes longer. Remove from skillet and place in a large bowl. Brown pork sausage in that skillet and add to the onions and celery. Add remaining stuffing ingredients and mix thoroughly. Set aside. Cover and chill. (This will make more stuffing than is needed to stuff the turkey; put the extra in a separate casserole.)

Season turkey with salt and pepper. Fill cavities with stuffing, and to avoid any bacterial growth, roast the turkey as soon as it has been stuffed. Place turkey in a large roasting pan and surround with the sliced onions. Spoon butter or oil over the turkey, then cover the whole turkey loosely with foil. Place in a preheated 325° oven and roast for 2 hours. Add the Marsala and continue to roast, basting occasionally, until browned and tender, approximately an additional 2 to 3 hours.

CHICKEN MAGNIFICENT

Makes 6 to 12 servings, depending on appetites

- 10 to 12 chicken thighs or breasts, or a combination
- 2 ½ cups fresh white bread crumbs; must be homemade (see below)!
- 2 ¼ teaspoons salt
- ½ teaspoon black pepper
- 1 cup grated Parmesan cheese
- ½ pound (2 sticks) melted butter
- 1 or 2 tablespoons garlic oil (p. 18)

WHEN NO ONE IS LOOKING
Assemble the crumb mixture 1 day ahead, cover and refrigerate. Bring to room temperature before using. Or, coat and assemble the chicken 1 or 2 hours ahead, cover lightly, and leave at room temperature until time to bake. Or, bake the chicken 2 or 3 hours before serving, cover lightly, leave at room temperature, then reheat in a preheated 375° oven.

FROZEN POWER
Prepare the fresh white crumbs any time and freeze them for a month or longer. Keep plenty of these crumbs available in the freezer and keep grated Parmesan in your freezer; then prepare this magnificent chicken on a moment's notice!

Trim away excess fat and the flat bony part of the breasts' ribs, but *do not remove skin or any other bones!* Make bread crumbs from day-old white bread. Remove crusts and whirl remaining bread in a food processor. Spread out crumbs to dry at room temperature for a few hours. Combine these crumbs in a large bowl with the salt, pepper, and grated Parmesan. Combine melted butter and garlic oil in another large container.

Preheat oven to 350°. Dip each chicken piece into the butter-oil mixture, then roll in the crumb mixture, coating all sides well. Arrange chicken skin sides up in a single layer in a large open roasting pan. Pat remaining crumbs on the top of the chicken pieces and spoon on any remaining butter. Bake uncovered, basting once, for 1 hour and 15 minutes, or longer, but only until tender and well browned. Do *not* overcook. Serve hot or at room temperature.

BAKED "FRIED" CHICKEN

Makes about 4 servings

- 1 frying chicken, cut into 6 to 8 pieces
- 1 cup flour
- 2 teaspoons dried oregano
- 2 teaspoons garlic salt
- ½ teaspoon salt
- ½ teaspoon black pepper
- ½ teaspoon cayenne
- 2 eggs beaten slightly with 1 tablespoon water
- ¾ cup dry bread crumbs
- ⅛ pound butter (½ stick), melted
- 2 tablespoons vegetable oil

WHEN NO ONE IS LOOKING
Mix the flour with the salts and spices 1 or 2 days ahead; keep covered. The chicken can be baked 1 or 2 hours ahead, but undercook slightly, then return to the 375° oven shortly before serving to reheat and cook a little longer.

Combine flour, oregano, garlic salt, salt, black pepper, and cayenne and mix well. Place this mixture in a paper or plastic bag and coat the chicken pieces by shaking them inside the bag. Place bread crumbs in a shallow dish. Arrange beaten egg in a large bowl and the bread crumbs in a shallow bowl. Dip seasoned chicken in the beaten egg, then roll in the bread crumbs. Place these prepared pieces in an oiled large roasting pan in a single layer. Combine butter and oil, then spoon over the chicken pieces. Bake in a preheated 375° oven for 30 minutes, then baste and return to the oven for about another 30 or 40 minutes—until tender and brown.

BALSAMIC CHICKEN WITH PORTOBELLO MUSHROOMS

Makes 4 to 6 servings

1 frying chicken split into halves
salt and pepper to season
2 chopped shallots
¼ cup balsamic vinegar
¼ cup sugar
3 tablespoons soy sauce
3 tablespoons vegetable oil

for the mushrooms:
1 pound portobello mushrooms
6 tablespoons butter (3 ounces)
2 chopped shallots
salt and pepper
2 tablespoons balsamic vinegar
1 tablespoon soy sauce
1 tablespoon sugar

WHEN NO ONE IS LOOKING
Prepare the mushrooms 1 day ahead; cover and refrigerate them. Prepare everything several hours ahead; cover and reheat later before serving.

Season chicken with salt and pepper. Combine the shallots, balsamic vinegar, sugar, soy sauce, and oil in a bowl, and mix well until sugar has dissolved. Pour over the chicken and marinate for several hours; if possible marinate in a large heavy-duty resealable plastic bag—turning the bag over from time to time.

Prepare the mushrooms: Halve the mushrooms and cut them into ¼-inch slices. In a very large skillet or large pot, cook the shallots in the butter over moderate heat for 1 minute, then add the mushrooms, salt and pepper, and cook over moderate heat, stirring occasionally, until mushroom liquid has evaporated. Remove from heat and set aside.

Prepare the chicken: Place chicken halves skin sides down in a roasting pan and brown under the oven broiler—about 3 to 5 minutes. Turn chicken and brown the skin sides—another 4 to 5 minutes. Add remaining marinade and a little water. Turn oven to 350° and bake for 45 minutes or longer, basting occasionally, until chicken is tender and browned—adding water to prevent burning.

To serve: Heat mushrooms in a skillet and add the juices remaining after cooking the chicken; stir until bubbling hot. Spoon over the chicken, or serve as an accompaniment at the side of the chicken.

MEAT

STEAKS WITH ONIONS AND SWEET RED PEPPERS

Makes 6 servings

- 3 New York sirloin steaks, 1-inch thick, fat and gristle removed
- 3 sweet red peppers
- 2 large onions, sliced
- 3 tablespoons vegetable oil
- garlic salt and black pepper
- ¼ pound butter, melted
- 6 slices of New York corn rye bread or French bread

WHEN NO ONE IS LOOKING
Prepare the peppers and onions 1 day ahead. Keep them covered and refrigerated, but bring to room temperature a few hours before serving and reheat while cooking the steaks.

Toast bread slices in a moderate oven until lightly browned and very crisp. Set aside. Cut peppers in half and broil skin sides up until charred. Place charred peppers in a paper or plastic bag and let them cool for 15 or 20 minutes. Remove skins and seeds, then cut into slices. Sauté onions in the oil until tender but not too brown. Add the sliced peppers, then season with salt and black pepper and set aside while you broil the steaks.

Season steaks with garlic salt and black pepper, then broil or barbecue them to your taste. Reheat onions and pepper slices while steaks are cooking. Arrange toast slices on individual dinner plates (warmed if possible) and spoon some onions and peppers on each. Carve steaks into ¼-inch slices and arrange on top of the onion mixture, then spoon butter over steak slices and serve at once.

ROAST PRIME RIB OF BEEF

Makes 12 to 16 servings

- 1 whole prime rib of beef (17 to 18 pounds after it has been trimmed and tied by your butcher)
- salt and pepper to taste

WHEN NO ONE IS LOOKING
This is delicious at room temperature and excellent for a buffet dinner. If you decide to serve it in this style, roast the beef 3 to 4 hours ahead, cover lightly, leave at room temperature, and carve it at the buffet. The Madeira sauce (p. 147) is excellent with slices of this roast, so prepare it up to two days ahead (prepare it independently, not as part of the process of deglazing a roasting pan) and keep it covered and refrigerated.

Preheat oven to 450°. Season the meat generously—top and bottom—with salt and pepper, then place it in a large shallow roasting pan, fat side up, and roast for 10 minutes. Reduce heat to 375° and roast an additional 2 to 2 ½ hours, or to your taste. Remove from the oven and let the roast rest 20 minutes before carving.

TWO BEEF WELLINGTONS

Makes 16 servings

You will need either 1 very large oven or 2 regular size ovens. The 2 tenderloins should not be crowded on 1 pan, nor should you use 2 levels in one oven. If you only have 1 regular oven, plan this treat for 8 guests instead of 16.

2 whole beef tenderloins (each weighing about 7 pounds before trimming)
olive oil or clarified butter
2 ½ to 3 pounds puff pastry, homemade (p. 356) or the commercial frozen variety available in supermarkets
1 egg beaten with 1 tablespoon of water (for egg wash)

for the stuffing:
2 tablespoons butter
1 clove garlic, mashed (or from garlic oil, p. 18)
1 small onion
1 pound fresh mushrooms, finely chopped
2 teaspoons flour
1 ½ teaspoons salt
¼ teaspoon black pepper
¼ cup milk
4 ounces "Chicken Liver Pâté" (p. 43)
1 tablespoon freshly chopped parsley
3 egg yolks
1 tablespoon cognac

WHEN NO ONE IS LOOKING
The stuffing should be prepared 1 day ahead. The beef tenderloins should be roasted in the morning, then chilled. Complete the Madeira sauce in the morning immediately after the meat has finished roasting. Wrap the beef tenderloins in pastry in the morning or early afternoon of the dinner party and keep chilled.

FROZEN POWER
Puff pastry freezes well.

for the Madeira sauce:
1 onion, finely chopped
2 carrots, finely chopped
½ cup chopped celery
⅛ pound butter (½ stick), or olive oil
2 tablespoons tomato paste
4 ½ cups rich beef stock
½ cup dry Madeira
salt and black pepper to taste
¼ cup cornstarch dissolved in ½ cup cold water

Prepare the stuffing 1 day ahead. It must be absolutely cold before using. Sauté chopped onion in the butter with the garlic for a few minutes. Add chopped mushrooms, stir, and cook a few more minutes. Cover and cook 2 additional minutes. Sprinkle with flour, and stir. Add milk, then cook and stir for a few minutes. Season with salt and pepper, add pâté, and stir. Beat in the egg yolks and cook over lowest heat, stirring constantly for 2 minutes. Remove from heat and add parsley and cognac. Taste for seasoning. Cool, then cover and chill.

Preheat oven to 450° and roast the beef tenderloins in the morning. Be sure meat is at room temperature before roasting. Trim beef of all fat, skin, and gristle. Cut off the thin tail ends (freeze and use them later as steaks). Each tenderloin should weigh about 4 pounds after trimming. Rub trimmed beef with oil or butter and season with salt and pepper. Place tenderloins in a large roasting pan (or pans) and roast for 10 minutes. Reduce heat to 400° and roast about 20 minutes longer, basting once or twice. Meat must be rare. Remove meat from roasting pan, but save the pan and its drippings to make the sauce. Cool the tenderloins, then cover and chill.

Prepare the sauce: Sauté onion, carrots, and celery in the butter or oil until tender. Add tomato paste and beef stock, stir, then simmer uncovered for 15 minutes. Add the Madeira and use this mixture to deglaze the roasting pan(s), scraping the browned bits inside the pan(s). Simmer for 2 or 3 minutes, then strain into a saucepan. Taste for seasoning. Thicken with the dissolved cornstarch by gradually adding it to the boiling sauce until it reaches the thickness you prefer. Set aside.

Assemble, wrap, and finish the beef Wellingtons: Divide puff pastry into two portions, then for *each* tenderloin, follow these instructions:

1. Cover each tenderloin with stuffing—putting most of it on the top side, which will be placed upside down on the pastry.

2. Roll pastry into a large rectangle about ⅛ inch thick. Brush with egg wash.

3. Place chilled tenderloin top side down on pastry. Wrap pastry around the meat and cut away excess pastry. Place wrapped tenderloin in an large, oiled shallow roasting pan. Egg wash entire top. Decorate with pastry leaves, and cut a small hole in top center. Egg wash again. Chill until time to bake (at least one hour, but longer is fine).

For the final baking, preheat oven(s) to 400°. Keep tenderloins chilled, then bake them in the preheated oven(s) for 40 to 50 minutes. Reheat the Madeira sauce, carve at the table or at a buffet, and serve with the sauce.

BRISKET

Makes 10 to 16 servings

8 to 9 pounds beef brisket (weight after trimming)
salt and pepper
2 packages dried onion soup
1 ½ cups beef bouillon (canned is okay)
2 cups dry red or white wine, or beer
4 medium-size onions, sliced
⅓ to ½ cup ketchup

WHEN NO ONE IS LOOKING
Be sure to start this 1 or 2 days ahead so the meat can chill (easier to slice) and the fat can be easily removed. Cover and refrigerate. Sauce can be made any time after the first day's roasting.

FROZEN POWER
An ideal dish for the freezer. Freeze the entire amount or divide it and freeze in small portions.

Season brisket with salt and pepper and place fat side up in a large roasting pan. Mix remaining ingredients together and pour this mixture over the meat. Cover pan tightly with a cover or use double foil, then place in a preheated 400° oven for 10 minutes. Reduce heat to 275° and roast an additional 3 hours or longer. The meat should be very tender. Remove and cool to room temperature, then cover and refrigerate overnight.

Next day: Remove fat, then lift meat out and place it on a slicing board. Taste juices for seasoning, then thicken either with a roux or with diluted cornstarch. Set aside. Cut brisket into slices and arrange as desired. Pour thickened sauce over the slices. Reheat before serving.

BEEF TENDERLOIN STEAKS WRAPPED IN CRÊPES

Makes 8 servings

8 beef tenderloin steaks, 1 ¼ inches thick, fat and skin removed
salt and cracked black pepper
8 large "Crêpes," 10 inches in diameter (p. 152)
olive oil or clarified butter
1 tablespoon grated Parmesan cheese
melted butter

for mushroom filling:
6 tablespoons chopped shallots (or use frozen shallots, p. 18)
6 tablespoons butter
1 pound fresh mushrooms, sliced
4 teaspoons flour
salt and pepper
½ cup heavy cream
½ cup Madeira or sherry

for Madeira sauce:
1 large carrot, chopped
1 onion, chopped
1 tablespoon butter
3 cups rich beef stock
2 teaspoons tomato paste
2 tablespoons cornstarch diluted in ¼ cup cold water
¼ cup Madeira or sherry
salt and pepper

WHEN NO ONE IS LOOKING
Make the mushroom filling, Madeira sauce, and the crêpes a day ahead. Cover and keep refrigerated separately. Bring all of them to room temperature before assembling and cooking the steaks. You can do the entire assembly of the steaks, except for the final baking, in the early afternoon; cover the crêpe-wrapped steaks with plastic wrap and leave at room temperature. Shortly before serving proceed with the final baking.

FROZEN POWER
The mushroom filling, the Madeira sauce, and the crêpes all freeze beautifully, making this both an elegant and an easy dish.

Prepare mushroom filling: Melt butter in a skillet, add shallots and sauté gently for a few minutes. Add mushrooms and sauté for 2 minutes. Sprinkle with the flour, stir, then add cream and continue to stir until mixture begins to bubble. Reduce heat, season with salt and pepper, then add Madeira and simmer for 1 or 2 minutes. Remove from heat and cool.

Prepare Madeira sauce: Sauté chopped carrot and onion in the butter slowly until tender and lightly browned. Add beef stock and tomato paste and simmer gently for 10 to 15 minutes, covered part of the time. Thicken to taste with the dissolved cornstarch. Strain. Add Madeira, adjust seasoning, then set aside.

Cook and assemble the steaks: Have the crêpes ready. If they were made ahead and refrigerated or frozen, make certain they are room temperature. To soften the crêpes, stack them with melted butter in between each, wrap in foil and place in a very low oven for 2 or 3 minutes.

Season steaks with salt and cracked pepper. Heat the oil or butter in a heavy skillet and sauté steaks until browned but still rare. Remove from skillet and set aside.

Place ⅛ of the mushroom filling on each crêpe, then top each with a steak. Wrap crêpes around the meat (like wrapping a package) and place seam sides down in 1 large well-buttered, shallow roasting pan (if necessary, use 2 pans). Do not crowd the steaks. Brush tops with melted butter, and sprinkle each with about ½ teaspoon grated Parmesan. Cover lightly and set aside.

Before serving, preheat oven or 2 ovens to 450°. Place pan(s) in the oven(s) long enough to thoroughly heat. This can take 8 to 15 minutes depending on the thickness of the steaks and their temperature when they go in the oven(s). Meat should be medium rare. Reheat sauce and serve with each portion, or let guests help themselves.

ALL-PURPOSE WONDERFUL CRÊPES

Makes about 24 7-inch crêpes

6 eggs
2 cups milk (plus some extra)
1 ½ cups flour
¼ teaspoon salt
¼ pound (1 stick) butter, melted
additional melted butter for stacking

WHEN NO ONE IS LOOKING
Cook these 1 to 2 days in advance. Stack the crêpes with melted butter between each, and wrap in foil with 6 or 7 to a package. Cool and refrigerate. Bring to room temperature before using, then reheat them in their foil wrapping in a very low oven—only long enough to allow you to separate them and to fold or roll them without cracking or breaking.

FROZEN POWER
Freeze the crêpes and keep them as frozen assets for various wonderful concoctions. Follow the instructions given above in "When No One Is Looking."

Beat the eggs, then gradually add the flour and milk alternately to the eggs. Add salt and melted butter and let the batter stand at least 1 hour (or overnight in the refrigerator). Batter should have the consistency of heavy cream; add more milk if necessary. Cook crêpes in a nonstick skillet.

MEATBALLS

Makes enough for 2 quarts of tomato sauce

- 2 pounds beef chuck—not too lean—ground twice
- 1 small onion, finely chopped or grated
- 2 tablespoons chopped parsley
- ½ cup milk
- ½ cup bread crumbs
- 2 ¼ teaspoons salt
- ½ teaspoon black pepper
- 1 garlic clove, mashed (or from garlic oil, p. 18), plus 1 tablespoon of garlic oil
- ½ cup grated Parmesan cheese
- ⅓ to ½ cup ketchup
- 2 eggs, slightly beaten
- canola or corn oil (for sautéing the meatballs)

WHEN NO ONE IS LOOKING
Combine the meat mixture 1 day ahead; cover and keep refrigerated.

FROZEN POWER
Perfect as frozen assets if you combine the meatballs with a fine quality tomato sauce, such as the one on page 183.

Combine all ingredients (except the oil for sautéing) in a large bowl and mix thoroughly—best done with your very clean hands. Form into meatballs—any size you prefer. Heat a large nonstick skillet , add oil, and sauté the meatballs until well browned. Eat them as is, or heat them in tomato sauce, such as the one on page 183.

MY BEST MEAT LOAF

- 1 ½ pounds ground beef (not too lean)
- 1 ½ teaspoons salt
- ¼ teaspoon ground black pepper
- 1 teaspoon dry mustard or 1 tablespoon of Dijon-style mustard
- 1 small onion
- 1 sweet pepper, green or red
- ¾ cup tomato juice
- ½ cup tomato ketchup
- ½ cup dry bread crumbs
- 2 eggs, lightly beaten with a fork

for later:

- ½ cup chile sauce or ketchup

optional:

- 2 large potatoes or 4 small ones
- a little oil

WHEN NO ONE IS LOOKING
Mix the ingredients together in the morning; cover and refrigerate. Bake later.

Place ground beef in a large bowl. Finely chop onion and sweet pepper in a food processor, then add to the beef. Add all remaining ingredients and mix thoroughly with your hands.

Mound the mixture in a large flat nonstick roasting pan, and bake in a preheated 450° oven for 15 minutes. Turn heat down to about 350° and bake an additional 30 minutes. Remove from oven and cover top with the chile sauce or ketchup, then return to oven for about another 15 minutes. Serve hot or cold.

Optional: Toss sliced potatoes with a little vegetable oil, then scatter them around the meatloaf after the first 15 minutes of baking. Continue to bake as usual, except about half way through, use a spatula and turn the potatoes so that they brown on both sides.

HOME-STYLE BEEF FAJITAS

Makes 2 to 4 servings

1 ½ pounds skirt steak (or flank steak)
2 to 3 onions, sliced
2 tablespoons oil
green chile salsa (homemade or bought)
guacamole
corn or flour tortillas

for the marinade:
½ cup wine vinegar (or part balsamic)
½ cup oil
½ teaspoon salt
¼ teaspoon black pepper
1 teaspoon dried oregano
1 teaspoon dried ground cumin

WHEN NO ONE IS LOOKING
Mix the marinade 1 day ahead. Cover and leave at room temperature.

Combine marinade ingredients and mix well. Pour over the skirt steak, and marinate for about 4 hours, turning the steak midway.

Sauté the onions in the 2 tablespoons of oil over high heat until browned, then set aside. Barbecue or broil the steak until well browned but still rare. Set aside.

Shortly before serving, carve steak on the diagonal into ¼-inch thick slices. Heat a large skillet and add the sautéed onions and the steak slices. Stir over high heat for about 1 minute, only long enough to heat. Bring skillet to table with the chile salsa, guacamole, and tortillas. Let guests help themselves.

OPEN-FACE BEEF TACOS WITH OLIVES AND RAISINS

Makes 4 to 6 servings

corn tortillas
vegetable oil for frying the tortillas

for the filling:
1 onion, chopped
1 clove garlic, mashed (or from garlic oil, p. 18)
3 tablespoons unflavored oil
1 pound lean ground beef
1 teaspoon salt or to taste
½ teaspoon black pepper
½ teaspoon ground cumin
½ teaspoon dried oregano
1 cup chile salsa (homemade or bought)
½ cup coarsely chopped pimento-stuffed green olives
½ cup dark raisins, rinsed in hot water, then drained

for the garnish:
chile salsa
grated Jack cheese
chopped green peppers
shredded green lettuce
chopped green onions

WHEN NO ONE IS LOOKING
Fry the tortillas 2 days ahead; place them in plastic bags and refrigerate. Reheat in a 350° oven. Prepare the beef mixture 1 day ahead; keep covered and refrigerated. Reheat gently before serving.

FROZEN POWER
Fry tortillas and freeze them in tightly sealed plastic bags. Defrost for a few minutes, then reheat in a 350° oven before serving.

Prepare tortillas: Heat oil in a skillet, then fry the corn tortillas until crisp and drain them on paper towels. Set aside until needed.

Prepare filling: Sauté the onion with the garlic in the oil until lightly browned, then add the beef and sauté over high heat, stirring frequently, until almost cooked through. Add salt, pepper, cumin, oregano, and chile salsa. Stir, cover, and cook over low heat for about 5 minutes. Add the olives and raisins and simmer another few minutes. Remove from heat and set aside until ready to serve, then reheat briefly.

Serve: Place crisp tortillas on dinner plates, then top each with some of the beef mixture. Let guests help themselves to the garnishes.

GREEK STEW

Makes 6 servings

- 3 pounds lean beef stew meat, cut in 2-inch chunks
- 4 large onions, sliced
- ½ cup olive oil
- 2 tablespoons flour
- 1 (6-ounce) can tomato paste
- 3 teaspoons salt, or to taste
- ½ teaspoon black pepper
- 1 teaspoon cinnamon
- ½ teaspoon cloves
- ½ teaspoon ground cumin
- ¾ cup dry red wine
- ¼ cup brown sugar
- ¼ cup dark raisins

WHEN NO ONE IS LOOKING
Cook this 1 or 2 days ahead. Cover and refrigerate. Reheat in a 300° oven.

Combine all ingredients in a large ovenproof casserole and stir until well combined. Cover and bake at 250° for 3 to 4 hours.

LEG OF LAMB WITH A MUSTARD-ROSEMARY COVER

Makes 8 servings

1 large leg of lamb (6 to 7 pounds after trimming)
salt and black pepper
1 onion, chopped
2 or 3 carrots, chopped
2 teaspoons mashed garlic (or from garlic oil, p. 18)
2 teaspoons dried rosemary
½ cup Dijon-style mustard
2 tablespoons soy sauce
4 tablespoons olive oil (or corn oil)
1 cup dry red wine
2 cups beef stock

WHEN NO ONE IS LOOKING
Chop the carrots and onions in the morning; keep covered and refrigerated until time to use. The leg of lamb can be coated with the mustard mixture in the morning and left at room temperature until time to roast.

Preheat oven to 350°. Remove all fat and skin from the lamb. Season with salt and pepper. Place chopped onion and carrots on the bottom of a roasting pan. In a bowl combine mashed garlic, rosemary, mustard, and soy sauce, then whisk in the oil. Spread this mixture first on the underside of the leg, then place the leg on the carrots and onions underside down and cover top and sides of the lamb with the remaining mixture. Roast uncovered for 1½ to 2 hours, depending on the weight of the meat and how well done you like it. Remove lamb from oven and place on a warm platter. Remove excess fat from roasting pan, then deglaze the pan with the red wine and beef stock. Serve some of this sauce with the sliced lamb.

Note: If you want to thicken the sauce, dissolve 2 tablespoons cornstarch in about ⅓ cup cold water and gradually add it to the boiling sauce, stirring constantly, until it reaches desired thickness. Reduce heat and simmer for 1 minute.

LEG OF LAMB WITH WHITE BEANS

Makes 6 to 8 servings

- 1 leg of lamb (5 or 6 pounds, trimmed)
- salt and black pepper
- 2 tablespoons of oil
- 2 large onions, chopped
- 3 to 4 fresh tomatoes, chopped or puréed (or substitute canned)
- 2 (1-pound) cans of white kidney beans (cannellini), rinsed and drained
- ½ cup dry red wine
- 1 cup rich beef stock

WHEN NO ONE IS LOOKING
Prepare this entire dish up to 4 hours ahead, but undercook slightly. Cover lightly and leave at room temperature. Return to a 350° oven to reheat and cook a little more.

Preheat oven to 400°. Season lamb with salt, pepper, and oil, then place the lamb on top of the chopped onions in a roasting pan. Roast uncovered for 20 minutes, then reduce heat to 350° and continue roasting another 20 minutes. Add tomatoes, wine, beef stock, and beans, and return to the oven to roast about 20 to 30 more minutes, basting once or twice. For medium rare the lamb will take approximately 1 ½ hours, but it depends on the size of the leg and how cold it is when you begin. Use your judgment or a meat thermometer. Remove from oven and let the lamb rest for 15 minutes before carving. Carve the lamb and serve the white beans and sauce on top of the slices, or at the side.

BUTTERFLIED LEG OF LAMB

Makes 6 to 8 servings

1 large leg of lamb, boned then butterflied and flattened

for the marinade:
2 tablespoons chopped shallots (or use frozen shallots, p. 18)
2 teaspoons mashed garlic (or from garlic oil, p. 18)
1 ½ teaspoons salt
½ teaspoon black pepper
3 tablespoons chopped fresh rosemary or 3 teaspoons dried
2 teaspoons sugar
juice of ½ lemon
1 cup dry red wine
⅔ cup olive oil (or corn oil)

WHEN NO ONE IS LOOKING
Mix the marinade 2 to 3 days ahead. Cover and refrigerate.

Combine ingredients for the marinade. Marinate the lamb at room temperature in this mixture for at least 3 hours or all day, turning it over once or twice. Broil or barbecue, turning and basting with the remaining marinade. This takes about 40 minutes.

LAMB STEW MY FAVORITE WAY

Makes 6 to 8 servings

- 4 pounds lean lamb stew meat, cut in 2-inch chunks
- ⅛ pound butter (½ stick)
- 2 large onions, coarsely chopped
- 5 tablespoons flour
- 2 cups canned tomatoes
- ½ teaspoon dried sweet basil
- ¼ teaspoon dried oregano
- ¼ teaspoon dried rosemary
- salt and black pepper
- 1 cup sour cream

WHEN NO ONE IS LOOKING
Prepare this 2 days ahead; keep covered and refrigerated. Reheat gently.

FROZEN POWER
This freezes well. If possible, freeze without the sour cream. Defrost completely, then reheat over low heat, stirring occasionally.

Melt butter in a large pot and sauté lamb for 2 minutes, turning pieces frequently. (It is not necessary to brown the meat.) Add the onions and sauté another minute. Sprinkle the flour over the meat and stir thoroughly. Reduce heat, then stir in the tomatoes. Add herbs, season with salt and pepper, then cook over low heat, stirring constantly, until sauce begins to boil. Cover, turn heat to lowest simmer, and cook for 2 hours, or until lamb is tender. If desired, the stew can be cooked in a 300° oven. When done, remove from heat and stir in the sour cream. Reheat gently.

BONED LAMB RACKS WITH PINE NUTS AND CURRANTS

Makes 4 to 6 servings

- 2 racks of lamb, boned, fat and skin removed (but save bones)
- garlic oil (p. 18)
- salt and black pepper
- ⅓ cup currants, washed, drained, and dried on paper towels
- ⅓ cup pine nuts, lightly toasted
- 2 cups lamb stock (made from the bones) or use canned beef bouillon

WHEN NO ONE IS LOOKING
Prepare the lamb stock 1 or 2 days ahead; keep covered and refrigerated. Prepare the currants and pine nuts 1 day ahead.

Preheat oven to 450°. Roll the two boned lamb racks in garlic oil, then season generously with salt and pepper. Roast uncovered for 15 minutes, then baste and return to oven for about 5 minutes. The lamb is meant to be rare, but you can roast it longer to suit your taste. Remove from oven and place lamb on an ovenproof platter. Cover loosely with foil and keep warm in a very low oven while you make the sauce. Remove oil left in the roasting pan, then add the stock and deglaze the pan. Reduce slightly, and if desired thicken lightly. Pour some of this sauce over the lamb and cover with the currants and pine nuts. Carve the lamb at the table, and serve additional sauce to each guest or pass it separately.

RACK OF LAMB WITH MUSTARD AND A RED WINE SAUCE

Makes 4 to 6 servings

- 2 racks of lamb, trimmed of all fat
- salt and black pepper
- ½ cup Dijon-style mustard

1 teaspoon dried rosemary
1 tablespoon soy sauce
1 teaspoon mashed garlic
(or from garlic oil, p. 18)
3 tablespoons olive oil
1 cup dry red wine
1 ½ cups beef bouillon
¼ pound (1 stick) cold butter,
sliced

WHEN NO ONE IS LOOKING
Prepare the mustard mixture 2 days ahead; keep covered at room temperature.

Preheat oven to 450°. Combine mustard, rosemary, soy sauce and garlic in a bowl, then whisk in the olive oil. Season racks of lamb with salt and pepper, then coat them with the mustard mixture. Roast the lamb for 15 minutes if meat is at room temperature (20 minutes if it is cold). Remove from the oven and baste, then return to oven for 5 to 10 minutes. Remove racks to a carving board. Add red wine and bouillon to the roasting pan and deglaze, then reduce the sauce by about half. Whisk in the butter slices over very low heat—only until combined—then remove from heat. The sauce will separate if you try to reheat it, so do not add the butter until you are ready to serve. Carve lamb and serve slices with the sauce.

RACKS OF LAMB WITH PARSLEY AND GARLIC

2 racks of lamb, trimmed of
all the fat, and bone ends
"Frenched"
2 tablespoons olive oil or
corn oil
salt and black pepper

for the parsley-garlic coating:
¼ cup olive oil or corn oil
1 clove garlic mashed
(or from garlic oil, p. 18)
½ teaspoon salt
½ cup freshly chopped parsley
1 cup dry bread crumbs

WHEN NO ONE IS LOOKING
Prepare the crumb mixture 2 days ahead; keep covered and refrigerated. Bring to room temperature before using.

Ask your butcher to prepare the racks for carving: to remove the chine bone and all the fat; to mark places for carving the ribs; and to French the ends by scraping away the fat and gristle from the ends of the bones.

Preheat oven to 450°. Mix together the ingredients for the parsley-garlic coating and set aside. Rub lamb racks with the 2 tablespoons of oil, and season them with salt and pepper. Roast them in the preheated oven for 15 minutes. Remove from oven, and pat parsley-garlic mixture on the top sides of the racks. Return to oven and roast approximately 5 to 10 minutes longer—depending on how well done you want the lamb.

MEDALLIONS OF LAMB WITH GARLIC AND ROSEMARY

Makes 4 to 6 servings

- 2 racks of lamb, boned and all fat removed
- salt and black pepper
- 4 tablespoons garlic oil (p. 18)
- 2 teaspoons dried rosemary
- 1 cup white wine (medium-dry)
- ¼ pound (1 stick) cold butter, sliced

WHEN NO ONE IS LOOKING
Bone and trim the lamb 1 day ahead; cover and refrigerate.

Cut boned lamb into slices about ½ to ¾ inch thick. Season them with salt and pepper. Heat garlic oil in a heavy large skillet and sauté these medallions over moderately high heat on one side for about 1 to 2 minutes. Sprinkle with the rosemary, then turn them and sauté them for another few minutes. They should remain rare or at least pink. Remove them to an ovenproof platter, cover lightly with foil, and keep warm in a low oven (150°). Add wine to the skillet and reduce over high heat to ⅓ of the original amount, then whisk in the butter over low heat. Do not add the butter until ready to serve. When ready, serve the lamb medallions with the prepared sauce.

INDONESIAN LAMB ROASTS

Makes 8 to 10 servings

4 racks of lamb, cut into portions of 2 or 3 chops joined together

for the marinade:
¼ cup vinegar
rind and juice of 1 lemon
1 garlic clove, mashed (or from garlic oil, p. 18)
¼ cup chopped onion (or 1 tablespoon dehydrated minced onion)
1 teaspoon celery seeds
1 teaspoon dried oregano
2 bay leaves
2 tablespoons soy sauce
1 teaspoon salt
1 tablespoon A-1 sauce
2 tablespoons curry powder
2 dashes Tabasco sauce
⅓ cup Dijon-style mustard
⅓ cup honey
¼ cup corn oil

WHEN NO ONE IS LOOKING
Prepare the marinade up to 2 weeks ahead. Keep tightly covered and refrigerated.

Combine marinade ingredients in a bowl and mix thoroughly. Set aside. Place lamb chops in a large roasting pan in a single layer and spoon marinade over them. Leave at room temperature for 2 hours or longer. Drain marinade from the chops and reserve. Preheat oven to 450°. Roast lamb, fat sides up, for 15 minutes. Remove and baste with reserved marinade, then return to oven for 10 additional minutes. Remove from oven. Reheat remaining marinade to a simmer and serve with the lamb.

HOME-STYLE CHORIZO

- 3 pounds fresh pork, not too lean
- 3 ¼ teaspoons salt
- 1 tablespoon ground cumin
- 5 to 6 tablespoons ancho chili powder
- 1 tablespoon dried oregano
- 1 tablespoon Hungarian sweet paprika
- 6 tablespoons vinegar (use part balsamic)
- 2 tablespoons mashed garlic (or from garlic oil, p. 18)

WHEN NO ONE IS LOOKING
Prepare this 2 to 3 days ahead; keep covered and refrigerated.

FROZEN POWER
Divide and freeze the chorizo in the amounts you are likely to use. If desired, make them them into sausagelike fingers, then double-wrap and freeze in plastic bags.

Use an old-fashioned meat grinder and grind the pork only once using a coarse "die"—or, ask the butcher to grind it coarsely. Place the ground pork in a large bowl, then add remaining ingredients and mix thoroughly with your very clean hands. Sauté a small bit to taste for seasoning, then adjust if needed. Cover and refrigerate for 24 hours to mellow.

BAKED HAM

- 1 raw ham (about 14 pounds)
- 1 cup brown sugar (packed to measure)
- ⅓ cup Dijon-style mustard
- ⅔ cup dry sherry

WHEN NO ONE IS LOOKING
Prepare this in the morning; cover and leave at room temperature. Reheat or serve as is. The ham can be baked 1 day ahead; if so, serve it cold or at room temperature.

Preheat oven to 325°. Place ham in a large roasting pan and cover it with heavy foil. Bake for about 3 to 3 ½ hours without basting. Remove foil, then cover ham with a mixture of the sugar, mustard, and sherry. Return to oven and bake another hour, basting every 20 minutes. Serve hot or at room temperature.

VEAL CHOPS ORLOFF STYLE

Makes 4 servings

4 veal chops (1 ¼ inches thick)
salt and black pepper
1 recipe of "Duxelles" (p. 42)
¼ cup corn oil
1 cup dry white wine

for the cheese sauce:
3 tablespoons butter
3 tablespoons flour
1 ½ cups milk, heated
½ teaspoon salt
¼ teaspoon black pepper
⅓ cup grated Swiss Gruyère cheese
1 egg yolk, lightly beaten

WHEN NO ONE IS LOOKING
Prepare the cheese sauce 1 day ahead; keep covered and refrigerated. Bring to room temperature before using. The chops can be assembled with the sauce in the morning. Cover and refrigerate; 2 to 3 hours before the final baking remove and bring to room temperature.

Prepare the cheese sauce: Melt butter in a saucepan and stir in the flour. Cook, stirring, without browning. Add hot milk and whisk mixture until it comes to a boil. Reduce heat to a simmer, then add the salt and pepper. Remove from heat, then add the cheese and stir to melt. Taste for seasoning and if needed, adjust. Beat in the egg yolk, then set aside.

Prepare the veal chops: Heat corn oil in a heavy skillet. Season veal chops, then sauté them for a few minutes on each side, but do *not* overcook. They should remain rare. Remove from skillet and place them in a large shallow roasting pan in a single layer. Spoon the duxelles on each chop and pat down.

Pour off fat in skillet, then add the wine, deglaze and reduce to ½ of the original amount. Spoon around the chops. Spoon cheese sauce over each chop. Cover until time to bake. Preheat oven to 400°. Place prepared chops uncovered in the oven and bake for about 15 minutes, until until tops have browned.

SPECIAL ENTRÉES

LASAGNA WITH TOMATO-MEAT SAUCE

Makes 12 to 16 servings

for the meat sauce:
2 very large onions, chopped medium fine
1 pound fresh mushrooms, cleaned, then sliced or chopped
3 tablespoons garlic oil (p. 18)
3 ½ pounds beef chuck, ground twice
3 tablespoons vegetable oil (for sautéing the beef)
3 cups canned tomatoes (1-pound, 12-ounce can)—mash the tomatoes
3 (6-ounce) cans tomato paste
5 cups beef stock (or beef bouillon)
1 ½ teaspoons sweet basil
1 ½ teaspoons oregano
salt and pepper to taste

for the lasagna:
1 pound lasagna noodles
2 pounds ricotta cheese
1 pound mozzarella cheese, thinly sliced
8 to 9 ounces grated Parmesan cheese

WHEN NO ONE IS LOOKING
You can perform a variety of preparations ahead of time. Assemble the entire lasagna 1 day ahead, then cover and refrigerate. Or, prepare the sauce 1 to 2 days ahead and keep covered and chilled. The sauce is easier to work with when cold.

FROZEN POWER
I devised this recipe for freezing because I found it is so wonderful to have this scrumptious lasagna on hand. Freeze before baking, defrost, then bake as directed.

First prepare the sauce: It is best if prepared a day ahead and chilled. Sauté the chopped onions in the garlic oil in a large pot for about 5 minutes, or until tender and lightly browned. Add the mushrooms and continue to sauté for 5 to 10 minutes longer. Remove this mixture from the pot and set aside. Add the vegetable oil to the pot, then sauté the ground beef until lightly cooked. Return the onion-mushroom mixture to the pot, add remaining ingredients, and stir well. Bring to a boil, then turn down and simmer covered for 1 ½ to 2 hours. Remove cover during the last half hour. Taste for seasoning, then cool and chill.

Prepare the noodles: Bring a very large pot of water to a boil and add a little oil and 1 tablespoon salt. When water boils, add the noodles and stir occasionally; cook until barely tender. Add cold water to the pot to stop the cooking, then drain. Lift noodles carefully onto a rack and layer them between paper towels to remove any excess water.

Assemble: This recipe should fill three 8-inch square pans—this is very handy if you plan to freeze the lasagna—or use one very large shallow casserole. For three square pans, follow these instructions:

1. Reserve about 5 to 6 cups of the sauce to use later to spoon over individual servings. If you plan to freeze the lasagna, I suggest dividing it into three portions and freezing the reserved sauce in three separate containers.

2. Put a small amount of sauce in the bottom of each of the pans. Cover with some noodles; sprinkle lightly with a little salt and black pepper. Top noodles with some ricotta, then with some grated Parmesan, and then with slices of mozzarella. Repeat the steps just described: (1) layer of sauce; (2) layer of noodles; (3) layer of ricotta; (4) layer of Parmesan. You may be able to repeat these 4 steps once again, depending on the depth of your pan(s). Top the casserole(s) with a layer of noodles and Parmesan.

Serve: Place pan(s) in a preheated 350° oven and bake covered until very hot—the amount of time will depend on the temperature of the lasagna when you put it in the oven (approximately 30 to 45 minutes for one small pan, 1 hour or longer for a large pan, and longer if it is cold). While the lasagna is baking, heat the reserved sauce. When ready, cut lasagna into squares and top each serving with extra sauce, or pass the extra sauce separately. If desired, serve additional grated Parmesan.

TURKEY OR CHICKEN TETRAZZINI

Makes 8 to 12 servings

6 or 7 cups diced cooked turkey or chicken
1 onion, chopped
2 tablespoons butter
1 sweet red pepper, coarsely chopped
salt and black pepper
4 tablespoons butter
3 tablespoons flour
3 ½ cups rich warm chicken stock (or part leftover gravy)
1 cup heavy cream
1 cup sliced water chestnuts (if canned, drained and diced)
⅔ cup diced marinated artichoke bottoms or hearts
2 cups grated Parmesan cheese
2 to 4 tablespoons dry sherry
1 pound thin spaghetti, cooked al dente and drained

WHEN NO ONE IS LOOKING
Assemble this 1 day ahead; keep covered and refrigerated until 2 hours before the final baking.

FROZEN POWER
Freeze this delicious concoction, but do so before the final baking. To serve, defrost completely, then bake as directed above.

In a large pot sauté the chopped onion in the 2 tablespoons of butter until tender and lightly browned. Add the chopped sweet pepper and cook for 1 or 2 minutes over moderate heat. Season. Add the 4 tablespoons of butter, and as soon as it has melted, stir in the flour. Cook and stir over moderate heat for 1 minute, then add the warm chicken stock and stir constantly until mixture comes to a boil. Add the cream, diced turkey (or chicken), water chestnuts, artichokes, and 1 cup of the grated Parmesan. Stir over moderate heat until combined and warmed through. Add salt and pepper as needed, and if desired, add the sherry.

Combine the spaghetti (cut into smaller pieces, if desired) with the turkey (chicken) mixture. Spoon into a large shallow casserole (or two smaller ones) and sprinkle top with remaining grated Parmesan. Set aside until 30 minutes before serving.

Preheat oven to 375°. Place casserole(s) in the oven and bake uncovered for about 25 to 30 minutes—until hot and top has browned.

BAKED FETTUCINE

Makes 10 to 12 servings as a first course, 4 to 6 as a main entrée

You will need a 12-inch nonstick skillet with the handle removed!

- 8 ounces dry fettucine noodles
- 5 ounces grated Swiss Gruyère cheese
- 6 ounces grated Parmesan cheese
- 2 cups heavy cream
- 1 ¾ teaspoons salt
- ½ teaspoon black pepper
- 2 extra large eggs
- 3 tablespoons butter
- extra grated Parmesan to be passed at table

WHEN NO ONE IS LOOKING
Assemble the fettucine—ready for the final baking—the day before or in the morning. Cover and refrigerate until 2 hours before baking.

FROZEN POWER
Freeze only for use as leftovers.

If desired, the fettucine can be broken into smaller pieces before cooking. Cook fettucine al dente. Drain, then return to the pot; add the cheeses, and mix well. Beat the eggs with the cream, salt, and pepper, then add to the pasta in the pot and toss well. Melt the butter in the nonstick skillet, then pour in the entire pasta mixture. Bake in a preheated 350° oven until golden brown—about 45 minutes or longer. Invert on a large round ovenproof platter. Reheat briefly in the oven and serve very hot.

Cut in wedges and serve on hot plates. Pass additional grated Parmesan and black pepper.

CANNELONI WITH A RICOTTA-SPINACH FILLING

Makes 12 servings

for the tomato sauce:
2 onions, finely chopped
1 or 2 garlic cloves, mashed (or from garlic oil, p. 18)
4 or 5 tablespoons oil
5 cups canned tomatoes, chopped
1 tablespoon chopped fresh thyme or 1 teaspoon dried
2 tablespoons chopped fresh basil or 1½ teaspoons dried
1 to 2 teaspoons salt (or to taste)
½ teaspoon black pepper (or to taste)

WHEN NO ONE IS LOOKING
Prepare the sauce 2 days ahead; keep covered and refrigerated. Prepare the ricotta-spinach filling 1 day ahead; keep covered and refrigerated. Completely assemble the canneloni-crêpes several hours before the final baking.

FROZEN POWER
This tomato sauce, like most tomato sauces, freezes beautifully.

for the ricotta-spinach filling:
1 pound whole-milk ricotta cheese
1 (10-ounce) package frozen chopped spinach
1 teaspoon salt
¼ teaspoon black pepper
2 eggs
¾ cup grated Parmesan cheese

to assemble:
12 "Crêpes" (7 inches in diameter; p. 152)
extra grated Parmesan for the final topping

Make the tomato sauce: Sauté onion and garlic in the oil until lightly browned. Add remaining sauce ingredients and simmer covered for one hour. Uncover and simmer about 30 minutes longer. Taste and adjust seasoning. Set aside.

Make the filling: Defrost spinach and drain thoroughly. Frozen chopped spinach is usually not sufficiently chopped. Place it in a food processor, then process it a few seconds. Add the ricotta and process again a few seconds. Add the remaining ingredients and process only until well mixed. Taste and adjust seasoning, then cover and refrigerate at least one hour.

Assemble and finish: Fill each crêpe with a heaping tablespoon of the chilled filling and roll up. Cover the bottom of a large shallow casserole (or two) with some of the sauce, then place the filled crêpes on the sauce, seam sides down. Cover with more of the sauce and sprinkle tops with grated Parmesan. Bake uncovered in a preheated 400° oven for 15 minutes or longer, depending on how cold the filled canneloni are.

FETTUCINE ALFREDO MY WAY

Makes 4 servings as a main course, 6 to 8 as a first course

for the sauce:
½ pound butter (2 sticks)
2 cups heavy whipping cream
1 teaspoon salt
½ teaspoon black pepper
½ pound grated Parmesan cheese

for the pasta:
12 ounces dry fettucine
8 quarts water
2 tablespoons oil
2 tablespoons salt

WHEN NO ONE IS LOOKING
Prepare the sauce many hours ahead; cover and leave at room temperature. Heat and stir gently before adding to the fettucine.

Make the sauce: Melt the butter in a saucepan, but do not let it cook. Add the cream over lowest heat, then immediately remove from the heat. Stir in the salt, pepper, and Parmesan. Set aside.

Cook the pasta: Bring water to a boil in a large pot, then add oil and salt. Add fettucine to the rapidly boiling water and cook until al dente, that is, tender but not mushy. Drain well, then return the fettucine to the large pot. Add the sauce and toss over lowest heat for 2 to 3 minutes. Serve on heated plates.

LASAGNA ROLLS WITH A SPINACH-CHEESE FILLING

Makes 14 to 18 rolls

1 pound commercial lasagna, about 18 strips, each 10 inches long

for the sauce:
1 large onion, chopped
1 garlic clove, mashed (from garlic oil, p. 18)
2 tablespoons oil
1 (1-pound) can tomatoes
3 (8-ounce) cans tomato sauce
½ teaspoon dried basil
¼ teaspoon dried thyme
salt and black pepper to taste

for the spinach-cheese filling:
1 (10-ounce) package of frozen chopped spinach
1 ½ pounds ricotta cheese
1 cup grated Parmesan cheese
2 eggs
1 ¼ to 1 ½ teaspoons salt
¼ teaspoon black pepper
¼ teaspoon nutmeg

WHEN NO ONE IS LOOKING
Prepare the sauce up to 3 days ahead; keep covered and refrigerated. Prepare the filling 1 day ahead; cover and refrigerate. Assemble the rolls 1 day ahead; keep covered and refrigerated. Remove from refrigerator about 2 hours before the final baking.

FROZEN POWER
Freeze these rolls! To serve, defrost completely, then proceed as directed in the recipe.

Make the sauce: Sauté the onion and garlic in the oil until lightly browned. Add remaining ingredients, cover and simmer for 30 minutes.

Make the filling: Defrost spinach and drain very thoroughly, squeezing out the liquid if necessary. Whirl spinach in a food processor to chop it a little more. Add remaining ingredients and process until combined. Chill.

Assemble: Cook lasagna noodles until barely tender in a very large pot of boiling water, then drain and rinse with cold water. Lay noodles on towels to dry them thoroughly. Place about 3 tablespoons of the filling on each strip and spread evenly. Roll up (jelly-roll fashion). Put a thin layer of sauce in a shallow casserole(s) and then place the filled rolls on top in single layers. Cover with remaining sauce.

Bake and serve: Preheat oven to 350°. Bake filled casseroles, uncovered, until very hot—20 to 45 minutes. If desired, pass additional grated Parmesan at the table.

COUSCOUS WITH ZUCCHINI, GARBANZOS, AND RAISINS

Makes 8 to 10 servings

5 cups cooked couscous (the quick-cooking kind)
⅔ cup raisins, soaked in hot water, then drained
1 cup cooked garbanzo beans
3 tablespoons butter or olive oil
3 small zucchini washed but not peeled
salt and pepper

WHEN NO ONE IS LOOKING
Prepare this 1 day ahead; cover and refrigerate. Bring to room temperature a few hours before serving, then reheat as directed.

FROZEN POWER
This freezes well. Defrost completely, then reheat as directed in the recipe.

Prepare couscous according to package directions and set aside. Cut zucchini into small cubes and sauté 1 or 2 minutes in the butter or oil. Toss the garbanzo beans with the zucchini for a few seconds, remove from the heat, then add to the couscous. Stir in the raisins and season to taste. Set aside until ready to serve, then reheat in a microwave oven or cover with foil and reheat in a 350° oven.

TAMALES IN FOIL

Makes 14 to 16 tamales

for the beef and stock:
1 onion, quartered
2 ½ to 3 pounds stewing beef
2 teaspoons salt
1 garlic clove, mashed (or from garlic oil, p. 18)
2 ½ to 3 cups water (or to barely cover meat)

for the sauce:
1 onion, finely chopped
1 clove garlic, mashed (or from garlic oil, p. 18)
⅓ cup vegetable oil
⅓ cup flour
2 ½ to 3 cups stock left from cooking the beef
2 cups tomato sauce
2 ½ cups enchilada sauce (canned is fine)
salt and pepper, only if needed

for the corn mixture:
4 cups white cornmeal
1 teaspoon salt
4 teaspoons baking powder
¾ cup vegetable shortening
4 cups cream-style canned corn

WHEN NO ONE IS LOOKING
The easiest way to prepare these tamales is in three steps. First day: cook the beef. Second day: prepare the sauce. Third day: assemble the tamales and steam them. To reheat the tamales remove foil wrapping and wrap each one in plastic wrap, then heat in a microwave oven one or two at a time. If reheating a large number of tamales, either steam them again, or wrap them together in double foil and heat in a moderate oven until very hot. Reheat sauce separately.

FROZEN POWER
These can be frozen. Freeze tamales and sauce separately. Defrost, then reheat as directed above.

Cook the beef: Bring all ingredients to a boil, reduce heat, cover, and simmer gently until beef is tender—1 ½ to 2 ½ hours. Cool, and if possible refrigerate overnight. Next day, drain, but save the stock. Cut the beef into small cubes.

Prepare the sauce: Sauté the onion with the garlic in the oil until tender. Sprinkle onion and garlic with flour and stir over moderate heat. Gradually add the stock, tomato, and enchilada sauces. Stir constantly until mixture comes to a boil, then reduce heat, cover, and simmer over low heat for 30 minutes. Add the cubed beef and taste for seasoning. Chill this sauce—if possible, overnight.

Prepare the corn mixture: Place cornmeal in a large bowl, then whisk in the salt and baking powder. Add the shortening and thoroughly cream it until well distributed. Beat or stir in the creamed corn.

Assemble: Cut foil into rectangles approximately 9 x 12 inches. Place about 2 heaping tablespoons of the corn mixture on one of the foil rectangles. Pat corn mixture into a rectangle about 4 x 6 inches and ¼ inch thick. Place a small spoonful of *cold* tamale sauce in the center of the corn mixture. Using a spatula, roll corn mixture from each long side to the center, forming a cylinder. Roll up the foil and twist ends. Repeat until corn mixture is used up. Keep remaining sauce separate.

Cook: Place wrapped tamales in a steamer, then cover and steam 1 to 2 hours. Or, put tamales on a rack in a large roasting pan. Pour ½ inch of hot water below the rack, then cover with a lid or cover tightly with heavy duty foil or double foil. Place in a preheated 350° oven and roast for approximately 1½ to 2 hours. Test doneness by unwrapping one of the tamales; if it loosens easily from the foil, it is ready. Serve hot with remaining meat sauce spooned over each tamale.

A FABULOUS GREEN CORN TAMALE CASSEROLE

Makes 12 to 16 servings

four (10-ounce) packages frozen whole-kernel corn, *exactly* 40 ounces!
2 ½ teaspoons salt (or to taste)
¼ pound (1 stick) melted butter
1 ⅔ cups yellow cornmeal
1 pound aged Cheddar cheese, sliced
1 pound Monterey Jack cheese, sliced
8 ounces diced mild green chiles (canned)

for a simple tomato sauce:
14 ounces green chile salsa (canned is fine)
2 (1-pound) cans tomatoes, mashed

WHEN NO ONE IS LOOKING
Prepare both the tamale casserole and the tomato sauce 2 days ahead; keep refrigerated. Bring to room temperature and then reheat tamale casserole by wrapping it again in double foil and placing it in a 350° oven (with a pan of hot water on the lower level) until piping hot. Reheat sauce, stirring gently.

FROZEN POWER
Freeze both the tamale casserole and the simple sauce. Defrost completely, then reheat the tamale casserole by wrapping it again in double foil and placing it in a 350° oven (with a pan of boiling water on the lower level) until very hot. Reheat sauce, stirring gently.

Defrost the corn, then chop it fine in a food processor, but do not purée. Remove this corn to a bowl and add the salt, butter, and cornmeal. Stir until well combined.

Oil a rectangular Pyrex casserole (about 9 x 14 x 1 ¾ inches). Place half of the corn mixture in the bottom of this casserole. Cover with all of the sliced cheese and with all of the chopped chiles. Top with the remaining corn mixture. Wrap the entire casserole dish—yes, the top, bottom, and sides—with double foil, or with heavy duty foil. It must be very heavily wrapped—like a package. Preheat oven to 350°. Place the wrapped casserole in the middle of the oven and place another pan with hot water on the lowest rack in the oven. Bake for 1 hour. Reduce oven to 300° and bake an additional hour. Always be sure there is hot water in the pan on the lower level of the oven. Once again reduce oven heat, this time to 275° and bake one more hour. *This dish bakes for a total of three hours!*

Serve hot with the simple tomato sauce made by combining sauce ingredients in a pan and simmering them together for 3 minutes.

INDIVIDUAL GREEN CORN TAMALES SIMPLIFIED

Makes about 12 tamales

- dried corn husks
- 3 (10-ounce) packages frozen whole-kernel corn, *exactly* 30 ounces!
- 2 teaspoons salt
- ⅛ pound (½ stick) melted butter
- 1 ¼ cups yellow cornmeal
- 12 strips of Cheddar cheese (about ½ x 2 inches)
- 12 strips of Monterey Jack cheese (about ½ x 2 inches)
- 1 (7-ounce) can whole green chiles, cut into strips

for the sauce:

- 1 (1-pound, 12-ounce) can plum tomatoes
- 1 (1 pound) can green chile salsa

WHEN NO ONE IS LOOKING
Prepare the tamales and the sauce 1 day ahead, but keep them covered and refrigerated separately. Reheat tamales by wrapping them in double foil and placing them in a preheated 350° oven until very hot. Reheat sauce, stirring gently.

FROZEN POWER
Freeze the tamales by first wrapping each one in foil, then placing them in plastic bags. Freeze the sauce separately. To serve, defrost both the tamales and the sauce, then reheat the tamales in their foil wraps in a preheated 350° oven until very hot. Reheat sauce, stirring gently.

Make the sauce: Remove tomatoes from the can and pour the juice into a saucepan. Place tomatoes in a food processor and purée them, then add to the saucepan along with the green chile salsa. Simmer together for 3 to 5 minutes. Set aside.

Make the tamales: Soak the corn husks in warm water for several hours or overnight, then drain them thoroughly. Defrost the corn, then whirl in a food processor until almost, but not completely, puréed. Place in a bowl and add the salt, butter, and cornmeal. Stir until well combined. Arrange 2 large corn husks so they overlap—one with the point upward and other with the point downward. Use a little of the corn mixture to hold them in place. Spread the center with 2 generous tablespoons of the corn mixture and top each with a strip of each of the cheeses and with 1 or more strips of the green chile. Fold in sides of husks and fold up so their points overlap. If tamales do not hold together, tie with string.

Place tamales on a rack in a large steamer or on a rack in a large roasting pan. Put about ½ inch of hot water below the rack, then cover with a lid or tightly using very heavy foil or double foil. Either cook them on top of your stove if using a steamer pot or in a preheated 350° oven if using a roasting pan; they need to cook about 1 to 2 hours in either case. Test for doneness by unwrapping one of them; if the tamale is easily loosened from the husk it is ready. Serve with the sauce.

BASIC TOMATO SAUCE MADE FROM FRESH TOMATOES

Makes about 4 quarts

- 10 pounds of fresh, ripe tomatoes
- 4 large onions, sliced
- 2 cups sliced celery
- 2 tablespoons fresh oregano (or 2 teaspoons dried)
- 1 cup fresh sweet basil (packed to measure)
- salt and black pepper to taste
- 2 teaspoons cracked red pepper (optional)
- 1 to 2 tablespoons sugar
- 1 cup fine quality olive oil

WHEN NO ONE IS LOOKING
Prepare this sauce 2 or 3 days ahead; keep covered and refrigerated.

FROZEN POWER
The sauce freezes beautifully and will keep at least a year—an ideal basic resource to have at hand.

Remove stem end of tomatoes, quarter them (but do not peel), and place in a large stainless steel pot. Add the onions, celery, oregano, sweet basil, salt, black pepper, sugar, and if desired, the cracked red pepper. Cover and bring to a boil, stir, reduce heat, and cook over moderate heat for 2 ½ to 3 hours, covered half the time and uncovered the last hour or longer. Remove from heat and cool 15 to 20 minutes, then put through a food mill to remove skins and seeds. Return the strained tomato mixture to a clean stainless steel pot and cook uncovered for another hour. Add the olive oil and continue to simmer uncovered for another 30 minutes, then taste and add more seasoning if needed. Simmer a few more minutes, then set aside to cool.

CASSOULET MY WAY

Makes 16 servings or more

- 6 cups navy beans (small white ones)
- 1 bottle dry white wine
- 2 ducklings (4 or 5 pounds each)
- 2 large onions, chopped
- 3 pounds large round-bone lamb chops, cut into 1-inch pieces (use bones and all)
- 3 pounds pork chops
- 4 teaspoons salt (or to taste)
- black pepper to taste
- 6 cloves garlic, mashed (or from garlic oil, p. 18)
- ½ teaspoon dried thyme
- 1 (8-ounce) can tomato sauce
- 1 ½ pounds garlic sausage (French, Italian, or Polish)

WHEN NO ONE IS LOOKING
This really must be started a day ahead. If you have room in your refrigerator to store it, completely prepare it 2 days ahead. To serve, bring to room temperature and reheat, covered, in a moderate oven.

FROZEN POWER
If you have sufficient freezer space, by all means freeze this cassoulet. To serve, defrost completely, then reheat, covered, in a moderate oven.

The night before, do the following:

1. Place the beans in a large bowl and pour white wine over them. Add water until beans are covered with liquid.

2. Roast ducklings until done. Save all the fat after roasting. Remove meat from ducklings and refrigerate.

Make the cassoulet the next day:

1. Put beans and any remaining liquid in a large pot. Add water so beans are covered. Simmer for 1 ½ to 2 hours or until beans are tender. Beans will absorb most of the liquid while cooking.

2. Sauté onions and garlic in the fat left from roasting the ducklings. Add lamb pieces and sauté about 5 to 10 minutes. Set aside.

3. Sauté pork chops in another skillet.

4. Add onion-garlic-lamb mixture to the beans with the salt, thyme, pepper, and tomato sauce, and mix well.

5. In a large casserole or roasting pan with a tight-fitting lid layer the bean mixture with the duck meat and pork chops. Top with slices of garlic sausage. If mixture seems dry, add a little white wine. Taste for seasoning and add more if needed.

6. Preheat oven to 350°. Cover the filled casserole or roasting pan and bake for 45 minutes. Remove cover and bake an additional 15 minutes.

FRENCH ROLLS FILLED WITH CHEESE AND OLIVES

Makes 6 servings

6 large French rolls
7 ounces Cheddar cheese, grated
1 cup pitted and sliced ripe olives
1 small bunch green onions, chopped
½ green pepper, chopped
1 jalapeño pepper, chopped (optional)
1 (8-ounce) can tomato sauce
2 tablespoons red wine vinegar
½ cup olive oil
salt to taste (about ½ teaspoon)
black pepper (about ¼ teaspoon)

WHEN NO ONE IS LOOKING These wonderful hot sandwiches are ideal "do-aheads." Assemble them completely 1 or 2 days ahead and keep refrigerated.

Cut a "lid" from the top of each roll. Scoop out some of the soft insides. Combine remaining ingredients in a bowl and mix well. Fill the rolls with this mixture and replace the tops. Wrap each filled roll in waxed paper (*not foil*) and refrigerate. When almost ready to serve, preheat oven to 300°. Place rolls still in their paper wrapping on a baking pan and heat them for about 30 minutes, or until very hot.

CROQUE-MONSIEUR (FRENCH SANDWICHES)

Makes 4 sandwiches

- 8 slices homemade-type white bread, crusts removed
- 1 ½ cups grated Gruyère cheese (about 5 ounces)
- ¼ cup mayonnaise
- 1 tablespoon Dijon-style mustard
- salt and black pepper—only if needed
- 8 thin ham slices or sliced beef knockwurst or salami
- 4 tablespoons melted butter

WHEN NO ONE IS LOOKING
Assemble these in the morning; keep covered and refrigerated. Bring to room temperature before baking.

Combine the grated cheese, mayonnaise, mustard, and salt and pepper to taste. Brush both sides of the bread slices with the melted butter. Divide one-half of the cheese mixture on four slices of bread, then top each with the ham slices, knockwurst, or salami. Cover with the other four bread slices to make four sandwiches. Spread remaining cheese mixture on the tops of the sandwiches. Cover with plastic until shortly before serving; they can be left at room temperature for several hours. Preheat oven to 375°. Place sandwiches on a nonstick baking sheet and first bake them for 10 minutes on the lowest level in the oven. Then move the pan to the highest level and bake another 5 to 10 minutes until hot and tops are well browned.

MONTE CRISTO SANDWICHES

Makes 4 servings

12 slices of best quality white bread, crusts removed
soft butter
sliced cooked chicken or turkey
salt and black pepper
sliced cooked ham
sliced Monterey Jack or Cheddar cheese
3 eggs
⅓ cup milk
butter for sautéing
strawberry jam (optional)

WHEN NO ONE IS LOOKING
Assemble the sandwiches a day ahead, wrap firmly in plastic wrap and keep refrigerated until time to dip and sauté them.

Butter 4 slices of bread on one side and cover them with the chicken or turkey slices. Season lightly. Butter four more bread slices, this time on both sides and place on top of the chicken or turkey. Now add a layer of ham and one of cheese on top of these slices. Butter four more bread slices on one side and place them butter sides down over the cheese. Cut these sandwiches into halves and fasten each half with a sturdy toothpick.

Beat the eggs with the milk. Dip the prepared sandwiches in the egg mixture and arrange them on a large platter or pan. Heat butter in a large, heavy skillet, then sauté the sandwiches in the butter until browned. If you prepare them in batches, keep them warm in a lowest possible oven. Serve hot with or without the strawberry jam at the side.

TORTILLA PIZZAS WITH SMOKED SALMON AND SOUR CREAM

Makes 4 to 8 servings

2 8-inch or 10-inch flour tortillas

for topping ingredients:
1/3 cup olive oil (or vegetable oil)
1/4 cup finely chopped green onion
4 ounces smoked salmon, cut into 1-inch squares, or diced
1/2 cup sour cream
1/4 cup finely chopped fresh dill
freshly ground black pepper
salt if needed

WHEN NO ONE IS LOOKING
Combine the sour cream mixture 1 day ahead and refrigerate. Chop the green onion and cut the salmon into pieces in the morning and refrigerate. Assemble the tortilla pizzas ready to bake 1 or 2 hours ahead; cover and leave at room temperature.

FROZEN POWER
Flour tortillas freeze beautifully, so keep them on hand in your freezer, ready to use as needed.

Mix the sour cream with the dill and set aside. Preheat oven to 500°. Brush tortillas generously with the oil—top and bottom. Place them on nonstick pan(s). Scatter the tortillas with the green onion and divide the smoked salmon pieces on each. Season with the pepper, and with salt if needed (will depend on the saltiness of the salmon). Bake in the preheated oven for 7 to 8 minutes. Remove from oven, then spread each with the sour cream dill mixture and serve at once.

TORTILLA PIZZAS WITH SMOKED TURKEY AND CHEESE

Makes 4 to 8 servings

2 10-inch or 12-inch flour tortillas

topping ingredients:
1/3 to 1/2 cup olive oil (or vegetable oil)
1 cup diced smoked turkey
1 cup shredded Monterey Jack or Swiss Gruyère cheese
4 tablespoons chopped green onions
1 cup diced fresh tomatoes
salt and black pepper

WHEN NO ONE IS LOOKING
Chop the topping ingredients in the morning and refrigerate. Bring them to room temperature before baking. Assemble the tortilla pizzas several hours before baking; cover lightly with plastic and leave at room temperature.

FROZEN POWER
Assemble, wrap and then freeze these tortilla pizzas. To serve, defrost for 10 minutes before baking, place on a nonstick pan and bake as directed but for an additional 1 or 2 minutes.

Preheat oven to 500°. Brush tortillas generously—top and bottom—with the oil. Place them on nonstick pan(s). Scatter the topping ingredients on each tortilla. Season to taste. Place prepared tortillas in the top third of the oven and bake for 7 to 8 minutes.

CHILES EN NOGADA

Makes about 30

30 canned whole green chiles
½ cup (or more) pomegranate seeds, fresh or frozen

for picadillo stuffing:
2 pounds lean pork, ground twice (or substitute beef)
2 onions, finely chopped
1 garlic clove, mashed (from garlic oil, p. 18)
1 (1-pound) can tomatoes, chopped or mashed
1 cup raisins, soaked in hot water, then drained
¼ cup dry sherry
½ teaspoon cinnamon
¼ teaspoon cloves
salt and black pepper to taste
¾ cup chopped almonds, lightly toasted

for cream cheese-walnut sauce:
1 pound cream cheese
1 cup milk
2 cups walnuts, toasted, then finely chopped
½ teaspoon mashed garlic (from garlic oil, p. 18)
salt to taste

WHEN NO ONE IS LOOKING
Prepare the picadillo stuffing and cream cheese-walnut sauce 2 days ahead. Cover stuffing and sauce separately and refrigerate. Bring to room temperature a few hours before serving. Briefly reheat the picadillo stuffing, stirring gently, then fill the chiles.

FROZEN POWER
Freeze the stuffing and sauce in separate containers; defrost completely then proceed as directed. Pomegranate seeds freeze wonderfully. Remove them from ripe pomegranates when in season and store them in plastic cartons with tight tops. They can be easily removed with a small spoon.

Prepare the stuffing: Lightly brown pork or beef (add a teaspoon of oil if using the beef) with the onion and garlic. Add tomatoes, raisins, sherry, spices, salt, and pepper. Simmer uncovered, stirring occasionally, for 15 to 20 minutes. Taste for seasoning, stir in almonds, then set aside.

Make the sauce: Bring cream cheese to room temperature, then whip it until smooth, gradually beating in the milk. Stir in the walnuts, garlic, and salt. Mix thoroughly, then cover and set aside at room temperature if serving the same day.

Assemble: Remove seeds from chiles, then drain them on paper towels. Fill each chile with a rounded tablespoon of the picadillo stuffing and roll up. Place filled chiles in a single layer on a large serving dish. Spoon cheese-walnut sauce over each chile and sprinkle tops with pomegranate seeds.

CHILES RELLENOS IN A CASSEROLE

Makes 10 to 12 servings

- 16 ounces canned whole green chiles
- 1 pound sharp Cheddar cheese, sliced
- 1 pound Monterey Jack cheese, sliced
- 4 tablespoons flour
- ½ teaspoon salt
- 1 (13-ounce) can evaporated milk
- 4 eggs
- 16 ounces tomato sauce

WHEN NO ONE IS LOOKING
This is an ideal casserole to assemble completely 1 day ahead. Keep covered and refrigerated. Bring to room temperature about 1 hour before the baking.

FROZEN POWER
Bake and cool this casserole, then wrap it in double foil and freeze. To serve, defrost completely, then reheat in a moderate oven.

Open chiles, drain, then remove seeds. Place half of them in the bottom of a large shallow casserole. Cover with all of the Cheddar slices. Top with remaining chiles, then cover with all of the Jack cheese slices. Beat the flour and salt with a small amount of the milk to make a paste, then beat in remaining milk. Add the eggs and beat again until combined, then pour over the chiles and cheese. Preheat oven to 325°. Bake casserole in the middle of the oven for approximately 1 hour. Pour the tomato sauce over the top and continue the baking 20 to 30 minutes.

EGGS CHIMAY MY WAY

Makes 4 servings

6 hard-cooked eggs
¼ pound fresh mushrooms, finely chopped
½ small onion, finely chopped
3 tablespoons butter
juice of half a lemon.
3 tablespoons finely chopped parsley
salt and black pepper to taste
¼ cup grated Parmesan cheese

for the Mornay sauce:
3 tablespoons butter
3 tablespoons flour
2 cups milk, heated slightly
salt and black pepper to taste
⅛ teaspoon nutmeg
¼ pound grated Swiss Gruyère cheese
3 egg yolks

WHEN NO ONE IS LOOKING
Cook the eggs and prepare the Mornay sauce 1 day ahead. Cover and refrigerate separately.

FROZEN POWER
Do *not* freeze! Hard-cooked eggs do not freeze well; they turn rubbery.

Make the Mornay sauce: Melt butter, stir in flour, then add the milk and stir constantly until mixture comes to a boil. Reduce heat and simmer gently for 2 minutes. Stir in the grated Gruyère and remove from heat. Beat the egg yolks slightly, then whisk them into the sauce. Stir in the nutmeg. Taste for seasoning and set aside.

Prepare the eggs: Cut eggs in half lengthwise. Remove yolks and put them through a sieve into a bowl and set aside. Sauté the onion in the butter for a few minutes. Add mushrooms, salt, pepper, and lemon juice, then sauté 1 or 2 minutes longer. Stir this mixture into the sieved egg yolks. Add the parsley and about 2 tablespoons of the Mornay sauce. Fill the halved hard-cooked eggs with the mixture and place them in a large shallow casserole or in individual ones. Cover each stuffed egg with some Mornay sauce. Let them stand a few minutes, then coat each egg again with sauce.

Pour remaining sauce around the eggs. Sprinkle tops with the grated Parmesan cheese.

Preheat oven to 375°, then bake the prepared eggs for 10 to 20 minutes; then, if possible, brown tops under the oven broiler.

CHEDDAR AND PARMESAN CHEESE SOUFFLÉ

Makes 4 servings

- ⅛ pound butter (½ stick)
- 4 tablespoons flour
- 2 cups warm milk
- ½ teaspoon salt (or to taste)
- 5 ounces sharp Cheddar cheese, grated
- 4 ounces Parmesan cheese, finely grated
- 4 egg yolks
- 6 egg whites

WHEN NO ONE IS LOOKING
Prepare the soufflé base (the cheese-egg mixture) in the morning and place it in a large bowl. Cover with plastic wrap and leave at room temperature. About 45 minutes before serving, preheat the oven, beat egg whites, and proceed as directed in the recipe.

Melt butter, stir in flour and salt, then cook, stirring, over low heat for 1 to 2 minutes. Add milk and stir constantly until mixture comes to a boil. Remove from heat and stir in the grated cheeses. In another bowl beat egg yolks slightly, then add the warm cheese mixture to the egg yolks and stir to combine. Cover and set aside.

Preheat oven to 375°. Beat egg whites until stiff but not dry. Fold whites gently into the egg-cheese mixture. Pour into a generously greased 1½-quart soufflé dish to which you have attached a wax paper collar (also greased). Bake soufflé for 35 to 40 minutes. Serve at once.

BAKED WILD RICE AND SHRIMP SALAD

Makes 12 to 16 servings

½ cup chopped green onions
1 green pepper, finely chopped
1 ½ cups finely chopped celery
1 ½ cups sour cream
3 cups mayonnaise, or more to taste
juice of 1 lemon
2 teaspoons curry powder (or to taste)
½ teaspoon dried oregano
½ teaspoon dried thyme
salt and black pepper to taste
2 quarts cooked wild rice (8 cups)
3 ½ to 4 pounds cooked and peeled shrimp

WHEN NO ONE IS LOOKING
Mix this 1 day ahead. Keep covered and refrigerated. Bring to room temperature about 2 hours before heating, then proceed as directed.

FROZEN POWER
You can freeze the cooked wild rice, which will save time when you are ready to prepare this dish.

Preheat oven to 350°. Combine all ingredients, taste for seasoning, then spoon into a large casserole. Cover with foil and place in the oven for about 1 hour—only until very hot.

GINGERED RICE

Makes about 4 servings

- 3 cups cooked rice
- 3 tablespoons butter
- ⅓ cup chopped candied ginger
- ¼ cup finely chopped green onions

WHEN NO ONE IS LOOKING
Prepare this dish 1 day ahead. Cover and refrigerate. Bring to room temperature and reheat either covered with foil in a preheated 325° oven for about 20 minutes, or in a microwave oven.

FROZEN POWER
Cooked rice freezes well. Add the ginger and onions after defrosting.

Melt butter, then add the cooked rice and stir over low heat until hot. Add chopped ginger and green onions, and stir briefly over low heat. Serve hot.

RICE WITH GREEN CHILES, JACK CHEESE, AND SOUR CREAM

Makes 6 to 8 servings

- 3 cups cooked rice
- 2 cups sour cream (or crème fraîche)
- 1 teaspoon salt
- ½ cup diced, roasted green chiles
- ½ pound sliced or grated cheese, Monterey Jack, fontina, Swiss, or Cheddar

WHEN NO ONE IS LOOKING
Assemble this 1 day ahead; keep covered and refrigerated. Bring to room temperature, then bake as directed.

FROZEN POWER
Assemble this, then freeze. To serve, defrost and bring to room temperature, then bake as directed.

Mix sour cream with the salt and chopped chiles. Place ⅓ of the cooked rice in the bottom of a 1½-quart casserole. Top with ⅓ of the sour cream mixture, then with a layer of the cheese. Repeat this procedure twice. Preheat oven to 350°. Cover casserole and bake for 20 minutes. Uncover and bake another 10 minutes or until hot.

MARY CULLIN'S BLACK-EYED PEAS

Makes about 8 servings

- ¾ pound smoked bacon in one piece
- 1 pound dried black-eyed peas
- 2 garlic cloves (or from garlic oil, p. 18)
- 1 teaspoon salt (will probably need more)
- 1 tablespoon sugar
- ¾ pound "Chorizo Sausage," homemade (p. 166) or purchased
- 5 cups boiling water

WHEN NO ONE IS LOOKING
Prepare this up to 2 days ahead; keep covered and refrigerated. Reheat in a moderate oven before serving.

FROZEN POWER
This is a superb dish for freezer storage. If desired, divide into smaller portions and freeze them.

Preheat oven to 350°. Cut bacon into large cubes and place them in a heavy casserole or large heavy pot. Pick over the peas and discard the bad ones along with foreign objects such as pebbles. Add peas to the bacon and pour boiling water over them. Add garlic, salt, and sugar. Cover and place in the oven for 1½ hours. Cut chorizo in chunks and add to the peas. Return to oven for about 45 minutes. Taste for seasoning and add more salt if needed. Now remove cover and return to oven for 45 minutes or a little longer. Remove from oven and skim off excess fat on the surface.

VEGETABLES

BAKED BABY ARTICHOKES

Makes 3 to 4 servings

6 to 8 baby artichokes
juice of 1 lemon
2 tablespoons garlic oil (p. 18)
1 teaspoon dried oregano
salt and black pepper
⅓ cup moderately dry white wine

WHEN NO ONE IS LOOKING
Prepare in the morning. Cover with plastic and leave at room temperature. Before serving, cover with foil and reheat in a moderate oven.

Cut off the outer leaves of the artichokes, trim tops and bottoms, then cut in half and place in water with some of the lemon juice to prevent darkening.

Preheat oven to 375°. Arrange artichokes cut sides down in a baking dish, sprinkle with a little more lemon juice, then dribble garlic oil over the artichokes. Crumble oregano on the tops, season, then add the wine. Cover with foil. Bake about 20 minutes. Remove from oven, turn pieces over, cover again, and return to oven until tender—10 to 20 additional minutes.

ASPARAGUS CHINESE STYLE

Makes 10 servings

5 pounds fresh asparagus
3 tablespoons peanut or corn oil
1 garlic clove, mashed, from garlic oil (p. 18)
1½-inch piece fresh ginger, peeled and finely minced
salt and black pepper to taste

WHEN NO ONE IS LOOKING
Clean, peel, and slice the asparagus 1 day ahead; keep refrigerated in a tightly sealed plastic bag.

Break or cut off the tough ends of the asparagus, then peel the stems with a vegetable peeler. Slice asparagus diagonally into ¾-inch pieces. Heat oil in a large heavy pot. Add garlic and ginger and heat for a few seconds, then add asparagus slices and stir-fry over highest heat for 1 or 2 minutes. Season, then remove from heat and serve.

A CAKELIKE CARROT PUDDING

Makes 8 to 10 servings

- ½ pound butter (2 sticks) at room temperature
- ½ cup brown sugar (pack to measure)
- 1 egg
- 1 tablespoon water
- 2 cups grated raw carrots
- 1 ½ cups flour
- ½ teaspoon baking soda
- 1 teaspoon baking powder
- ½ teaspoon cinnamon
- ½ teaspoon nutmeg
- ½ teaspoon salt

WHEN NO ONE IS LOOKING
Cover and refrigerate the mixture 1 day ahead. Pour or spoon into the ring mold the next day and proceed with the baking; or, bake the carrot pudding and refrigerate. Wrap it in foil and reheat in a 350° oven.

FROZEN POWER
Freeze this carrot pudding after baking it. Cool, then wrap well and freeze. To serve, completely defrost, then wrap in foil and reheat in a 350° oven.

Cream butter with the sugar, then add the egg and water and beat very well. Stir in the grated carrots. Sift dry ingredients together twice, or mix them together with a whisk in a bowl, then add to the carrot mixture. Grease a ring mold about 9 or 10 inches in diameter, spoon in the mixture, and chill for 2 or more hours. Remove from refrigerator about ½ hour before baking. Preheat oven to 350°. Bake for about 1 hour, then remove from oven and turn out upside down on a platter.

FRESH CARROT PURÉE

Makes 4 to 6 servings

1 pound fresh carrots, peeled and sliced
⅛ pound (½ stick) butter
salt and black pepper to taste
1 teaspoon sugar
¼ cup heavy cream

WHEN NO ONE IS LOOKING
Prepare this in the morning. Cover and leave at room temperature. Reheat in a microwave oven or in a conventional oven (covered), but only until hot; avoid overcooking.

Sauté carrots in the butter over low heat, stirring occasionally for 15 to 20 minutes, or until very tender. Season with salt, pepper, and sugar, then place in a food processor and add the cream. Process to a purée. Taste for seasoning and consistency; you may want to add another tablespoon or so of cream

JULIENNED SWEET PEPPERS CHINESE STYLE

Makes 4 servings

3 large sweet peppers, use a mix of red, green, yellow, or orange
1 tablespoon finely chopped or grated fresh ginger
3 tablespoons garlic oil (p. 18)
salt and black pepper to taste

WHEN NO ONE IS LOOKING
Prepare ginger 1 day ahead; keep it sealed and refrigerated. Peel the peppers and julienne them 1 day ahead, store them in a sealed plastic bag and keep refrigerated. Bring to room temperature 2 or 3 hours before you plan to cook them, then proceed as directed.

Peel the peppers using a potato peeler, removing as much of the peel as possible; do *not* roast the peppers! Remove stems and seeds, then julienne (thinly slice) and set them aside. Heat ginger and garlic oil together in a large skillet or large pot. When very hot add the julienned peppers and quickly stir-fry, tossing well for 30 seconds. Season with salt and pepper and toss another 15 to 30 seconds. Immediately remove from heat and serve.

CAULIFLOWER CUSTARDS

Makes 6 to 8 servings

- 1 fresh cauliflower (3 cups of cooked flowerettes)
- 1 pound ricotta cheese (whole milk)
- ¼ teaspoon ground nutmeg
- salt and black pepper to taste
- ¾ cup grated Parmesan cheese
- 1 teaspoon garlic oil (p. 18)
- 3 eggs

WHEN NO ONE IS LOOKING
Prepare these 1 day ahead. Wrap them in plastic and keep them refrigerated. Reheat in a microwave oven only until very hot.

Cook the cauliflower, then process it in a food processor until almost puréed. Add the ricotta, nutmeg, salt, pepper, and Parmesan and process again. Add the eggs and again process. Remove to a bowl, stir in the garlic oil and taste for seasoning.

Preheat oven to 350°. Butter individual Pyrex baking cups or ceramic ones, then spoon in the cauliflower mixture. Place filled cups in a large baking pan. Fill baking pan with hot water until reaches up to ⅓ of the sides of the filled cups. Place in the oven and bake 25 to 35 minutes or until they test done (a knife inserted will come out clean, like a custard). Remove, cool briefly on a rack, then unmold and serve.

BAKED SUMMER SQUASH

Makes 8 to 10 servings

2 pounds small, green summer squash
2 tablespoons butter
2 tablespoons flour
1 cup cream (or milk)
1 clove garlic, mashed, from garlic oil (p. 18)
1 tablespoon chopped green onions
salt and black pepper to taste
2 hard-cooked eggs, chopped
2 egg yolks

WHEN NO ONE IS LOOKING
Assemble the casserole mixture 1 day ahead; keep it covered and refrigerated. Bring to room temperature before baking.

Boil squash until tender, drain, then put through a food mill or a sieve and set aside. Preheat oven to 350°. Melt butter and stir in flour. Gradually add the cream, stirring constantly until sauce comes to a boil. Simmer 2 minutes, then stir in the garlic, green onions, salt, pepper, and chopped eggs. Remove from heat, then stir in the egg yolks. Combine this mixture with the puréed squash and pour into a buttered casserole. Bake for 30 minutes.

A FAVORITE CORN AND GREEN CHILE CASSEROLE

Makes about 6 servings

- 20 ounces frozen whole kernel corn, 2 (10-ounce) packages
- ¼ pound butter (1 stick), melted
- 2 eggs, lightly beaten
- ½ cup yellow cornmeal
- 1 ¼ teaspoons salt
- 1 cup sour cream
- 1 ¼ cups diced Monterey Jack cheese (7 or 8 ounces)
- 1 (7-ounce) can diced green chiles

WHEN NO ONE IS LOOKING
Bake this corn casserole 1 day ahead but do not overbrown. Cool, then cover and refrigerate. Remove from refrigerator 2 hours before serving, then reheat uncovered in a 350° oven.

FROZEN POWER
By all means, do freeze this for wonderful future dining. Underbake slightly—only until lightly browned. Cool, then wrap (or double-wrap) in heavy foil and freeze. To serve, defrost completely and then reheat in a 350° oven.

Exact amounts are crucial. Do *not* increase amount of the whole kernel corn. To bake, use a 8 x 11½ x 2-inch Pyrex casserole or close to that size. If the casserole is too large, the ingredients will dry out, and if it is too small and deep, they will burn on the outside and be too wet inside.

Defrost corn, then place it in a food processor and pulse it until finely chopped but not puréed. Preheat oven to 350°. Grease the casserole with butter or shortening. Combine processed corn with the remaining ingredients. Pour into casserole and bake about 45 minutes or until firm to the touch and lightly browned.

CREOLE CORN

Makes 4 to 6 servings

- 1 (10-ounce) package frozen corn kernels
- ½ onion, chopped
- ½ sweet red or green pepper chopped
- ½ cup finely chopped celery
- 3 tablespoons butter
- salt and black pepper to taste
- 2 tablespoons heavy cream
- 2 fresh, ripe tomatoes, peeled, seeded, and diced

WHEN NO ONE IS LOOKING
Prepare this 1 day ahead. Cover and refrigerate. Bring to room temperature before reheating. Reheat either in a microwave oven or in a preheated 350° oven, but only until hot.

Defrost the corn, then place it in a food processor and process until almost a purée. Remove and set aside. Sauté onion, sweet pepper, and celery in the butter until tender and lightly browned. Add corn and cook for 1 or 2 minutes, then season and add the cream. Cook again for 2 minutes, stirring occasionally. Add diced tomatoes and cook uncovered for 2 more minutes. Taste for seasoning, then serve hot.

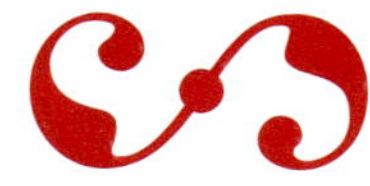

POTATO GRATIN THE FRENCH WAY

Makes 6 to 8 servings

- 2 pounds boiling potatoes
- 2 teaspoons salt (approximate)
- black pepper to taste
- 3 cups whole milk
- 2 cups heavy whipping cream
- 1 cup grated Swiss Gruyère cheese

WHEN NO ONE IS LOOKING
Assemble the gratin 8 hours in advance, except for the final 1 cup of cream and grated cheese.

FROZEN POWER
This is not as perfect in taste after it has been frozen, but it is nonetheless delicious as a defrosted leftover.

Peel and slice the potatoes. Place them in a buttered oblong casserole (about 9 x 14 inches). Do *not* make more than two layers, and season each as you arrange it; add the milk. Preheat oven to 375° and bake in the lowest level of the oven for 30 minutes. Remove from oven and gently turn the potatoes with a spatula.

Return to oven and bake 15 additional minutes, and again remove from oven and turn them. Return to oven for 15 more minutes (this making a total of 1 hour). Remove from oven, pour 1 cup of the cream over the top and set aside for at least ½ hour or as long as 8 hours. Leave at room temperature covered with plastic wrap.

Later: Preheat oven to 350°. Add the remaining 1 cup of cream and bake in the middle of the oven for 30 or 45 minutes. Remove from oven, sprinkle with the grated cheese, then return to the top level of the oven for 15 to 20 minutes. By this time the sauce will have thickened and the top will be well browned.

TWICE-BAKED YUKON GOLD POTATOES

Makes 8 servings

4 medium-size Yukon Gold potatoes
2 to 4 tablespoons soft butter
¼ to ½ cup warm milk
salt and pepper to taste
2 tablespoons melted butter
sour cream (optional)

WHEN NO ONE IS LOOKING
Prepare the potatoes 1 day ahead, but separately refrigerate the mashed potatoes and skins. Reheat the mashed potatoes in a microwave oven, then proceed as directed. (If skins are cold, they may take 3 to 5 minutes longer in the oven.)

Preheat oven to 400°. Bake potatoes for approximately one hour or until tender. Remove from oven and halve, then carefully scoop out the flesh and put it through a ricer. Place the intact skins on a baking sheet. Whip riced potatoes with the soft butter and milk to desired consistency and season with salt and pepper. Brush skins with melted butter and bake them for about 20 minutes, until golden and crisp. Spoon warm mashed potatoes into the skins and bake about 10 minutes, or until heated through. If desired, top each with two teaspoons of sour cream.

BAKED STUFFED POTATOES

Makes 10 servings

5 extra-large baking potatoes
¼ pound butter (1 stick), soft or melted
salt and white pepper to taste (about 1½ teaspoons salt and ½ teaspoon pepper)
2 extra large eggs
½ to 1 cup warm milk

WHEN NO ONE IS LOOKING
Prepare these 1 day ahead. Cover and refrigerate until time to bake. Baking will take a little longer.

FROZEN POWER
These freeze beautifully. First freeze them on a tray. When they are solidly frozen, wrap each separately and place in plastic bags that can be tightly sealed. To serve, defrost the stuffed potatoes for about 45 minutes (do *not* completely defrost). Preheat oven to 375°, and bake for 30 to 40 minutes.

Bake potatoes, then cut them in half lengthwise and scoop out the insides. Reserve the intact skins. Place scooped out potatoes through a food mill, then into a large bowl. Add butter, salt, pepper, and beat with an electric mixer. Add the eggs and beat again, then gradually beat in the milk until desired consistency—they should be very moist but *not runny.* Taste for seasoning.

Preheat oven to 375°. Spoon mixture into the potato skins, and press the sides of each together so they have a better appearance. If desired, decorate tops with some of the potato mixture put through a pastry tube. Bake until hot and lightly browned—about 10 to 15 minutes.

FRENCH-FRIED POTATO BASKETS

Makes about 10

8 large baking potatoes
oil or vegetable shortening for frying
salt

WHEN NO ONE IS LOOKING
Prepare these in the morning. Leave them at room temperature lightly covered. Before serving, reheat as directed.

FROZEN POWER
These are amazingly good after freezing. Freeze each potato basket in a small plastic bag, then group two or three together in larger plastic bags. To serve, defrost, then reheat as directed.

These are most easily done with a French potato-basket fryer. Although somewhat more difficult, you can construct a fryer by combining two fine metal sieves—one about 3 ½ inches in diameter and the other about 4 ½ inches in diameter.

Plan to make one potato basket at a time. Ideal for this production is a thermostatically regulated deep fat fryer—otherwise use a deep fat thermometer. Fill fryer or other pot with oil and heat to 375°. Peel potatoes and keep them in cold water. Drain and shred one potato at a time and prepare one basket at a time. Dip both parts of the potato-basket fryer (or your 2 sieves) in the hot oil. Line the larger part of the basket (or sieve) with shredded potatoes. Fit smaller basket on top and fasten closed. Fry in the oil until very well browned. Remove, drain, then unfasten and remove basket. If potatoes stick, don't hesitate to hit the basket (or sieve) firmly on your table. If the fryer-baskset was deep in oil before being filled, and if the potatoes have been cooked until brown, you won't have any problem.

Continue with the other potatoes and remember to dip the basket fryer in hot oil each time before filling. When all baskets have been made, sprinkle them with salt. Set aside at room temperature. Just before serving place potato baskets on a baking sheet and reheat uncovered in a preheated 400° oven—only until hot. Watch that they do not burn.

POTATOES ANNA IN A NONSTICK SKILLET

Makes 4 to 6 servings

5 large baking potatoes
¼ pound melted butter (1 stick)
salt and black pepper

WHEN NO ONE IS LOOKING
These do extremely well when prepared in the morning. Leave the potatoes at room temperature, lightly covered. Preheat oven to 400° and reheat the potatoes uncovered until very hot—30 to 45 minutes.

The important trick to preparing these delicious potatoes is the skillet. Buy a 9- or 10-inch nonstick skillet with a removable handle because the handles are plastic and will not take intense oven heat. Remove the handle and reserve the skillet for this kind of preparation.

Peel potatoes and slice thin—if possible use a Feemster slicer (see p. 17) or a similar cutter. Arrange potatoes in a decorative flower pattern (only the bottom layer need be arranged). Season with salt and pepper and spoon melted butter over the layer. Continue layering potatoes in the same way, ending with melted butter. Preheat oven to 425°. Bake uncovered for 1½ to 2 hours—until very well browned. Remove from the oven, drain off excess butter, then turn potatoes upside down on an ovenproof dish or platter. Shortly before serving return to a 425° oven to reheat.

SCALLOPED POTATOES

Makes 6 servings

4 cups sliced boiling potatoes
salt and black pepper for potatoes
⅛ pound butter (½ stick)
4 tablespoons flour
½ teaspoon salt
½ teaspoon black pepper
2 ½ cups hot milk

WHEN NO ONE IS LOOKING
Prepare this 1 day ahead, but underbake it slightly. Cover and refrigerate. To finish, bring to room temperature, then finish the baking in a preheated 350° oven.

FROZEN POWER
Underbake and freeze this casserole. Cool it and then wrap for the freezer. To serve, defrost completely, then finish baking in a preheated 350° oven.

Preheat oven to 350°. Melt butter, then stir in the flour. Add the salt, pepper, and hot milk, and stir constantly over moderate heat until sauce comes to a boil. Reduce heat and simmer 2 minutes. Remove from heat and set aside. Arrange a layer of half of the potatoes in a large shallow casserole. Season to taste with salt and pepper. Pour half the sauce over these potatoes. Arrange remaining potatoes on top, season, then cover with the rest of the sauce. Bake in the upper part of the oven for about an hour—until potatoes are tender and the top is brown and bubbling.

DUCHESSE POTATOES WITH MUSHROOMS

Makes 6 to 8 servings

for the potato mixture:
3 extra-large baking potatoes
4 egg yolks
salt and white or black pepper, to taste
⅛ pound butter (½ stick), melted
2 to 4 tablespoons milk

for the mushroom mixture:
1 large onion, chopped
6 tablespoons butter
1 pound fresh mushrooms, sliced

WHEN NO ONE IS LOOKING
Assemble this completely in the morning; cover it with plastic wrap, and leave it at room temperature until time to bake.

Prepare the duchesse potatoes: Peel potatoes, cut them in pieces, and cook them in boiling salted water until tender but not mushy. Drain them well, then put them through a food mill or ricer. Place in a large bowl, then add the egg yolks and beat with an electric beater. Add the melted butter, salt and pepper, and enough milk to achieve a whipped consistency that holds its shape. (Do *not* add too much milk.) Set aside.

Prepare the mushroom mixture: Sauté the chopped onion in the butter until golden and tender, then add the mushrooms and cook for a few minutes, stirring frequently. Remove from heat and set aside.

Assemble: Butter a casserole. Either line the bottom with half the potatoes, fill with the mushroom mixture, then top with remaining potatoes; or, line casserole with all of the mushroom mixture and top with all of the potatoes.

Bake and serve: Preheat oven to 375°. Bake casserole for 30 minutes or longer, until very hot and browned. Serve hot.

POTATOES MACAIRE

Makes 4 servings

4 baking potatoes
¼ pound (1 stick) butter (soft)
salt and black pepper

WHEN NO ONE IS LOOKING
Bake the potatoes in the morning and arrange them in casseroles. Cover lightly and leave at room temperature until time for the final baking.

Bake potatoes. Scoop out insides and mash them roughly with a fork. Do not sieve them or whip them. Add butter, salt, and pepper. Butter 4 individual shallow casseroles—or 1 large casserole—and fill with the potatoes. Preheat oven to 400°. Bake the potato casseroles uncovered until well browned—10 to 15 minutes. Serve very hot.

YAMS WITH PECANS AND RAISINS

Makes 6 to 8 servings

4 cups mashed cooked yams
½ teaspoon salt (or to taste)
⅛ pound melted butter (½ stick)
½ cup brown sugar (packed to measure)
1 teaspoon nutmeg
1 teaspoon cinnamon
¾ cup raisins, soaked in hot water, then drained well
1 ½ cups toasted pecans
3 eggs, beaten

WHEN NO ONE IS LOOKING
Prepare the yam mixture in the morning or 1 day ahead; keep covered and refrigerated. Bring to room temperature before baking.

Combine all ingredients and spoon into a large casserole. Preheat oven to 350°. Bake, uncovered, for 45 minutes to 1 hour.

SWEET POTATOES WITH PINEAPPLE

Makes 4 to 6 servings

- 2 extra-large sweet potatoes or 4 smaller ones
- ⅛ pound butter (½ stick), or more
- 2 tablespoons brown sugar
- ½ cup canned crushed pineapple, measured after draining
- ½ teapoon salt (or to taste)
- 4 tablespoons light or medium rum (preferably Haitian Barbancourt)
- grated nutmeg

WHEN NO ONE IS LOOKING
Prepare these 1 day ahead. Wrap completely with plastic or foil and refrigerate. Bring to room temperature before the final baking.

FROZEN POWER
These freeze well. First freeze them on a tray; then when firm, wrap each individually in plastic and again in foil. To serve, defrost, then bake as directed.

Bake the potatoes, then cut them in half lengthwise and scoop out the contents (save the potato skins intact). Put the potato flesh through a food mill or ricer and place in a bowl. Add the butter (melt it if potatoes have cooled), and add remaining ingredients except for the nutmeg. Mix well and taste for seasoning. Spoon into the potato skins and sprinkle with nutmeg, cover with plastic wrap, and set aside at room temperature. Shortly before serving preheat oven to 375° and bake potatoes for 10 minutes, or long enough to heat and brown slightly.

YAM POTATO PUFFS

Makes 15 to 16 small puffs

2 ½ pounds yams, cooked, then peeled and mashed
2 to 4 tablespoons brown sugar
¼ teaspoon salt
1 teaspoon cinnamon
1 teaspoon nutmeg
¼ cup cornflake crumbs
⅛ pound butter (½ stick), melted
2 egg yolks
large marshmallows

for rolling the puffs:
2 cups cornflake crumbs
⅛ pound (½ stick) butter, melted

WHEN NO ONE IS LOOKING
Prepare the yam mixture 1 day ahead; keep covered and refrigerated. Prepare the yam balls the day of your party, but remember to freeze them before baking

FROZEN POWER
Freezing is a necessity, so keep them as frozen assets.

Prepare mixture for rolling the puffs by combining the crumbs and melted butter. Set aside.

Combine mashed yams with the brown sugar, salt, cinnamon, nutmeg, cornflake crumbs, butter, and the egg yolks. Wrap a small tablespoonful of this mixture around a marshmallow, then roll this yam ball in the crumb mixture. Place on a tray to freeze. When all have been prepared, place tray in freezer and when all have frozen hard, wrap each yam puff in double foil or plastic wrap. To serve, preheat oven to 350°. *Do not defrost.* Remove yam puffs from freezer, unwrap, then bake in their frozen state for 25 to 30 minutes.

SPINACH CRÊPES

Makes 12 servings

24 "Crêpes" (p. 152), 6 or 7 inches in diameter
3 (10-ounce) packages frozen chopped spinach
⅛ pound butter (½ stick)
¼ cup flour
1 cup light cream
½ cup milk
2 teaspoons salt (or to taste)
½ teaspoon black pepper
¼ teaspoon nutmeg
½ cup grated Parmesan cheese
additional melted butter
additional grated Parmesan cheese
finely chopped parsley

WHEN NO ONE IS LOOKING
Assemble these in the morning. Cover with plastic wrap and leave at room temperature until time to bake.

FROZEN POWER
Crêpes freeze beautifully. Remember to soften them when they are still in their foil wrapping by placing them in a very low oven just long enough to roll them without cracking.

Defrost spinach and drain very thoroughly; set aside. In a large skillet, melt the butter, stir in the flour and cook over low heat for 1 minute. Remove from heat and stir in the cream and milk. Return to heat and cook, stirring constantly, until mixture comes to a boil. Reduce heat and simmer slowly for a few minutes. Add salt, pepper, and nutmeg and stir in the ½ cup grated Parmesan. Add spinach and stir over low heat for 1 or 2 minutes. Taste for seasoning. Remove from heat, cool, and chill.

Preheat oven to 350°. Fill each crêpe with some spinach mixture, roll up, and place the rolls seam sides down in buttered, shallow casseroles. Brush tops with melted butter and sprinkle with grated Parmesan. Bake until very hot and tops are lightly browned. Remove from oven, sprinkle with chopped parsley and serve.

SPINACH PHYLLO STRUDEL

Makes 2 rolls, serves 10 to 12

- 2 (10-ounce) packages frozen chopped spinach, thawed, drained, and squeezed dry
- 3 onions, finely chopped
- ¼ cup butter (⅛ pound)
- ½ pound Feta cheese
- 6 ounces farmers cheese or 8 ounces cream cheese
- 3 eggs
- ¼ cup finely chopped fresh dill
- salt and black pepper to taste
- ¼ teaspoon nutmeg
- ½ pound phyllo pastry sheets (14 to 16 sheets)
- ½ pound melted butter
- 1 cup dry bread crumbs

WHEN NO ONE IS LOOKING
Assemble the rolls (before baking) 1 day ahead. Keep covered and refrigerated. Bake before serving.

FROZEN POWER
These freeze extremely well, but freeze them before baking. To finish, defrost them for about 1 hour (do not over-defrost), then bake as directed. They will need to bake 10 to 15 minutes longer. Watch that they do not burn; if necessary, reduce oven heat.

Sauté chopped onions in the butter until tender and lightly browned. Add spinach and cook over moderate heat for 3 minutes. Set aside. Place cheeses, eggs, and dill in a food processor, then process until well combined. Remove and add to the spinach mixture and season with salt, pepper, and nutmeg. Remove, cool, then chill at least for 4 hours or overnight.

Assemble and bake: Using the phyllo sheets, prepare to make 2 rolls. For each roll, place 1 phyllo sheet on a board, brush with butter and sprinkle with crumbs. Repeat the procedure with 6 to 8 more phyllo sheets. Divide chilled spinach mixture into two portions. Place one of the portions along the longest side of the prepared phyllo dough and roll up jelly-roll style. Lift roll, using spatulas, and place seam side down in a lightly greased baking pan with sides. Repeat entire process to make a second roll. Preheat oven(s) to 375°. Bake rolls for 15 minutes, then remove from oven and score rolls through the top (not the filling) into 2-inch slices. Reduce oven heat to 350° and bake another 20 to 30 minutes—until well browned. Finish slicing and serve hot or warm.

ZUCCHINI, TOMATO, AND ONION CASSEROLE

Makes 6 servings

6 medium-size zucchini
3 fresh, ripe tomatoes
(if tomatoes are not ripe, use canned)
1 small onion, sliced
salt and black pepper

WHEN NO ONE IS LOOKING
Assemble and bake 1 day ahead; keep covered and refrigerated. Reheat in a 350° oven before serving.

FROZEN POWER
This freezes very well. Defrost, then reheat in a 350° oven.

Cut ends off the zucchini, but do *not* peel; then slice them ⅛ to ¼ inch thick. Layer the zucchini with the tomatoes and onions, and season layers with salt and pepper. Preheat oven to 350°. Bake, covered, for 45 minutes. Uncover and bake about 30 more minutes.

MUSHROOMS SUPER EASY

Makes 8 to 10 servings

3 to 4 dozen large fresh mushrooms, cleaned (see p. 15)
½ pound melted butter (2 sticks)
salt and black pepper to taste

WHEN NO ONE IS LOOKING
Dip the mushrooms in the butter and arrange them in a baking dish. Lightly cover and leave them at room temperature until time to bake.

Dip mushrooms in the melted butter one-by-one, then place them in a single layer in a large baking dish or roasting pan. Preheat oven to 400°, then bake the mushrooms uncovered for about 10 minutes. Do not overcook.

GLAZED SHALLOTS

Makes 6 to 8 servings

24 large shallots, peeled
3 tablespoons butter
¼ cup honey
1½ cups chicken stock
1 cup Madeira

WHEN NO ONE IS LOOKING
Prepare these 1 day ahead; keep covered and refrigerated. To serve, bring to room temperature and reheat in a preheated 300° oven, stirring frequently.

Melt butter in a skillet over moderate heat. Add shallots and sauté until golden, stirring occasionally, for 5 to 10 minutes. Add remaining ingredients and simmer gently, mostly uncovered, for 40 minutes or longer, or until almost all the liquid is reduced to form a glaze.

GLAZED PEARL ONIONS WITH RAISINS AND ALMONDS

Makes about 6 servings

2 ½ pounds pearl onions
¾ cup raisins, soaked in hot water, then drained
1 cup dry sherry
⅓ cup honey
2 tablespoons butter
½ teaspoon dried thyme
salt and black pepper to taste
1 tablespoon red wine vinegar
1 cup slivered almonds, lightly toasted

WHEN NO ONE IS LOOKING
Prepare these 1 or 2 days ahead without adding the almonds. Reheat before serving, then top with the toasted almonds.

Bring a pot of salted water to a boil, add onions and cook exactly 3 minutes, then drain. Cool slightly, then cut root ends off the onions and squeeze onions out of their outermost layer at the stem end. Combine peeled onions, raisins, sherry, honey, butter, thyme, salt, and pepper in a large, deep skillet with a cover. Bring to a boil, reduce heat to low, cover and simmer, stirring occasionally, until liquid has almost evaporated and onions have begun to caramelize; this will take about 45 minutes. Stir in vinegar and correct seasoning. Shortly before serving, reheat gently, sprinkle with toasted almonds, and serve hot.

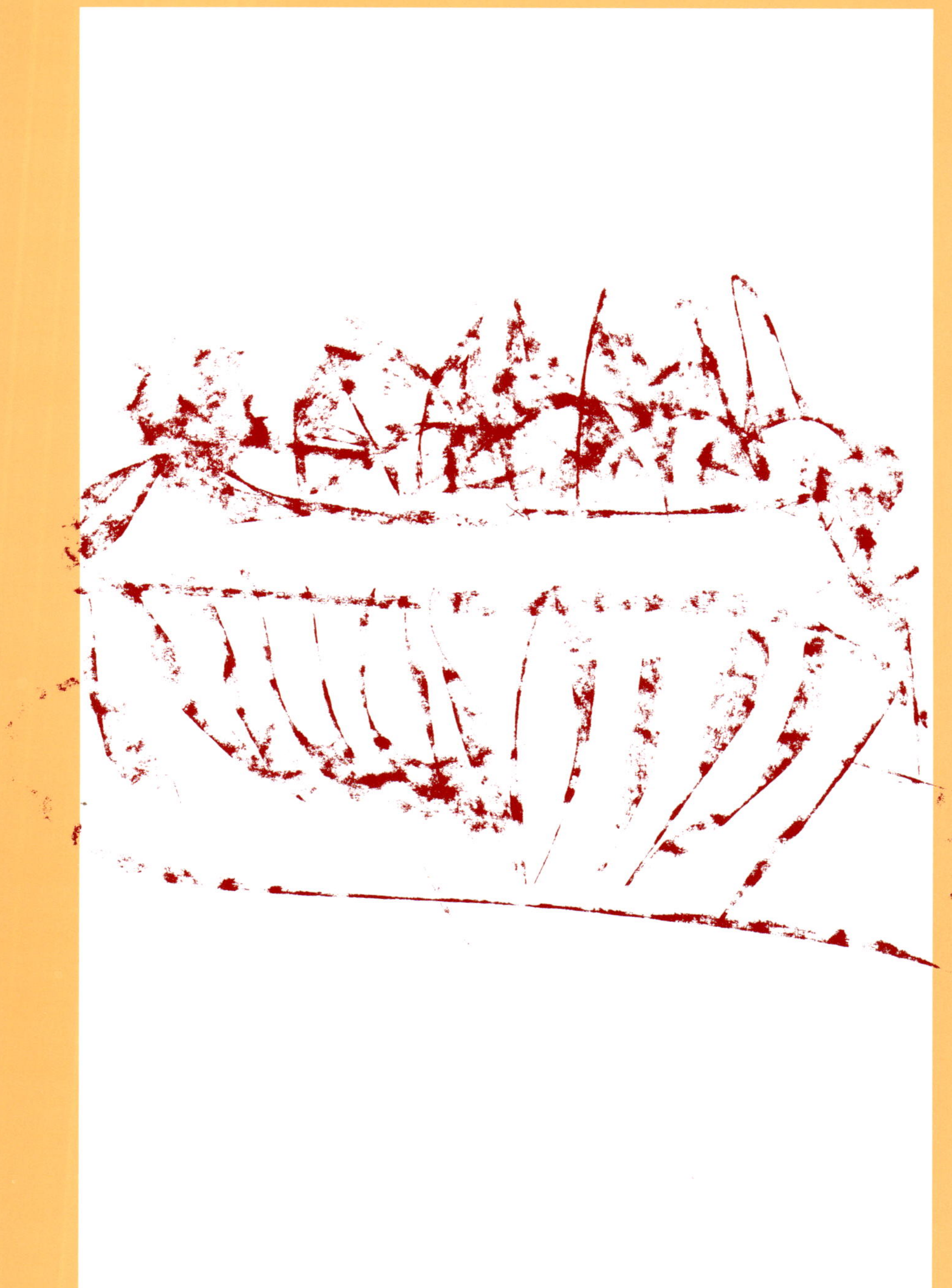

SALADS,
SALAD DRESSINGS,
SALSAS, AND
SPECIAL SAUCES

BELGIAN ENDIVE SALAD WITH GRAPES, HAZELNUTS, AND BLUE CHEESE—SERVED WITH A HAZELNUT VINAIGRETTE

Makes 8 to 10 servings

1 cup hazelnuts (filberts)
1 to 2 cups diced or crumbled blue cheese
6 to 10 Belgian endives, cut crosswise into ½-inch pieces
½ of a small red cabbage, finely chopped
2 cups seedless grapes

for the hazelnut vinaigrette:
2 tablespoons balsamic vinegar
3 tablespoons rice vinegar
2 teaspoons kosher salt
¾ teaspoon cracked black pepper
1 cup hazelnut oil
¼ cup olive oil

WHEN NO ONE IS LOOKING
Prepare the hazelnuts any time. They can be toasted, skinned, and kept refrigerated (covered) one or two weeks ahead. Make the vinaigrette 7 to 10 days ahead; store in a jar with a tight-fitting cover and keep refrigerated.

FROZEN POWER
Prepare the hazelnuts and store them in the freezer for up to one year.

Make the vinaigrette: In a bowl whisk together the vinegars, salt, and pepper, then whisk in the oils. Toast the hazelnuts by placing them in a pan in a 325° oven for about 10 minutes. Remove nuts from oven and wrap in a kitchen towel to cool for 1 or 2 minutes. Rub the nuts in the towel to remove as much of their skins as possible. Or, rub off the skins with your fingers. Chop the nuts, or easier, place nuts in a plastic bag and crush them. Set aside.

Arrange endives in a large bowl with the cabbage and grapes, cover with plastic and keep refrigerated. When ready to serve, toss with as much of the hazelnut vinaigrette as you like. Scatter some of the blue cheese and the chopped or crushed hazelnuts on each serving.

ENDIVE, APPLE, AND WALNUT SALAD

Makes 8 to 10 servings

6 or 7 large Belgian endives
1 bunch watercress, leaves only
4 green onions, finely sliced
1 sweet red pepper, julienned
1 cup toasted walnuts, halved
½ cup fresh orange juice
2 or 3 Golden Delicious apples, peeled and sliced
"Basic Vinaigrette" to taste (p. 237)

WHEN NO ONE IS LOOKING
Prepare the vinaigrette 1 week ahead. Place in a jar with a tight-fitting cover; keep refrigerated. Prepare the salad—except for the apples, walnuts, and vinaigrette—in the morning; cover with plastic and keep refrigerated. Before serving add the apples and walnuts, then toss the salad with the vinaigrette.

Combine endives, watercress, green onions, and sweet pepper in a large salad bowl. Cover tightly with plastic and refrigerate. Combine apples and orange juice. When ready to serve, drain apples and add them to the salad. Add walnuts and vinaigrette, toss and serve.

OLD-FASHIONED CARROT AND RAISIN SALAD

Makes about 5 cups

4 cups grated raw carrots
pinch of salt
1 cup raisins, soaked in hot water, drained, and dried on paper towels
2 to 4 tablespoons lemon juice
¾ cup mayonnaise (or to taste)

WHEN NO ONE IS LOOKING
The flavors blend much better if prepared a day ahead. The salad will keep, covered and refrigerated, for three to five days.

Combine all ingredients and mix well. Cover and chill. Serve cold.

SPINACH, ROMAINE, AND SESAME SEED SALAD

Makes about 8 servings

- 2 bunches of fresh spinach, washed, dried, stems discarded
- 1 large head of romaine lettuce
- ½ to 1 pound bacon, cooked crisp, then crumbled
- 1 cup coarsely grated Monterey Jack cheese
- 4 tablespoons toasted sesame seeds

for special salad dressing:

- 1 ½ tablespoons sugar
- ½ teaspoon salt
- ½ teaspoon dry mustard
- 2 tablespoons finely grated onion (or finely chopped in a food processor)
- ¼ cup white wine vinegar
- 1 cup corn or canola oil (*not* olive oil)

WHEN NO ONE IS LOOKING
Prepare the special salad dressing up to 1 week ahead; store in a jar in the refrigerator. Assemble the salad in the morning (*without the dressing*). Cover tightly with plastic wrap and refrigerate until time to serve, then add dressing and toss.

Prepare the salad dressing first: Combine sugar, salt, mustard, onion, and vinegar and stir until sugar has dissolved. Gradually beat in the oil. Refrigerate in a tightly sealed jar.

Combine spinach and romaine (torn into bite-size pieces) in a large salad bowl. Scatter grated cheese over the greens, then sprinkle with crumbled bacon and top with sesame seeds. Just before serving, add salad dressing and toss.

CAESAR SALAD, MY VERSION

Makes about 4 servings

- 6 cups romaine lettuce, broken into pieces or sliced
- 1 cup "Basic Vinaigrette" (p. 237)
- 1 teaspoon Dijon-style mustard
- 1 teaspoon mayonnaise
- 6 anchovies, drained and finely minced
- 1 to 2 cups croutons (homemade or purchased)
- ⅓ to ½ cup grated Parmesan cheese

WHEN NO ONE IS LOOKING
Please note that the basic vinaigrette, p. 237, can be made up to 2 weeks ahead if kept refrigerated. Prepare this dressing with the anchovies and mustard up to 5 days ahead; cover and keep refrigerated. Prepare the croutons up to 1 week ahead; keep sealed in a plastic bag and refrigerated.

FROZEN POWER
Freeze the croutons (homemade or purchased).

Place the mustard, mayonnaise, and minced anchovies in a small bowl, then whisk in the vinaigrette; cover and set aside.

Place the romaine lettuce in a salad bowl, then cover with plastic wrap and refrigerate. When ready to serve add the croutons, grated Parmesan, and the prepared dressing then toss.

CHICKEN SALAD IN PAPAYA HALVES

Makes 4 to 8 servings

4 ripe papayas, halved and seeds removed
2 cups diced, cooked chicken
¼ cup chopped sweet pepper (green or red or orange)
¾ cup finely chopped celery

for the dressing:
3 tablespoons chopped ginger from ginger preserved in syrup
1 tablespoon syrup from the ginger
2 tablespoons lemon juice
½ cup mayonnaise
½ cup sour cream
salt to taste

for the garnish:
1 small can mandarin oranges, drained
½ cup toasted macadamia nuts

WHEN NO ONE IS LOOKING
Prepare the dressing 2 days ahead; keep covered and refrigerated. Cook the chicken 1 day ahead, and keep it covered and refrigerated. Prepare the chicken mixture in the morning; a few hours before serving spoon it into the papaya halves, cover and refrigerate.

Combine all dressing ingredients, then cover and chill. Combine chicken, sweet pepper, and celery, then chill. When ready to serve, spoon chicken mixture into the papaya halves and spoon on the dressing. Garnish with the mandarin oranges and macadamia nuts.

CANTALOUPE RINGS FILLED WITH APPLE-TUNA CHUTNEY

Makes about 6 servings

- 2 medium-size cantaloupes, peeled and seeds removed, then cut in thick rings
- 1 ½ cups diced peeled apple
- 1 ½ cups finely chopped celery
- 2 tablespoons lemon juice
- 1 ½ teaspoons curry powder
- ¼ teaspoon salt, or to taste
- ½ cup mayonnaise (approximately)
- 1 cup canned tuna, well drained
- 2 tablespoons chopped chutney
- Boston lettuce leaves

WHEN NO ONE IS LOOKING
Prepare the cantaloupe rings and the apple-celery mixture 1 day ahead; keep them separately covered and refrigerated.

Combine apple, celery, lemon juice, curry, salt, and mayonnaise. Cover with plastic and refrigerate. Refrigerate cantaloupe rings. Shortly before serving, line individual plates with lettuce leaves, then place cantaloupe rings on top. Fill each ring with apple-celery mixture, then top each with tuna and 1 tablespoon chopped chutney.

WALDORF SALAD WITH CANDIED GINGER

Makes about 6 servings

- 2 large apples, peeled and diced (about 2 cups)
- 2 cups finely chopped celery
- ½ cup candied ginger, finely chopped
- 1 cup toasted walnuts, chopped
- pinch of salt
- 2 to 4 tablespoons lemon juice (to taste)
- ½ cup or more of mayonnaise

WHEN NO ONE IS LOOKING
Prepare this 1 day ahead; cover and keep refrigerated. Stir gently before serving.

Combine ingredients and chill.

SHRIMP AND CASHEW NUT SALAD

Makes 2 to 3 servings

- ½ pound cooked bay shrimp or dice larger shrimp
- ½ cup toasted, unsalted cashew nuts
- 1 cup seedless grapes (red or green)
- 2 green onions, finely chopped
- 4 tablespoons chopped green pepper
- ½ cup mayonnaise
- 2 tablespoons lemon juice
- ¾ teaspoon curry powder
- ¼ teaspoon salt, or to taste
- ⅛ teaspoon black pepper
- Boston lettuce leaves

WHEN NO ONE IS LOOKING
Prepare this salad 1 day ahead. Cover and refrigerate.

Combine ingredients, cover and chill. Serve on Boston lettuce leaves.

HERRING SALAD WITH APPLE AND ONION

Makes about 4 servings

12 ounces wine herring snacks
1 large onion, chopped or finely sliced
1 ½ cups diced or shredded tart apple, about 1 large apple
1 cup sour cream (or unflavored yogurt)
½ teaspoon salt
1 tablespoon lemon juice (or to taste)
2 teaspoons freshly chopped dill

WHEN NO ONE IS LOOKING
Prepare this salad 1 or 2 days ahead. Stir before serving.

Drain herring and discard liquid, spices, and onion. Cut herring into small pieces. Place prepared onion in a bowl, cover with boiling water, and let stand for 3 minutes, then drain. Spread onion on paper towels to remove excess moisture. Combine onion with the herring pieces and add remaining ingredients. Mix together gently, then cover and chill.

CUCUMBER-TOMATO SALAD

Makes 4 to 6 servings

2 cups diced fresh, peeled and seeded tomatoes
2 cups diced, peeled and seeded cucumbers
2 tablespoons olive oil
salt and black pepper to taste

WHEN NO ONE IS LOOKING
Prepare this in the morning; cover and keep refrigerated.

Combine ingredients, cover and chill for 2 hours or longer.

CUCUMBER-MINT SALAD

Makes about 4 servings

- 4 small cucumbers or 2 large ones, peeled, seeded, then diced
- salt
- 1 cup sour cream
- 1 teaspoon finely minced garlic from garlic oil (p. 18)
- ½ teaspoon salt
- ¼ teaspoon black pepper, or to taste
- 3 tablespoons finely chopped fresh mint

WHEN NO ONE IS LOOKING
Prepare the sour cream dressing 1 or 2 days ahead, but do not mix with the cucumbers until ready to serve.

Sprinkle diced cucumbers lightly with salt and refrigerate for 2 to 3 hours. Combine remaining ingredients in a separate bowl to make the sour cream dressing, then cover and refrigerate. Drain cucumbers, then combine with the sour cream dressing and serve.

TOMATOES CONCASSÉ

Makes 1½ to 2 cups

- 6 fresh ripe tomatoes
- ¼ cup chopped fresh sweet basil
- 1 teaspoon salt
- ½ teaspoon black pepper
- 2 tablespoon balsamic vinegar
- 1 teaspoon sugar
- ½ cup olive oil

WHEN NO ONE IS LOOKING
Prepare this in the morning; cover and refrigerate.

Peel and seed the tomatoes, then dice them and place in a bowl. Place remaining ingredients in a blender or food processor and process until the basil is finely chopped. Pour over the diced tomatoes. Cover and chill for a few hours, or serve at room temperature.

Serve as a salad on lettuce or as a side dish to accompany fish, poultry, or meat.

FRESH TOMATO SALSA

Makes about 3 cups

- 4 or 5 fresh, ripe tomatoes, peeled and seeded
- 1 medium-size onion, finely chopped
- 2 jalapeños, seeded and finely chopped
- 2 or 3 tablespoons chopped cilantro
- 1 tablespoon balsamic vinegar
- 1 tablespoon olive oil
- ½ to 1 teaspoon salt
- ¼ teaspoon black pepper

WHEN NO ONE IS LOOKING
This should be prepared several hours ahead; cover and keep chilled. Or, prepare it 1 day ahead; keep covered and refrigerated.

Combine all ingredients and chill.

OLIVE AND TOMATO SALSA

Makes about 2 cups

- 1 ½ cups pitted Kalamata olives, chopped
- 3 tomatoes, peeled, seeded, and diced
- ¾ cup finely chopped onion
- grated zest and juice of 1 lemon
- 2 tablespoons balsamic vinegar
- 3 tablespoon olive oil
- salt and black pepper to taste

WHEN NO ONE IS LOOKING
Prepare this 1 or 2 days ahead; keep covered and refrigerated.

Mix ingredients together, then chill at least 2 hours or overnight. Serve cold or at room temperature.

COOKED TOMATO SALSA

Makes about 1 quart

1 large onion, chopped
2 garlic cloves, mashed, from garlic oil (p. 18)
2 tablespoons vegetable oil
1 large can of peeled plum tomatoes (3 ½ cups)
2 cups tomato juice
2 to 4 jalapeños, seeded and chopped
salt to taste
Tabasco (or other hot sauce), to taste

WHEN NO ONE IS LOOKING
Prepare this up to 1 week ahead; keep covered and refrigerated.

FROZEN POWER
Yes indeed, freeze this cooked salsa.

Sauté onion and garlic in oil over moderate heat until tender. Purée the canned tomatoes in a food processor, then add them with their juice and with the 2 cups of tomato juice to the onions. Add the chopped jalapeños, then cover and simmer for 10 minutes. Uncover and simmer about 10 more minutes. Add salt to taste and Tabasco if a spicier salsa is desired.

TOMATO AND SWEET PEPPER SALSA

Makes 6 to 8 servings

8 fresh, ripe tomatoes, seeded and diced
1 sweet pepper, red or green, finely chopped
3 green onions, finely chopped
½ cup olive oil
2 tablespoons balsamic vinegar
salt and black pepper to taste
Boston lettuce leaves

WHEN NO ONE IS LOOKING
Prepare the tomato mixture in the morning; keep covered and refrigerated until time to serve.

Combine all ingredients except lettuce leaves, mix well, then chill. Spoon onto Boston lettuce leaves.

PAPAYA-CUCUMBER-GINGER SALSA

Makes 2 to 3 cups

- 2 large papayas, peeled and chopped
- 4 small pickling cucumbers, peeled and chopped
- ⅓ to ½ cup minced fresh ginger
- ¼ cup lime juice (or part lemon juice)
- 3 to 4 tablespoons brown sugar
- 2 tablespoons Thai fish sauce
- 1 teaspoon Chinese chili sauce, to taste (or Tabasco)

WHEN NO ONE IS LOOKING
This is best eaten the same day, but it is quite good the next day. So, if you prefer, prepare it 1 day ahead, but keep it covered and refrigerated.

Combine all ingredients, cover and chill. Serve cold.

TOMATILLO SALSA

Makes 2 to 3 cups

- 6 to 8 fresh tomatillos
- 2 jalapeño chiles, seeded and coarsely chopped
- ½ to ¾ cup fresh cilantro
- ⅓ cup coarsely chopped onion
- 3 tablespoons water
- ½ teaspoon salt (or to taste)

WHEN NO ONE IS LOOKING
Prepare this salsa 1 day ahead; keep covered and refrigerated.

Remove husks from the tomatillos, then rinse them in warm water to remove any stickiness and dry with paper towels. Quarter them, then combine with the other ingredients in a food processor. Process to the desired consistency. Cover and chill. Serve cold or at room temperature.

CUCUMBER AND ONION SALSA

Makes 1½ to 2 cups

WHEN NO ONE IS LOOKING
Make this 1 day ahead, then keep covered and refrigerated. Stir gently before serving.

- 4 to 6 small pickling-size cucumbers, peeled and grated—you need about 1 cup grated—or the equivalent from larger cucumbers but with the seeds removed
- 1 small onion (or half a large one), peeled and grated—you need ⅔ to 1 cup grated onion
- 1 ¼ teaspoons salt
- 1 tablespoon sugar
- 1 tablespoon rice vinegar (or mild white vinegar)
- ½ cup mayonnaise

Combine grated cucumbers and grated onion in a bowl. Sprinkle with the salt and let stand 15 minutes, then drain in a sieve—pushing down on the vegetables to release liquid. Let stand 30 minutes to 1 hour, then place drained mixture in a bowl. Add the sugar, vinegar, and mayonnaise and mix well. Cover and refrigerate.

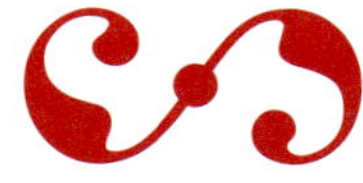

MANGO AND SWEET RED PEPPER SALSA

Makes about 2 cups

1 ripe mango, peeled and diced
1 sweet red pepper, chopped
¼ cup lemon juice
¼ cup orange juice
3 tablespoons finely chopped onion
⅓ cup finely chopped cilantro
1 small clove garlic, mashed or from garlic oil (p. 18)
½ teaspoon salt (or to taste)
½ teaspoon black pepper (or to taste)

WHEN NO ONE IS LOOKING
Prepare this 1 day ahead; cover and keep refrigerated.

Combine all ingredients, cover and chill.

MY BASIC VINAIGRETTE

Makes about 1 quart

1 tablespoon salt
½ teaspoon black pepper
1 teaspoon dry mustard
2 teaspoons sugar
1 or 2 garlic cloves, mashed, from garlic oil (p. 18)
1 cup vinegar (or less)
2 ¼ cups salad oil, part olive

WHEN NO ONE IS LOOKING
This vinaigrette keeps well for 2 weeks if tightly sealed and refrigerated. If possible, bring the vinaigrette to room temperature before using it.

Combine all ingredients except the salad oil and whisk them together thoroughly. Then whisk in the salad oil. Store in tightly sealed jars in the refrigerator.

SWEET BASIL VINAIGRETTE

Makes about 1 quart

1 tablespoon salt
1 ¼ teaspoons white pepper
2 ½ teaspoons dry mustard
12 to 18 fresh sweet basil leaves (no stems)
2 teaspoons mashed garlic from garlic oil (p. 18)
1 cup white vinegar flavored with green peppercorns (the peppercorns are optional)
1 cup olive oil
1 ¼ cups corn or canola oil

WHEN NO ONE IS LOOKING
Flavor the vinegar with the peppercorns weeks in advance. Keep the flavored vinegar in a tightly covered jar at room temperature. Prepare the basil vinaigrette up to 1 week ahead, but keep it covered and refrigerated.

Prepare the white vinegar at least 1 week ahead of preparing this vinaigrette —green peppercorns are available in most markets. Combine the salt, white pepper, dry mustard, sweet basil leaves, garlic, and vinegar in a blender. Blend until the basil is finely chopped or puréed. Gradually add the oils, then pour at once into jars that can be tightly sealed. Store in the refrigerator, but bring to room temperature before using.

RUSSIAN DRESSING

Makes about 1½ cups

1 cup mayonnaise
¼ cup ketchup
¼ cup chili sauce
2 teaspoons Dijon-style mustard
2 teaspoons grated horseradish (bottled is fine)
1 teaspoon Worcestershire sauce
2 teaspoons red wine vinegar
dash of Tabasco sauce

WHEN NO ONE IS LOOKING
If this is made with commercial mayonnaise, you can safely prepare it 7 to 10 days ahead; keep it tightly covered and refrigerated.

Whisk all ingredients together. Store, covered, in the refrigerator.

REMOULADE

Makes about 1½ cups

1 cup mayonnaise
3 green onions, finely chopped
3 small sweet pickles, finely chopped
1 tablespoon chopped capers
3 large pimento-stuffed green olives, chopped
2 tablespoons Dijon-style mustard
2 tablespoons lemon juice
salt and black pepper

WHEN NO ONE IS LOOKING
If this is made with commercial mayonnaise, it will keep 1 to 2 weeks if tightly covered and refrigerated.

Combine all ingredients, then season to taste.

RUTH MELLINKOFF'S VERSION OF SCANDIA DILL SAUCE

Makes about 2 cups

1 cup snipped fresh dill
3 tablespoons sugar
3 tablespoons white wine vinegar
¼ cup mayonnaise (commercial)
½ cup (generous) Dijon mustard
1 cup flavorless vegetable oil, e.g., corn oil

WHEN NO ONE IS LOOKING
Prepare this up to 1 week ahead; keep covered and refrigerated.

Combine dill and sugar in a food processor and process until dill is chopped. Add vinegar, mayonnaise, and mustard to the dill and process until well mixed. Add the oil in a very fine stream, very slowly at first. Spoon into a sterile glass jar, cover, and refrigerate.

MAYONNAISE IN A FOOD PROCESSOR

Makes a generous quart

2 large eggs
¼ cup lemon juice
2 teaspoons salt
½ teaspoon black pepper
2 teaspoons sugar
1 teaspoon dry mustard
3 cups salad oil, part olive

WHEN NO ONE IS LOOKING
Since this is not prepared with preservatives, do not store it more than a week. It should always be kept covered and refrigerated.

Place all ingredients, except the oil, in a food processor and process until well blended. Pour a tiny bit of oil in the feed tube and process. Continue to process, adding the oil gradually. Remove, stir well, then place in a sterile jar in the refrigerator.

GREEN MAYONNAISE

Makes about 1 quart

- 3 egg yolks
- 1 whole egg
- 1 ½ teaspoons salt
- 1 ½ teaspoons sugar
- 1 ½ teaspoons dry mustard
- ½ teaspoon paprika
- ¼ teaspoon black pepper
- ¼ to ½ teaspoon dried tarragon
- ¼ cup chopped fresh dill
- ¾ cup chopped fresh parsley
- 4 to 5 green onions, cut in small pieces
- ⅓ cup white wine vinegar
- 2 ½ cups salad oil, all or part olive oil

WHEN NO ONE IS LOOKING
Prepare this up to 3 or 4 days ahead; keep covered and refrigerated. Unlike commercial mayonnaise, homemade versions should *not* be kept more than a week.

Combine all ingredients except oil in a food processor and whirl them together until everything is finely chopped and well mixed. Start adding the oil very slowly—a few drops at a time—then gradually add the rest of the oil. Store in jars that can be tightly covered in the refrigerator.

HORSERADISH CREAM

- ½ cup heavy whipping cream
- 2 tablespoons freshly grated horseradish (bottled is okay if recently purchased)
- 1 teaspoon lemon juice
- 1 teaspoon sugar (scant)

WHEN NO ONE IS LOOKING
Prepare this up to 2 days ahead; keep covered and refrigerated.

Combine all the ingredients and mix well; cover and refrigerate.

HORSERADISH CREAM WITH APPLE

add to the horseradish cream (above):

- 1 apple, peeled and shredded
- 2 teaspoons lemon juice

Mix grated apple with the lemon juice. Cover and refrigerate.

Note: This will keep 6 to 8 hours without the apples turning brown.

SECRET STEAK SAUCE

Makes about 2 cups

1 cup chutney (Major Grey style)
½ cup Heinz ketchup
½ cup Heinz chili sauce
2 tablespoons Worcestershire sauce
1 tablespoon Dijon-style mustard
1 tablespoon cognac or California brandy
several drops of hot Chinese pepper sauce (or to taste)

WHEN NO ONE IS LOOKING
This will keep for many weeks in a tightly sealed jar in the refrigerator.

Combine all ingredients in a food processor and process until smooth—or at least until no large chutney chunks remain. Serve cold or at room temperature.

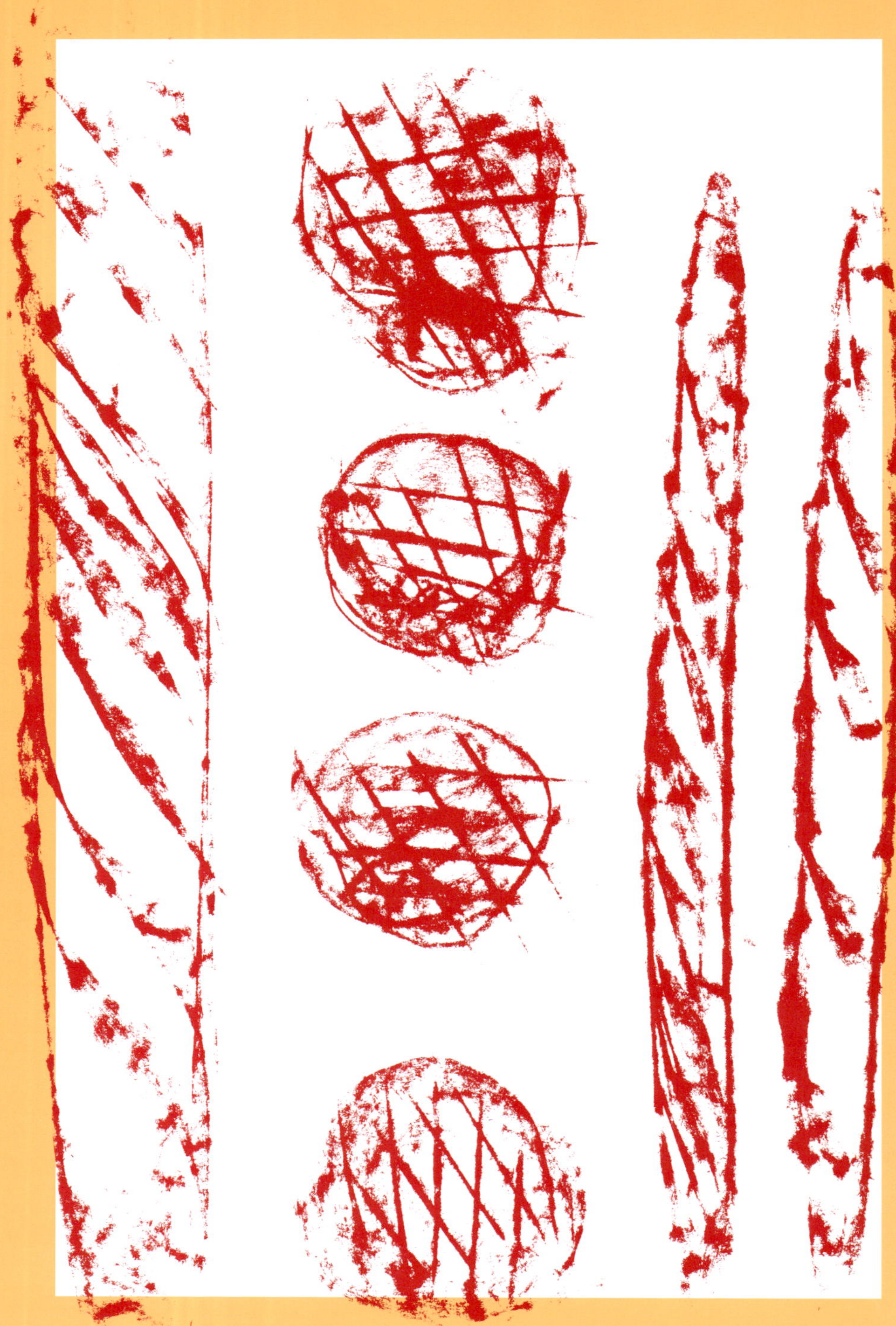

BREADS AND COFFEE CAKES

OLIVE BREAD, MY VERSION

Makes 2 large or 4 smaller loaves

- 2 packages dry yeast
- ⅔ cup warm water
- 1 tablespoon sugar
- 1 tablespoon flour
- 2 cups warm water
- 2 tablespoons olive oil
- 1 tablespoon salt
- 2 pounds flour (about 8 to 9 cups)
- 2 cups (or less) pitted Kalamata olives, or pitted oil-cured black olives

WHEN NO ONE IS LOOKING
Bake these 1 or 2 days ahead. Wrap them in foil and refrigerate. Either reheat in a moderate oven lightly wrapped, or slice and toast before serving.

FROZEN POWER
Perfect for freezing. Be sure to double-wrap them. I like this bread even better after it has been frozen. Defrost, then bake in a preheated 375° oven for approximately 10 minutes.

Place the ⅔ cup warm water in a small bowl and sprinkle yeast on the water. Add the 1 tablespoon of sugar and the 1 tablespoon of flour and stir until yeast has dissolved. Let it stand for several minutes until it begins to foam. Place the 2 cups warm water in a large mixing bowl. Add the salt, olive oil, and the dissolved yeast. Beat in the flour, either with an electric dough hook or with a heavy wooden spoon. Knead thoroughly until the dough becomes very elastic. Turn out on a floured board then pat into a circle. Sprinkle with the olives and roll up, then knead again thoroughly. Place in an oiled bowl, cover and let rise until doubled—about 45 minutes, plus or minus. Turn out on a floured board and divide into either two or four portions. Knead briefly and shape into round or oblong loaves. Place them on lightly greased heavy, flat baking pans. Let rise again until doubled—about 30 to 45 minutes. Brush with water and bake in a preheated 400° oven for 20 minutes. Reduce oven to 350° and bake approximately 20 to 30 minutes. Cool, then wrap until ready to serve. Reheat briefly before serving.

FLOUR TORTILLAS

Makes 4 tortillas

- 1 cup all-purpose flour
- 2 tablespoons vegetable shortening or lard
- ½ teaspoon salt
- 4 to 6 tablespoons water

WHEN NO ONE IS LOOKING
Prepare these tortillas up to 2 days ahead; keep refrigerated, sealed in a plastic bag. Bring to room temperature before using. To serve warm, reheat wrapped in plastic in a microwave oven for 15 to 20 seconds. If using them for quesadillas, it is not necessary to reheat them.

FROZEN POWER
These freeze perfectly. Place them in a plastic bag that you can seal, or double-wrap them in foil.

Mix flour and salt together. Cut shortening or lard into the flour with your hands until a coarse meal is formed. Blend in 4 tablespoons of water using a fork, adding more water only as needed until mixture sticks together. Turn dough out on a floured board and knead for 4 to 5 minutes. Wrap dough in plastic and let it rest for 45 minutes or up to 2 hours.

Divide the dough into 4 pieces and form each into a ball. Roll each ball into a thin circle 7 to 8 inches in diameter. Try to keep the tortillas circular and thin.

Cook tortillas one at a time in an ungreased, moderately hot skillet. Cook the first side for 15 to 20 seconds, until it begins to bubble and the underside develops a few light brown spots; turn, then cook the other side a shorter time, about 10 seconds. Place cooked tortillas one on top of the other. Cool at room temperature and then place them in a plastic bag until ready to use.

Note: If you plan to use these in quantity, do not hesitate to double, triple, or quadruple the recipe.

CRISP FRENCH ROLLS

Makes 1 to 2 dozen, depending on size

- 2 packages dry yeast
- ½ cup warm water
- 2 tablespoons sugar
- 1 ½ cups lukewarm water
- 1 tablespoon salt
- 2 tablespoons melted butter or oil
- 4 egg whites, slightly beaten
- 6 ¼ cups sifted flour (28 ounces)
- cornmeal

WHEN NO ONE IS LOOKING
Slightly underbake these rolls 1 day ahead, and as soon as they are cool, wrap them in foil and refrigerate. To serve, unwrap the rolls, then reheat them briefly in a preheated 350° oven.

FROZEN POWER
Slightly underbake these rolls, then cool them. Wrap them in foil, then seal them in plastic bags and freeze. To serve, defrost rolls briefly, then reheat them (unwrapped) in a preheated 350° oven.

Dissolve yeast in the ½ cup warm water, then stir in the sugar; set aside. Place the 1 ½ cups lukewarm water, salt, melted butter or oil, and egg whites in a large bowl. Stir in the dissolved yeast and gradually beat in part of the flour with an electric dough hook or with a wooden spoon, then knead in the rest with your hands. The dough should become smooth and blistered. Cover and let rise for about 1 hour, or until doubled in bulk.

Turn dough out on a floured board and knead for a minute, then divide dough into 4 parts. Cut each into 6 portions (or fewer) and shape them into rounds. Let them rest for 3 minutes, then shape them into ovals. Grease baking pans and sprinkle generously with cornmeal. Place ovals on the pans and let rise for 20 to 30 minutes. Preheat oven to 425°. Brush tops of rolls with cold water, then bake for 15 minutes. Remove, brush again with cold water, reduce oven to 300°, and then return rolls to oven for about 10 minutes more.

CRUSTY FRENCH-STYLE RYE BREAD

Makes 2 to 4 loaves

- 2 packages dry yeast
- ⅔ cup warm water
- 1 tablespoon sugar
- 1 tablespoon salt
- 2 cups lukewarm water
- 2 ½ cups rye flour (spoon lightly to measure)
- 6 cups sifted white flour (27 ounces)
- 3 tablespoons caraway seeds
- 1 egg white mixed with 1 tablespoon cold water
- kosher salt
- cornmeal

WHEN NO ONE IS LOOKING
Bake these 1 day ahead and when cool, wrap in foil and refrigerate. Reheat the bread (unwrapped) in a preheated 350° oven.

FROZEN POWER
Like most breads this one freezes well. After the breads are cool, double-wrap them in foil and freeze. To serve, defrost in the foil wrapping, then reheat uncovered in a preheated 350° oven.

Dissolve yeast in the ⅔ cup warm water. Stir in sugar and salt. Place the lukewarm water in a large bowl and add dissolved yeast. Beat in the rye flour and as much of the white flour as needed to make a stiff dough. (Use an electric dough hook or a wooden spoon and finally your hands.) Turn out on a floured board and knead in the caraway seeds. Place dough in a greased bowl and cover. Let rise until doubled in bulk—45 minutes or longer. Punch down the dough and turn it out on a floured board. Divide either into 2 or 4 portions (depending on size of loaves desired) and let them rest for 5 minutes.

Preheat oven to 400°. Grease flat baking pans and sprinkle generously with cornmeal. Shape dough into long loaves and place them on the prepared pans. Score tops of loaves with a sharp knife and brush with egg white mixture. Let rise about 30 minutes. Brush loaves again with egg white and sprinkle with the kosher salt. Bake for 30 minutes. Reduce oven to 300° and bake 20 to 25 minutes longer. Remove breads from pans and cool on racks.

CRESCENT BUTTER ROLLS

Makes 32 rolls

1 package dry yeast
¼ cup warm water
1 tablespoon sugar
¾ cup milk
½ cup sugar
3 extra-large eggs, slightly beaten
½ pound butter (2 sticks), melted
4 ½ cups sifted flour (21 ounces)
½ teaspoon salt
cold milk

WHEN NO ONE IS LOOKING
Bake these 1 day ahead but underbake slightly, that is, do not let them brown too much. Cool the rolls, then wrap in foil and refrigerate. Reheat them loosely wrapped in foil in a preheated 375° oven.

FROZEN POWER
Perfect for power in your freezer, but underbake them slightly. Cool the rolls, then freeze them in plastic bags that can be tightly sealed. To serve, defrost, wrap loosely in foil, and reheat in a preheated 375° oven.

Dissolve yeast in warm water and sprinkle with the 1 tablespoon sugar; set aside. Combine the milk, ½ cup sugar, eggs, and ½ of the butter (¼ pound) in a large bowl, then add dissolved yeast and stir. Beat in flour and salt. Cover with a damp cloth or with plastic wrap and let rise 1 ½ hours or until double in bulk.

Preheat oven to 400°. Divide dough into 2 parts. Roll out each part on a floured board into a large circle ¼ inch thick. Spread each with the half of the remaining butter and cut into 16 wedges. Roll up wedges from the wide ends to the tips. Place on nonstick baking pans or on greased pans and let rise again until doubled—about 1 ½ hours. Brush tops of rolls with cold milk, then bake about 12 minutes. Serve hot.

CORNMEAL SPOON BREAD

Makes about 4 servings

- 1 cup yellow cornmeal (stone-ground, if possible)
- 3 cups milk
- 1 teaspoon salt
- ⅛ pound butter (½ stick)
- 4 eggs
- 2 teaspoons baking powder
- ⅓ cup grated Parmesan cheese

WHEN NO ONE IS LOOKING
Prepare the cornmeal base in the morning; cover tightly with plastic wrap and leave at room temperature. Beat eggs and baking powder just before baking, then proceed as directed in the recipe.

Heat 2 cups of the milk to simmering, then remove from heat and slowly add the cornmeal while you stir or whisk vigorously. Return to low heat and add the salt, the remaining milk, and the butter, then continue to stir until thickened—about 2 minutes. Remove from heat and set aside until ready to bake.

Butter or oil a 1½ quart casserole (or soufflé dish). Preheat oven to 375°. Place eggs in a large bowl and sprinkle with the baking powder, then whisk them until light and frothy (or use an electric beater). Fold or gently stir the egg mixture into the cornmeal mixture only until combined—do not beat. Stir in the Parmesan cheese. Pour or spoon into the prepared casserole and bake for 40 to 45 minutes.

CHEESE AND GREEN CHILI BRIOCHES

Makes 12 to 16

- 2 packages dry yeast
- ⅓ cup warm water
- 4 whole eggs
- ⅓ cup milk
- 3 tablespoons sugar
- 1 tablespoon salt
- ½ pound butter (2 sticks), melted then cooled to room temperature
- 5 cups sifted flour (22 to 23 ounces)
- 1 (7-ounce) can diced green chilies, drained
- 2 cups diced Monterey Jack or Cheddar cheese, or a mixture (about 9 ounces)

for egg wash:
egg mixed with 1 tablespoon water

WHEN NO ONE IS LOOKING
Prepare the dough one day ahead; cover and refrigerate. Remove from refrigerator 1 hour ahead of forming into the brioche rolls, then proceed as directed above.

FROZEN POWER
Underbake these a little, then cool them and freeze by wrapping each brioche in foil, then storing them in sealable plastic bags. To serve, defrost briefly, then heat in a 375° oven.

Place warm water in a bowl, then sprinkle the dry yeast on the water and stir until yeast has dissolved; set aside. Place eggs in a large bowl with the milk, sugar, and salt, then beat until well combined. Add the dissolved yeast and stir. Add melted butter and combine, then gradually beat in the flour either with a dough hook or by hand using a strong wooden spoon. Beat until the dough is elastic. Add the green chilies and the diced cheese and mix until combined—either with your hands or with a dough hook. Place this dough in a large, greased bowl and cover with a damp cloth or with plastic wrap. Let rise 45 to 60 minutes or until double in bulk.

Preheat oven to 400°. Turn dough out onto a floured board and knead briefly. Divide into 12 to 16 pieces (depending on desired size) and form into round-shaped rolls. Place them on nonstick parchment-lined pans and let rise for approximately 30 minutes. Brush tops with the egg wash.

Bake the brioches for 10 minutes, then reduce oven heat to 350° and bake another 10 to 20 minutes, depending on size. (Watch that bottoms do not burn; if necessary place another pan below.)

GARLIC-PARMESAN TOASTED BREAD

Makes 4 to 6 servings

- 1 1-pound sourdough bread, cut in half horizontally
- 2 to 4 tablespoons soft butter
- ½ cup mayonnaise
- ½ cup grated Parmesan cheese
- 1 to 2 teaspoons garlic oil (p. 18)

WHEN NO ONE IS LOOKING
Prepare the mayonnaise mixture 1 day ahead; cover and keep refrigerated. This can be broiled several hours ahead. Cover lightly and leave at room temperature. Preheat oven to 375° and reheat the prepared bread until hot, but not dried out.

Mix mayonnaise, Parmesan cheese, and garlic oil together; set aside. Butter cut sides of the bread and place under a broiler unit to brown lightly. Remove from oven and spread the prepared mixture on both pieces. Broil again until top has puffed and is golden brown. Watch that they do not burn! Cut in wedges and serve hot.

PULL-APART MONKEY BREAD

Makes 8 to 10 servings

1 package dry yeast
¼ cup warm water
1 teaspoon sugar
⅛ pound butter (½ stick), melted
1 cup milk
¼ cup sugar
1 teaspoon salt
2 extra-large eggs, slightly beaten
4 ½ cups sifted flour (18 ounces)
⅛ pound butter (½ stick), melted and cooled to room temperature

WHEN NO ONE IS LOOKING
Bake this 1 day ahead and after cooling it, turn it out on an oven-proof plate or platter; wrap bread and platter together in foil and then refrigerate. Reheat the bread in its foil wrapping in a preheated 375° oven for about 20 minutes—longer if it is cold.

FROZEN POWER
A wonderful treasure to have waiting for you in your freezer. After the monkey bread has cooled, turn it out upside down, double-wrap in foil and freeze it. To serve, defrost completely, then reheat in its foil wrapping in a preheated 375° oven.

Sprinkle yeast on the warm water in a small bowl and stir with the 1 teaspoon of sugar until dissolved; set aside. Combine the ⅛ pound melted butter, milk, sugar, salt, and eggs in a large bowl and beat until combined. Add dissolved yeast and stir well. Beat in the flour with an electric dough hook or by hand with a wooden spoon until dough is smooth. Cover and let rise until double in bulk—45 minutes to 1 hour.

Preheat oven to 375°. Lightly oil a bundt pan (or angel food cake pan). Turn risen dough onto a floured board and knead for 1 minute. Pat out about ½ inch thick and then cut into 2-inch pieces. Dip each in the melted and cooled butter and arrange them in the prepared pan, pressing the dough pieces down gently. Let rise until double—20 to 30 minutes. Bake for 35 to 40 minutes (if it browns too fast, turn oven to 350°), then remove from oven and cool on a rack. If you want to serve the bread immediately, turn out upside down and serve, but be warned, turning it out upside down just out of the oven often causes it to fall apart. A better way is to bake it several hours ahead, cool it completely in the pan set on a rack—about one hour—then unmold it upside down on an ovenproof plate or platter. Then wrap the whole thing—bread and platter—in foil and set aside until almost time to serve. Reheat in its foil wrapping in a preheated 375° oven—about 20 minutes if it is at room temperature or longer if it is cold.

COLD-OVEN POPOVERS

Makes 4 to 6

- 1 cup sifted flour (sift before measuring)
- ¾ teaspoon salt
- 1 cup milk (room temperature)
- 2 extra-large eggs, slightly beaten
- 1 teaspoon melted butter or oil

WHEN NO ONE IS LOOKING
Make the batter one day ahead. Cover and refrigerate. When batter stands overnight, it will have thickened some, so add a few more tablespoons of milk before baking.

Combine flour and salt in a bowl. Mix milk, eggs, and oil together, then gradually add to the flour, stirring until well mixed. Grease cold glass custard cups with vegetable shortening and fill them about half full of the batter. Place cups on a baking pan and place in a cold oven—yes, a cold oven! Immediately turn oven to 400° and bake 45 to 60 minutes, or until well puffed and browned. Serve hot.

WALNUT AND RAISIN COUNTRY BREAD

Makes 2 loaves

- 1 envelope dry yeast
- ½ cup warm water
- 1 tablespoon sugar
- 2 ½ cups lukewarm water
- 4 ½ cups all-purpose white flour
- 1 tablespoon salt
- 2 cups whole wheat flour (preferably stone-ground)
- 1 cup rye flour
- ½ cup bran flakes
- 1 cup raisins, soaked in hot water, then drained and dried
- 3 cups walnuts, lightly toasted and coarsely chopped

WHEN NO ONE IS LOOKING
Bake the breads one day ahead. Cool, wrap in foil, and refrigerate. They are best if reheated briefly in a 350° oven; then serve warm or at room temperature. The bread will be delicious for several days, sliced and toasted.

FROZEN POWER
These are wonderful breads to have on hand in your freezer. Cool them on racks, then double-wrap them in foil. To serve, defrost at room temperature or overnight in the refrigerator, then reheat briefly in a 350° oven and serve warm or at room temperature.

Dissolve yeast in the ½ cup warm water and 1 tablespoon sugar. Place the 2 ½ cups of lukewarm water in a large bowl, then stir in the dissolved yeast, followed by the white flour and salt. Gradually beat in the whole wheat and rye flours, using a dough hook if possible—or by hand with a heavy wooden spoon. Add bran flakes, raisins, and walnuts and knead until a soft dough forms. Add more white flour if needed. Place dough in a large greased bowl and cover with a damp cloth or with plastic wrap and let rise until doubled in volume, 45 minutes or longer.

Oil a large baking sheet. Turn dough out on a lightly floured surface and knead for 1 minute. Divide the dough into two pieces and form each into a round or oblong loaf. Place these on the prepared pan. Let rise until doubled in volume, or until the dough is no longer springy to touch—30 minutes to 1 hour.

Preheat oven to 475°. Fill a large pan with about 1 cup of hot water and place it on the lowest level of the oven. Place pan with breads on the next level above and bake for 5 minutes, then immediately reduce oven to 375° and bake for 30 minutes. Remove pan with the water. Reduce oven to 350° and bake about another 30 minutes or until the bottom of each loaf sounds hollow when tapped. Remove and cool on racks.

FAUX DOUGHNUTS

Makes about 8

1 ¾ cups flour (sift before measuring)
¾ cup sugar
2 teaspoons baking powder
½ teaspoon salt
⅓ cup melted butter
½ cup milk
1 teaspoon vanilla
1 egg

for after baking:
¼ pound butter (1 stick), melted
1 cup sugar combined with 1 tablespoon cinnamon (or to taste)

WHEN NO ONE IS LOOKING
Bake these 1 day ahead; wrap and refrigerate overnight. Reheat before serving.

FROZEN POWER
Freeze these "doughnuts" but do *not* roll them in the melted butter and sugar-cinnamon mixture. To serve, defrost, reheat, then roll in the sugar-cinnamon mix.

Combine flour, sugar, baking powder, and salt and mix thoroughly (or sift together several times). Combine the milk, melted butter, vanilla, and egg, then beat together slightly. Preheat oven to 400°. Grease muffin pans. Stir liquid ingredients into dry ones and stir until moistened and combined. Do not beat. Spoon into prepared pans and bake for 20 minutes. Remove at once and dip each "doughnut" in the melted butter, then roll each in the sugar-cinnamon mixture.

DANISH PASTRY FOR BEAR CLAWS AND PECAN ROLLS

This pastry can be used to make 8 "Bear Claws" and 18 "Pecan Rolls" (see the recipes for these that follow, pp. 259, 261)

for the basic dough:
1 pound butter (slightly cooler than room temperature)
⅓ cup sifted flour (1½ ounces)
2 packages dry yeast
⅓ cup warm water
1 cup eggs (4 or 5)
⅓ cup sugar (3 ounces)
½ cup milk
1 teaspoon salt
2 tablespoons honey
¼ teaspoon mace
¼ teaspoon cinnamon
1 teaspoon vanilla
1 teaspoon lemon extract
4 cups sifted flour (1 pound)
1 ¾ cups sifted cake flour (6 ounces)

FROZEN POWER
Double-wrap and freeze the Danish pastry dough for up to one week after completing all of the rollings and after chilling it. To use, defrost the dough overnight in the refrigerator.

Prepare the dough: With a wooden spoon or an electric mixer paddle, mix the 1 pound of butter and ⅓ cup sifted flour to form a butter-paste. Spread it in a plastic-lined 9 x 9-inch square pan and chill about 20 minutes. Dissolve yeast in the warm water and set aside. Beat eggs with the sugar, milk, salt, honey, mace, cinnamon, vanilla, and lemon extract, then add dissolved yeast and stir well. Gradually beat in both kinds of flour using either a dough hook or a wooden spoon. Cover and chill 20 minutes. This is the flour-dough.

Roll: Do not hesitate to use plenty of flour to roll out the dough, but remove excess with a pastry brush before folding. Roll out flour-dough into a rectangle about 12 inches by 18 inches and mark in thirds. Remove butter-paste from refrigerator and cut it in half. Spread one half of the butter-paste in the center of the rolled-out dough. Fold one third of the flour-dough on top of this. Spread the other half of the butter-paste on top of the folded-over dough, and then fold over the remaining third of the flour-dough. Press down, wrap in plastic, and refrigerate for 30 minutes.

Remove folded dough from refrigerator and place on a floured board with one of the open ends facing you. This time roll out into a rectangle about 18 inches by 24 inches, then fold both ends to the middle and close like a book. Turn dough again so ends face you and repeat this last step. Wrap in plastic wrap (or waxed paper) and chill for 45 minutes.

Repeat the two rollings described in the previous paragraph. Now wrap again and chill overnight. Check occasionally because the dough may begin to rise; press it down firmly.

BEAR CLAWS

Makes 8

"Danish Pastry" (p. 258)

for the filling:
2 ⅛ cups sliced or slivered blanched almonds, lightly toasted
½ cup sugar
½ teaspoon salt
¼ pound butter (1 stick)
1 egg
¾ teaspoon almond extract

for the egg wash:
1 egg
1 tablespoon water

for the icing:
2 cups sifted powdered sugar
water, only enough to give a thin-spreading consistency
1 teaspoon vanilla extract
sliced blanched almonds for decoration

WHEN NO ONE IS LOOKING
Bake the bear claws one day ahead; wrap them in foil and keep them refrigerated. Unwrap and reheat in a 350° oven before serving.

FROZEN POWER
Freeze the bear claws after baking and after they have cooled. Wrap them in foil, then store in sealable plastic bags. To serve, defrost, then reheat in a 350° oven.

Make the filling: Finely chop the toasted almonds in a food processor. Place butter and sugar in a bowl and beat with an electric mixer until creamy. Beat in the finely chopped almonds, then the eggs, salt, and almond extract. Set aside.

Prepare the icing: Mix powdered sugar with water, heat gently, then add vanilla extract for flavoring; set aside.

Prepare the egg wash: Beat one egg with one tablespoon water; set aside.

Use half of the prepared Danish pastry dough for these bear claws. Divide it into two equal pieces. Roll each into a rectangle approximately 8 x 16 inches. Divide each rectangle into 8 squares, 4 x 4-inches each, and brush with egg wash. Place one tablespoon of filling in the middle of each square and fold over. Make three cuts on the smooth side, but *not* all the way through to the seam side. Arrange the "claws" on baking pans lined with nonstick parchment paper. Let rise 20 to 25 minutes. Preheat oven to 375°. Brush rolls with egg wash and sprinkle tops with sliced almonds. Bake rolls for 20 to 25 minutes. Remove to a rack, then drizzle with the prepared icing.

PECAN ROLLS

Makes 18 rolls

"Danish Pastry" (p. 258)
whole toasted pecans
(1 to 2 cups)

for the filling:
1 cup chopped toasted pecans
½ cup sugar mixed with
2 tablespoons cinnamon
1 beaten egg

for the syrup:
6 ounces butter (1½ sticks)
½ pound brown sugar
2 tablespoons water

for the egg wash:
1 egg
1 tablespoon water

for the cinnamon sugar:
cinnamon
sugar

WHEN NO ONE IS LOOKING
Bake pecan rolls one day ahead; wrap them in foil and keep them refrigerated. Unwrap and reheat in a 350° oven before serving.

FROZEN POWER
Freeze the pecan rolls after baking and after they have cooled. Wrap them in foil, then store in sealable plastic bags. To serve, defrost, then reheat in a 350° oven.

Make the syrup: Combine syrup ingredients in a saucepan and bring to a gentle boil, stirring to dissolve sugar. Simmer 1 minute, then cool.

Spoon prepared syrup into 18 muffin tins (nonstick if possible), then press the whole pecans into syrup. Divide half of the prepared Danish pastry dough into 2 pieces. Roll each portion into a rectangle about ¼ inch thick. Brush with some of the egg wash, then cover thickly with cinnamon-sugar mixture and chopped pecans. Roll up and cut each roll into 9 slices. Place slices cut sides down in the muffin tins on top of the whole pecans and press down. Brush with egg wash and let rise until slightly puffy, about 25 to 35 minutes. Bake in a preheated 375° oven for about 20 minutes. Turn out upside down onto nonstick parchment paper or greased foil.

WALNUT-FILBERT COFFEE CAKES

Makes 2 (9-inch) coffee cakes

for the dough:
1 package dry yeast
¼ cup warm water
1 teaspoon sugar
¼ pound (1 stick) melted butter
1 cup milk
½ cup sugar
1 teaspoon salt
3 eggs
5 cups flour

for the walnut-filbert filling:
¼ pound (1 stick) soft butter
⅔ cup sugar
1 egg
⅛ teaspoon salt
2 teaspoons vanilla
1 cup walnuts, toasted
1 cup filberts, toasted

WHEN NO ONE IS LOOKING
Bake the coffee cakes one day ahead. Cool, then wrap them in foil and keep refrigerated. Before serving, reheat wrapped lightly in foil in a preheated 375° oven.

FROZEN POWER
Yes, do freeze these coffee cakes. And if desired they can be divided into smaller portions before freezing.

Prepare the filling: Place the nuts in a food processor and finely chop them. Cream the soft butter and sugar together until thoroughly combined and fluffy. Beat in the egg, salt, and vanilla. Stir in the chopped nuts, then set aside.

Prepare the dough: Sprinkle yeast on the warm water in a small bowl and stir with the 1 teaspoon sugar until dissolved. Meanwhile in an electric mixer bowl combine the melted butter, milk, sugar, salt, and eggs and beat until combined. Add the dissolved yeast and stir well. Beat in the flour until dough is smooth with an electric dough hook or by hand with a wooden spoon. Cover and let rise until double in bulk—45 minutes to 1 hour or longer.

Assemble and finish the coffee cakes: Preheat oven to 375°. Grease 2, 9-inch round baking tins. Divide dough into two portions. Roll out one portion into an oblong about 8 x 12 inches and spoon on half of the nut filling.

Spread filling over the dough, then roll up (like a jelly roll) and cut into 8 or 9 pieces and place them in one of the pans. Repeat the procedure with the second dough portion and filling. Let rise until double—about 30 minutes. Bake coffee cakes for 20 minutes; reduce heat to 350° and bake another 5 or 10 minutes or until browned and baked through. Remove and cool on racks, then remove from pans.

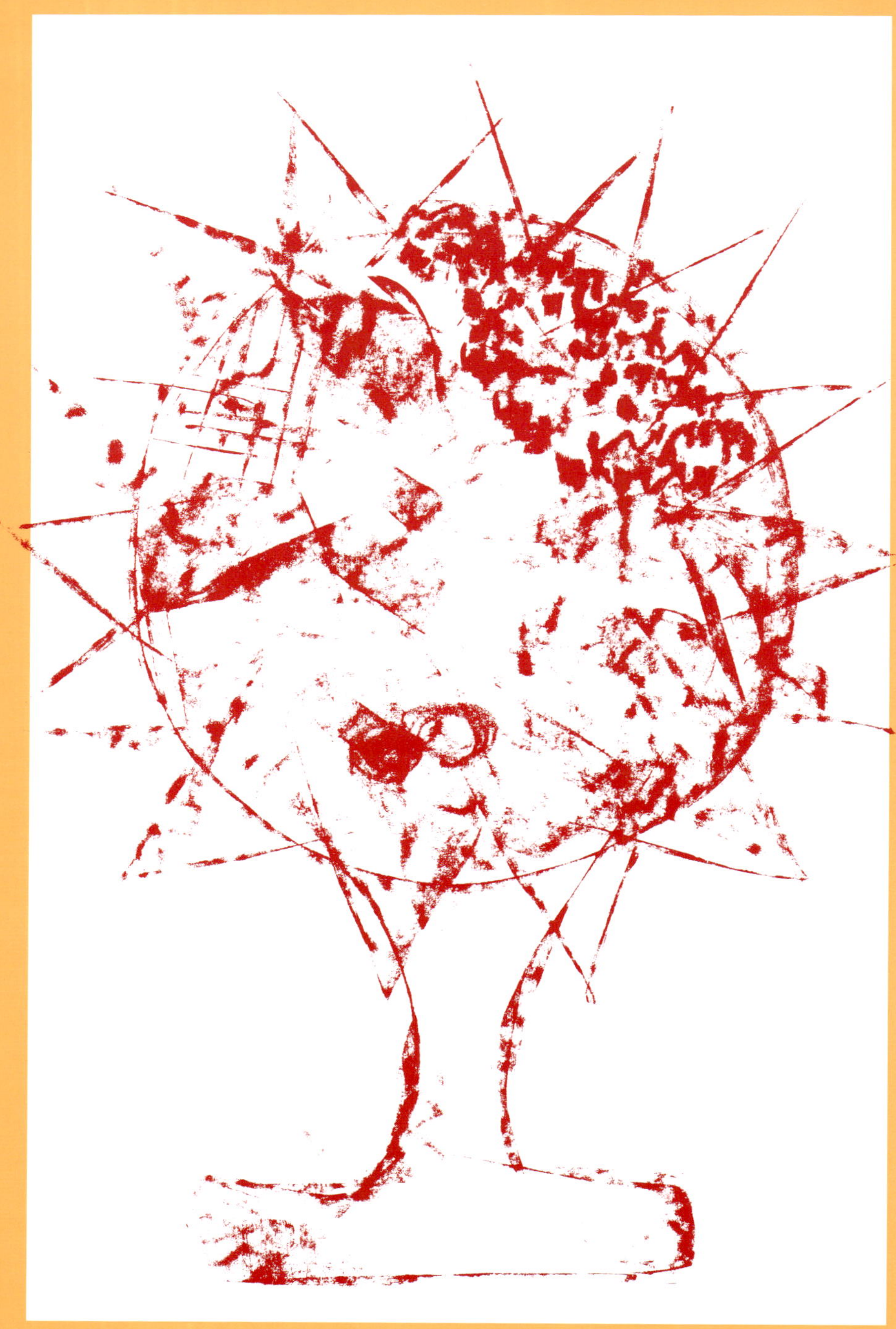

CAKES

DELUXE ORANGE-ALMOND CAKE

Makes about 12 servings

8 eggs, separated
1 ¼ cups sugar
grated zest of 2 oranges
2 teaspoons cinnamon
1 cup almonds, toasted, then ground
1 cup slivered almonds, toasted, then coarsely chopped
pinch of salt

for the orange syrup:
grated rind of 2 oranges
2 ½ cups freshly squeezed orange juice
1 cup sugar

WHEN NO ONE IS LOOKING
Prepare this cake up to 3 days ahead. Keep covered and refrigerated, but bring it to room temperature before serving.

FROZEN POWER
Freeze this cake unwrapped until very firm, then wrap it completely.

Prepare the syrup: Combine the syrup ingredients and bring to a boil, stirring constantly. As soon as the sugar has dissolved, remove from the heat and set aside at room temperature.

Prepare the cake: Preheat oven to 350°. Beat egg yolks with 1 cup of the sugar until light and fluffy. Add the grated orange zest, cinnamon, ground and chopped almonds, and salt; then stir gently until combined. In a separate bowl, beat egg whites until frothy, then sprinkle on the remaining ¼ cup sugar and beat until stiff. Fold this egg-white mixture into the almond mixture. Pour into a greased and floured 11- or 12-inch springform pan. Bake in the preheated oven for 15 minutes. Reduce heat to 325° and bake 15 minutes more. Reduce heat again, this time to 300°, and bake 15 to 20 minutes more, or until cake tests done. Cool on a rack, then poke holes in the top with a fork. Turn cake out into a large deep dish or casserole, Pour syrup over the cake and let it soak for several hours, or overnight. Serve at room temperature.

ORANGE, WALNUT, RAISIN CAKE

Makes 8 to 12 servings

1 large orange
1 cup raisins, rinsed in hot water, then drained
½ cup toasted walnuts
1 cup flour (sift then measure)
1 teaspoon baking soda
1 teaspoon salt
1 cup sugar
½ cup butter (soft but not melted)
1 ¼ cups milk (room temperature)
2 eggs (warmed in their shells in a bowl of hot water)

for the topping:
½ cup toasted walnuts, chopped
⅓ cup sugar
1 teaspoon cinnamon

WHEN NO ONE IS LOOKING
Bake this cake 1 or 2 days ahead. Cover with plastic wrap or foil and leave at room temperature.

FROZEN POWER
Yes, freeze this cake.

Squeeze orange and save the juice for later. Remove seeds from the orange, then cut both pulp and rind into quarters or smaller pieces. Place the orange pieces, raisins, and toasted walnuts in a food processor and pulse until chopped, but do not overdo. These ingredients should be chopped but *not* mushy. Set aside.

Sift the flour, baking soda, salt, and sugar together and place in a mixing bowl. Add the soft butter and mix until the butter is well distributed. Combine the eggs and milk, then add them to the flour and butter mixture and beat with an electric mixer on low for a minute or so. Fold in the chopped orange, raisins, and walnuts. Preheat oven to 350°. Pour or spoon mixture into a greased square, 9 x 9-inch baking pan. Bake in the preheated oven for 35 to 45 minutes, or until cake tests done. Cool on a rack for 10 minutes.

Spoon the reserved orange juice over the top of the cake. Combine topping ingredients, then sprinkle them over the cake.

ALMOND TORTE WITH EGG WHITES

Makes 10 to 12 servings

- ¼ pound butter (1 stick), melted
- 2 to 3 teaspoons vanilla
- 1 ⅛ cups blanched, toasted almonds—whole, slivered, or sliced
- ½ cup flour
- ½ teaspoon salt
- 1 cup sugar
- 8 egg whites
- 1 cup sliced, blanched almonds, lightly toasted

WHEN NO ONE IS LOOKING
Bake this cake 1 day ahead. Cover and leave it at room temperature.

FROZEN POWER
Freeze this cake until firm, then wrap it in foil or store in a plastic bag.

Preheat oven to 375°. Place the 1 ⅛ cups of almonds with the flour, salt, and ½ cup sugar in a food processor and process until finely ground; set aside. Beat egg whites in a large bowl until whites form soft peaks. Gradually beat in remaining sugar, until meringue forms stiff peaks but is not dry. Fold in the nut mixture, the vanilla, and then the melted butter. Line a very deep 9-inch round pan (or a springform) that you have greased and floured or lined with nonstick paper (greasing the paper and flouring it). Spoon mixture into the pan and top with the sliced toasted almonds, pressing them down gently. Bake in the preheated oven for 8 minutes, reduce heat to 350° and bake another 20 minutes; reduce heat again to 300° and bake another 5 minutes or until cake tests done. Do not overbake. Cool briefly on a rack then turn out and finish cooling.

FILBERT CAKE WITH EGG WHITES

Makes one deep 10-inch cake

- 1 ½ cups filberts (hazelnuts)
- 1 ½ cups sugar
- 1 cup flour
- 5 ounces butter (1 ¼ sticks), melted and cooled to room temperature
- 4 tablespoons rum (Haitian Barbancourt, if possible)
- 2 teaspoons vanilla
- 8 egg whites
- ¼ teaspoon salt
- powdered sugar (for garnish)

WHEN NO ONE IS LOOKING
Bake this cake 1 day ahead; cover and refrigerate, or leave it well covered at room temperature.

FROZEN POWER
Yes, freeze this cake, but double-wrap it. Or, freeze the cake until firm, then wrap it in plastic or foil and store it in a plastic bag that can be tightly sealed.

Toast the filberts in a preheated 325° oven for about 15 minutes, then remove them from the oven and rub off the loose brown papery covering. Do not be concerned about any brown skin that remains.

Butter a 10-inch springform pan and line it with a parchment or wax paper disk; then butter the paper. Preheat oven to 350°.

Coarsely chop ½ cup of the filberts and set them aside. Place the remaining 1 cup of filberts with ⅔ cup of the sugar in a food processor and pulse until the mixture is finely ground. Combine this mixture with the flour in a bowl and mix well; set aside. Beat egg whites with the salt in an electric mixer until they begin to thicken, then gradually beat in the remaining sugar, whipping only until the mixture forms a soft peak. Fold in the filbert-flour mixture, then the melted butter, rum, and vanilla. Pour into the prepared pan, then scatter the chopped filberts on top. Bake approximately 45 to 55 minutes or until top is golden brown and the cake feels firm when pressed gently in the center. Remove and cool briefly on a rack, then remove pan and the paper. If filberts fall off, put them back on the cake's top. Sprinkle top with the powdered sugar.

MAGNIFICENT COCONUT CUSTARD CAKE

Makes about 16 servings

2 10-inch genoise cake layers (p. 285 or p. 287)
4 cups angel flake coconut, toasted

for the coconut filling:
3 tablespoons cornstarch
3 tablespoons flour
¼ teaspoon salt
¾ cup sugar
1 (14-ounce) can coconut milk plus whole milk to total 2 ½ cups
⅛ pound butter (½ stick)
6 egg yolks
1 teaspoon vanilla
2 teaspoons coconut extract
1 tablespoon light rum

for the special syrup:
¾ cup canned pineapple juice
½ cup canned coconut cream (such as Coco Lopez)
5 tablespoons light rum

for the whipped cream frosting:
2 cups heavy whipping cream
1 tablespoon sugar
1 teaspoon vanilla
½ teaspoon coconut extract
¾ cup canned coconut cream (such as Coco Lopez)
1 ½ teaspoons unflavored gelatin soaked in 3 tablespoons cold water

WHEN NO ONE IS LOOKING
Toast the coconut 1 or 2 days ahead, but keep it tightly covered and leave at room temperature. Bake the genoise cake layers 1 day ahead, wrap them in foil and either refrigerate or leave at room temperature. Prepare the coconut filling 1 day ahead, but be sure to keep it covered and refrigerated. Prepare the syrup 1 or 2 days ahead, then cover and refrigerate.

FROZEN POWER
By all means, do freeze the genoise cake layers. Do not freeze the assembled cake because it will become soggy. However, freeze for use as leftovers after first cutting the remaining cake into slices and wrapping each separately; then serve the slices partly frozen.

Make the filling: Sift the cornstarch, flour, sugar, and salt together, then place in a saucepan. Add the coconut milk mixed with whole milk and the butter. Stir until very smooth. Cook over moderate heat, stirring constantly, until mixture comes to a boil. Remove from heat. Beat egg yolks in a separate bowl; then gradually beat the thickened coconut milk mixture into the egg yolks. When ingredients are well combined, return them to the saucepan. Cook over low heat, stirring constantly, until very thick. Remove from heat and cool over iced water, stirring occasionally. Add the vanilla, coconut extract, and rum. Add 2 cups of the toasted coconut. Cool, cover, and chill.

Make the special syrup: Combine the pineapple juice, coconut cream, and rum; set aside.

Prepare whipped cream frosting: Put the gelatin in the 3 tablespoons of cold water and dissolve it by placing it in a Pyrex container and setting the container in simmering water. As soon as it is dissolved, beat the heavy cream with the sugar, vanilla, and coconut extract until thick, then add the coconut cream. Beat in the dissolved gelatin all at once, continuing to beat it as you add it. Keep this frosting chilled until ready to use.

Assemble and finish: Slice each cake layer into two horizontal layers, thereby making a total of four. Place one layer on a large serving plate and sprinkle with ⅓ of the special syrup and cover with ⅓ of the coconut filling. Place second cake layer on top and sprinkle with another ⅓ of the syrup and ⅓ of the coconut filling. Place the third cake layer on top and repeat with the final ⅓ of the syrup and the last third of the filling. Place the fourth cake layer on top and press down gently. Keep chilled until ready to frost. Frost top and sides with the prepared whipped cream frosting and generously cover the whole cake with the remaining toasted coconut.

PINEAPPLE-COCONUT CUSTARD CAKE

Makes about 16 servings

Deliciously different from the Coconut Custard Cake

2 10-inch genoise cake layers (p. 285 or p. 287)
2 cups angel flake coconut

for the pineapple-coconut filling:
1 can crushed pineapple (1 pound, 4 ounces), well drained, but save the syrup!!
3 tablespoons cornstarch
3 tablespoons flour
¼ teaspoon salt
¾ cup sugar
2 ½ cups whole milk
⅛ pound butter (½ stick)
6 egg yolks
1 teaspoon vanilla
2 teaspoons coconut extract
1 tablespoon dark rum

for the special syrup:
½ cup coconut cream (such as Coco Lopez)
½ cup pineapple juice (reserved after draining the pineapple for the filling)
5 tablespoons dark rum

for the frosting:
2 cups heavy whipping cream
1 tablespoon sugar
1 teaspoon vanilla
¾ cup coconut cream (such as Coco Lopez)
1 ½ teaspoons unflavored gelatin soaked in ¼ cup cold water

WHEN NO ONE IS LOOKING
Prepare the entire cake 1 day ahead; keep covered and refrigerated. Or, prepare the pineapple filling and syrup 1 day ahead and assemble the cake on the day you plan to serve it.

FROZEN POWER
Freeze the cake layers since genoise freezes well. Do not freeze the assembled cake because it tends to become soggy. Leftovers, however, can be frozen. Freeze leftover cake in slices, each wrapped separately, then serve them partly frozen.

Make the filling: Sift the cornstarch, flour, salt, and sugar together, then place in a saucepan. Add the cold milk and stir until smooth. Add the butter, then cook over moderate heat, stirring constantly, until mixture comes to a boil. Remove from heat. Beat egg yolks in a bowl; then gradually beat the thickened milk mixture into the yolks. When combined, return this yolk mixture to the saucepan. Cook over low heat, stirring constantly, until very thick. Remove from heat and cool over ice water. Chill, then stir in the crushed pineapple, vanilla, coconut extract, and rum.

Make the special syrup: Combine the coconut cream, pineapple juice, and rum and stir well. Cover and set aside until ready to use.

Prepare whipped cream frosting: Dissolve the gelatin by placing it in the ¼ cup water in a Pyrex container and then setting the container in simmering water. Keep it liquid. Beat the heavy cream with the sugar and vanilla until it begins to thicken, then add the coconut cream. Add the dissolved gelatin all at once and beat until thick.

Assemble and finish: Slice each cake layer horizontally into two layers, thereby making a total of four. Place one layer on a large serving plate and sprinkle with ⅓ of the special syrup and cover with ⅓ of the filling. Place second layer on top and sprinkle with another ⅓ of the syrup and ⅓ of the filling. Place third cake layer on top and repeat with ⅓ of the syrup and the last third of the filling. Top with the fourth cake layer and press down gently. Keep chilled until whipped cream frosting has been prepared. Frost top and sides, then cover the whole cake—top and sides—with the coconut. Chill, and when very cold, cover carefully with plastic wrap.

NEW TOSCA CAKE

Makes 8 to 10 servings

1 9- or 10-inch layer of genoise (p. 285 or p. 287; or "Basic Yellow Cake," p. 289)
1 cup strawberry jam or seedless raspberry jam

for the topping:
½ cup sugar
2 tablespoons flour
¼ pound butter (1 stick)
2 tablespoons milk
1 ¼ cups sliced blanched almonds, lightly toasted
2 teaspoons vanilla

WHEN NO ONE IS LOOKING
Prepare this cake in the morning or 1 day ahead. Cover and leave at room temperature.

FROZEN POWER
Keep genoise layers or basic yellow cake layers hidden in your freezer as frozen assets; they are terrific for preparing this delicious cake.

Slice cake layer in half horizontally. Place the bottom half on an oven-proof dish. Spread with the strawberry jam. Top with the second cake layer. Set aside.

Prepare the topping: Mix sugar and flour together in a saucepan. Add the butter and milk and stir over low heat until sugar has dissolved and mixture comes to a gentle boil Reduce heat and simmer 1 minute. Stir in the almonds and heat very gently for 1 or 2 minutes. Remove from heat and stir in the vanilla.

Finish: Spread the almond topping on top of the cake, leaving one inch around the edge uncovered. Place under a broiler until the glaze is golden brown. It takes only 1 or 2 minutes so, watch that it does not burn!

CHOCOLATE WALNUT CAKE

Makes 8 to 10 servings

- 1 cup toasted walnuts, finely chopped
- ¾ cup unsweetened cocoa powder
- 1 tablespoon instant coffee
- 1 ½ cups sugar
- 8 large egg whites
- ¼ teaspoon salt
- ⅛ pound (½ stick) butter, melted and cooled to room temperature
- "Chocolate Ganache" (p. 283)

WHEN NO ONE IS LOOKING
Bake and frost this cake 1 day ahead. Cover and refrigerate, but bring it to room temperature before serving.

FROZEN POWER
Freeze this cake before icing. Add the chocolate ganache icing after defrosting the cake.

Place chopped walnuts in a large bowl, then stir in the cocoa powder, instant coffee, and ¾ cup of the sugar. Mix well and set aside.

Place egg whites in the bowl of an electric mixer and sprinkle with the salt. Beat whites until they begin to hold very soft peaks; then gradually beat in the remaining ¾ cup sugar, continuing to beat until the meringue forms stiff, but not dry, peaks. Stir about ¼ of this meringue into the walnut mixture, then fold in the remaining meringue followed by the butter.

Grease a 9-inch springform pan. Preheat oven to 350°. Pour cake mixture into the pan and bake for 30 to 40 minutes. Cool briefly on a rack, then cut around the sides, remove the sides from the springform pan, and lift the cake out. Place on a rack until cool, then frost with the chocolate ganache icing.

CHOCOLATE ALMOND CAKE

Makes 8 to 12 servings

- 9 ounces semisweet chocolate
- 6 ounces butter (1 ½ sticks), room temperature
- 1 cup sugar plus 2 tablespoons
- 9 ounces almonds (1 ½ cups), toasted then finely ground
- 6 eggs, separated
- ⅛ teaspoon salt
- 2 teaspoons vanilla

WHEN NO ONE IS LOOKING
Bake and frost this cake 1 day ahead; cover and refrigerate. Bring to room temperature before serving.

FROZEN POWER
Freeze this cake frosted or unfrosted.

Melt chocolate in a double boiler or in a microwave oven, then set aside. Beat butter in an electric mixer and gradually beat in the 1 cup of sugar, salt, and vanilla. Add egg yolks and beat again, scraping down the bowl, and continue to beat until mixture is light and fluffy, then beat in the melted chocolate. Add the almonds and beat on low speed only until incorporated.

Preheat oven to 375°. Beat the egg whites in a separate bowl until stiff but not dry, gradually beating in the 2 tablespoons of sugar. Stir a large spoonful of these whites into the chocolate mixture, then fold in the remaining whites. Butter a 9- or 9 ½-inch springform pan and line with wax paper or with nonstick parchment paper. Butter again. Spoon in the cake mixture and bake for 10 minutes in the preheated oven; reduce heat to 350° and bake about 15 minutes; then reduce heat again, this time to 325°, and bake about another 15 minutes. Remove from oven and place on a rack. Cool 10 minutes, then remove sides of springform. Cool completely, then turn cake out upside down on a rack, remove paper, then invert again to finish cooling right side up. If desired, frost with ganache (p. 283).

ANOTHER CHOCOLATE GÂTEAU

Makes 10 to 16 servings

1 10-inch layer of "Chocolate Genoise" (p. 280)
1 ½ dozen "Almond Macaroons" (p. 317, or purchase them)
1 cup strawberry jam
½ cup Grand Marnier liqueur

for chocolate coating:
12 ounces semisweet chocolate
⅛ pound butter (½ stick)
¼ cup light corn syrup

for the chocolate-orange filling:
1 tablespoon unflavored gelatin
¼ cup cold water
12 ounces semisweet chocolate
¼ cup sugar
¼ cup water
⅛ teaspoon salt
4 egg yolks
grated rind of 2 oranges
1 tablespoon Grand Marnier liqueur
4 egg whites
2 tablespoons sugar
1 cup heavy whipping cream

WHEN NO ONE IS LOOKING
Prepare this splendid creation 2 or 3 days ahead; it should be at least partly prepared 1 day ahead. Keep it well covered and refrigerated.

FROZEN POWER
Freeze the completely assembled gâteau, but move it into your refrigerator 2 days before serving to slowly defrost.

Make the chocolate coating (see diagram on p. 278): Cut 5 pieces of waxed paper each 7 x 8 inches; and cut 1 piece of waxed paper 5 x 17 inches. Place them on large, lightly oiled baking tins. Melt the chocolate, butter, and corn syrup in a Pyrex or stainless steel bowl placed over simmering water, and stir until smooth; then remove from heat and cool to room temperature. Spread ½ cup of the mixture on the one long strip of paper, then divide remaining coating on the other 5 pieces. Chill until firm—several hours.

8"
8"
7"
7"
8"
8"
7"
7"
8"
7"
17"
5"
5"
17"
2½"
17"

Make the chocolate-orange filling: Soak gelatin in the ¼ cup of cold water and set aside. Combine the 12 ounces of chocolate, ¼ cup sugar, ¼ cup water, and salt in a heavy saucepan over lowest heat, stirring until chocolate has melted. Beat egg yolks in a bowl; then gradually whisk the melted chocolate mixture into the egg yolks. Return mixture to the saucepan and stir over lowest heat for 3 to 4 minutes. Add the soaked gelatin and stir until dissolved. Remove from heat, add orange rind and Grand Marnier. Cool and stir over ice water until room temperature. In another bowl, beat egg whites until barely stiff, then beat in the 2 tablespoons of sugar and fold into the chocolate mixture. Beat cream until stiff and fold it into the chocolate mixture too. Chill until ready to assemble.

Assemble: Soak macaroons in the ½ cup Grand Marnier. Cut the "Chocolate Genoise" in half horizontally. Place 1 layer in a 10-inch springform pan and cover it with half the jam and half the soaked macaroons. Top this with half the chocolate-orange filling. Place remaining cake layer on the top and repeat with jam, macaroons, and remaining filling. Completely cover the gâteau with plastic wrap or foil and chill for at least 5 hours or overnight. When chilled remove sides of springform but leave bottom of pan and then place the gâteau on a platter. Remove the 5 small pieces of chocolate coating from refrigerator and as they start to soften, remove waxed paper and place chocolate around the cake sides, pressing with your hands, folding and pleating as needed (refer to diagram, p. 278). Then, to make a flower topknot, remove the long chocolate strip and when it starts to soften, remove paper and roll the chocolate strip loosely into a spiral about 4 inches in diameter. Place on top center of cake, then arrange it to look like a flower. Refrigerate cake until 1 hour before serving. *Note:* If chocolate strips soften too much, return them to the refrigerator briefly.

CHOCOLATE GENOISE

Makes 2 9-inch layers or 1 10-inch layer baked in a springform pan

- 6 eggs, warmed in their shells in a bowl of hot water
- 1 cup sugar
- ¼ teaspoon salt
- 1 teaspoon vanilla
- ½ cup sifted flour (2 ⅛ ounces)
- ½ cup Dutch-style unsweetened cocoa
- ¼ pound butter (1 stick), melted and cooled to room temperature

WHEN NO ONE IS LOOKING
Bake these cakes 1 day ahead; wrap them in foil or plastic wrap and refrigerate.

FROZEN POWER
First chill the cakes unwrapped for 1 hour in the freezer to avoid mashing them when you wrap them. When cold and firm, wrap them in foil or seal them in plastic bags.

Be sure to use a springform pan if preparing a 10-inch cake. Grease and flour pans, or grease and cover bottoms with circles of nonstick parchment. Preheat oven to 350°. Place unshelled eggs in a large bowl of hot water to warm them, then break the eggs into a large mixing bowl and beat until frothy. Gradually beat in sugar, salt, and vanilla (best done with an electric beater). Beat until mixture is the consistency of whipped cream. Sift flour and cocoa together twice, then gradually fold into the egg mixture. Fold in the butter with a few strokes; do not overmix or the sponge will break down. Pour or spoon mixture into pans and bake for 15 minutes. Reduce heat to 300° and bake 10 to 15 minutes longer (even longer for a 10-inch cake), or until tops spring back when gently touched. Remove cakes from oven and place on racks for 5 minutes, then remove cakes from pans and finish cooling on cake racks.

CHOCOLATE CHANTILLY CAKE

Makes 10 or more servings

2 9-inch layers of "Chocolate Genoise" (p. 280)
"Ganache" (p. 283)

for rum syrup:
½ cup water
½ cup sugar
3 tablespoons dark rum

for chocolate chantilly filling:
8 ounces dark sweet chocolate
½ cup milk
2 cups heavy whipping cream
1 teaspoon vanilla

WHEN NO ONE IS LOOKING
Prepare the cakes, syrup, and chocolate chantilly filling 1 or 2 days ahead; keep the cakes wrapped, and the syrup and chantilly filling covered; refrigerate all components. Or, assemble the entire cake, cover and keep refrigerated for 1 to 2 days.

FROZEN POWER
Freeze the entire assembled cake until firm, then double-wrap and return to the freezer.

Make the rum syrup: Combine sugar and water in a saucepan and stir over moderate heat until sugar has dissolved. Remove from heat and cool slightly, then stir in rum and set aside.

Make the chocolate chantilly filling: Melt the chocolate with the ½ cup milk over low heat, stirring constantly. Remove from heat and add the vanilla. Cool the mixture; it should be room temperature. Whip cream until stiff, then fold in the melted chocolate. Keep chilled until ready to use.

Assemble: Cut each cake layer in half horizontally, thus creating a total of 4 layers. Place 1 layer on a serving dish and brush on ¼ of the syrup. Spread with ⅓ of the chocolate chantilly filling. Do the same with 2 more cake layers. Top with the fourth layer, then chill cake for several hours—if possible in a freezer. After completely chilled, pour the "Ganache" icing over the entire cake.

CHOCOLATE GENOISE WITH CHOCOLATE-FILBERT CREAM

Makes about 8 servings

- 1 9-inch "Chocolate Genoise" layer (p. 280)
- 1 cup filberts (hazelnuts), toasted, skins rubbed off, then coarsely chopped
- ¼ cup Frangelico liqueur
- 1 cup heavy whipping cream
- ½ cup Nutella (Ferrero label), a cream made with filberts
- 1 cup "Ganache" (p. 283)

WHEN NO ONE IS LOOKING
Prepare this cake 1 day ahead; cover and keep refrigerated.

FROZEN POWER
Freeze the genoise cake layers. Or, freeze the completely assembled cake. Defrost overnight in the refrigerator.

Cut the chocolate genoise layer in half horizontally and place one half on a serving plate. Sprinkle with half the Frangelico. Whip cream until stiff, then fold in the Nutella and the chopped filberts. Spread ⅔ of this mixture on the cake layer.

Top with the second half of the cake. Sprinkle it with the remaining Frangelico and cover with the remaining cream mixture. Place in the freezer for ½ hour or longer—until top mixture has hardened. Remove from freezer and frost top and sides of the cake with the ganache. Refrigerate until firm, then cover with plastic wrap until about 1 hour before serving.

GANACHE (CHOCOLATE ICING OR FILLING)

Makes about 2 cups

12 ounces semisweet chocolate, chopped
1 cup heavy whipping cream

WHEN NO ONE IS LOOKING
Prepare this up to 7 days ahead if you keep it tightly covered and refrigerated. To use, heat gently and stir until softened to desired consistency.

FROZEN POWER
Yes, do freeze the ganache in tightly sealed containers. To use, defrost, then reheat gently and stir until softened to desired consistency.

Melt chocolate in a Pyrex container placed in simmering water or in a microwave oven. Remove from heat. Heat the cream, then add it to the chocolate and whisk until smooth. Cool, stirring occasionally.

If you have a microwave oven you can combine the chopped chocolate and cream in a bowl, then place in the microwave oven for 1 or 1 ½ minutes. Stir and whisk. If chocolate lumps remain, heat another ½ minute or so, that is, heat and whisk until mixture is smooth, but do not overheat.

DAVID'S FAVORITE PRUNE TORTE

Makes 8 to 16 servings

½ pound butter (2 sticks), room temperature
1 cup sugar
2 eggs (room temperature)
3 cups flour
½ teaspoon salt
1 teaspoon baking soda
1 teaspoon lemon juice
2 teaspoons vanilla

for the filling:
12 ounces pitted prunes
⅓ cup raisins, rinsed in hot water, then drained
2 tart apples, peeled and quartered
½ cup seedless raspberry jam

WHEN NO ONE IS LOOKING
Bake this 1 or 2 days ahead, then cover tightly and leave at room temperature. Or, keep it covered and refrigerated for 4 to 6 days ahead.

FROZEN POWER
This freezes beautifully.

Make the filling: Place the prunes, raisins, and apples in a food processor and pulse until very finely chopped, but not puréed. Place in bowl, add jam, and mix until well combined. Set aside.

Make the dough: Cream butter and sugar together until light and fluffy. Beat in the eggs. Sift together (or mix well) the flour, salt, and baking soda. Add to the butter mixture and beat slowly until combined. Add lemon juice and vanilla. *Do not overbeat.*

Finish: Set aside about ¼ of the dough to be used for a topping lattice. Divide remaining dough into two pieces. Grease a 9-inch square Pyrex baking pan. Pat one of the two pieces into the bottom and then cover with half the filling. Spread the second large piece of dough on top, then cover with remaining filling. Combine the dough you set aside earlier with a bit more flour. Roll out and cut into strips. Use these to form a lattice top for the torte. Do not worry about the regularity of the strips; they spread during the baking and invariably make a pleasing pattern.

Preheat oven to 350°. Bake torte for 15 minutes. Reduce oven to 325° and bake an additional 20 minutes. Reduce heat to 300° and bake 10 minutes, then reduce heat to 275° and bake for 10 minutes. Remove from oven and cool on a rack. When cold, wrap in foil and refrigerate or leave at room temperature.

VANILLA GENOISE

Makes 2 9-inch round layers or 1 deep 10-inch layer

6 eggs, warmed in their shells in a bowl of hot water
1 cup sugar
¼ teaspoon salt
1 ½ teaspoons vanilla
1 cup sifted flour (4 ½ ounces)
6 tablespoons melted butter, cooled to room temperature

WHEN NO ONE IS LOOKING
Bake this vanilla genoise 1 day before; wrap in plastic and either refrigerate or leave at room temperature.

FROZEN POWER
Yes, by all means, do freeze the genoise. Chill first until firm, then wrap and freeze. Genoise only needs about 10 minutes to defrost.

Line two 9-inch pans with nonstick parchment (or one 10-inch springform pan), then grease and flour the parchment. Preheat oven to 350°. After measuring the flour, sift it together with the salt and with 2 tablespoons of the sugar. Beat the warmed eggs in a large bowl with an electric mixer, then gradually add the remaining sugar, beating until mixture is about three times its original bulk and looks like soft whipped cream. Beat in the vanilla. Fold in the flour-sugar mixture by thirds, being careful not to overmix. Then fold in the melted butter with a few quick strokes, again being careful not to overmix. Divide batter into the prepared pans and bake for 15 minutes. Reduce heat to 325°. Bake 8 to 10 additional minutes for the two layers, but about 20 minutes or longer for the deep 10-inch cake. When done, cakes should shrink from pan edges and tops should spring back when gently pressed.

MACADAMIA NUT-PINEAPPLE-RUM CAKE

Makes a large cake or several small ones

1 pound candied pineapple, the dry, sugared type
½ to ¾ cup of quality medium-dark rum (if possible use Haitian Barbancourt)
1 pound butter, room temperature
2 cups sugar
7 eggs, warmed in their shells in a bowl of hot water
3 ½ cups flour (15 ¾ ounces)
1 teaspoon baking powder
½ teaspoon cream of tartar
10 ounces roasted, salted macadamia nuts (if unsalted, add 1 teaspoon salt to the dry ingredients)

WHEN NO ONE IS LOOKING
Bake this cake up to 5 or 6 days ahead; wrap and refrigerate. Bring to room temperature before serving.

FROZEN POWER
This is an ideal cake for the freezer. Double-wrap it in foil; it should keep at least 6 months in a freezer that holds an even, cold temperature. Defrost overnight at room temperature in the foil wrapping.

Dice the pineapple and place it in a bowl with the rum. Cover and leave at room temperature for at least 4 hours, but better overnight, or even longer. Stir once or twice. Set aside until needed.

Cream butter and sugar together until light and fluffy, then beat in the eggs one at a time. Combine the dry ingredients and sift together to mix thoroughly. Add them to the creamed butter mixture and stir until combined. Do not beat after adding the flour since overbeating will make the cake tough and dry. Now stir in the diced pineapple with any rum that has not been absorbed and the macadamia nuts.

Generously grease and flour a loaf pan or pans (or use nonstick pans with parchment paper in the bottoms). Preheat oven to 325°. Bake cake or cakes for 30 minutes, then reduce heat to 300° and bake 30 to 45 minutes longer—time will depend on the size of the cake or cakes. Remove from oven and place on racks to cool for 5 minutes, then remove cake(s) from pan(s) and cool them completely on the racks.

ANOTHER KIND OF GENOISE

Makes 3 9-inch or 2 10-inch layers

- 5 tablespoons butter, melted and cooled to room temperature
- 6 eggs, warmed in their shells in a bowl of hot water
- 1 ½ cups sugar
- 1 teaspoon vanilla
- 1 ½ cups cake flour (sift, then measure!)
- ¼ teaspoon salt
- 1 ½ teaspoons baking powder

WHEN NO ONE IS LOOKING
Bake 1 or 2 days ahead; wrap cakes carefully in foil and leave at room temperature.

FROZEN POWER
By all means, do freeze. First freeze the cakes for a few hours unwrapped to avoid squashing; when firm, double-wrap in foil or seal in plastic bags.

Preheat oven to 350° for the 9-inch layers or to 325° for the 10-inch layers. Prepare pans (3 9-inch or 2 10-inch) by greasing them with butter or vegetable shortening, then lining them with parchment or waxed paper, then greasing and flouring the parchment. Combine the sifted and measured cake flour with the salt and baking powder by sifting together three times. Beat eggs until light, then gradually beat in the sugar and vanilla, beating until about tripled in volume and almost the consistency of whipped cream. Sift the dry ingredients in 3 parts over the egg mixture and fold in gently. Do not overmix. Then, fold in the cooled butter with a few quick strokes.

Spoon or pour batter into the prepared pans. Bake the 9-inch layers for 15 to 20 minutes. Bake the 10-inch at 325° for 30 to 35 minutes. Remove from oven, cool for a few minutes; then invert and remove the cakes from pans and the papers from the cakes. Finish cooling on cake racks.

APPLESAUCE SPICE CAKE WITH A BROWN SUGAR CARAMEL ICING

Makes 16 or more servings

for the cake:
½ pound butter (2 sticks), room temperature
2 ¼ cups sugar
3 eggs, room temperature
2 teaspoons vanilla
3 cups sifted flour, measure after sifting (12 ½ ounces)
1 tablespoon baking soda
½ teaspoon salt
1 tablespoon cinnamon
1 ½ teaspoons nutmeg
1 teaspoon cloves
2 cups applesauce
1 cup walnuts, toasted then chopped
1 to 2 cups raisins (to your taste), soaked in hot water, then drained

for the icing:
6 ounces butter (1 ½ sticks)
¾ cup heavy whipping cream
1 pound brown sugar (light or dark)
1 ½ teaspoons vanilla
toasted walnut halves for garnishing or sprinkle with powdered sugar

WHEN NO ONE IS LOOKING
This cake tastes best if it ages at room temperature for at least 24 hours; even better if it ages 2 to 3 days; keep it wrapped as directed in the recipe.

FROZEN POWER
This cake has wonderful frozen power. Defrost it in its wrapping for 24 to 36 hours at room temperature before serving.

Make the cake layers: Grease two square pans (9 x 9 inch), or two 10-inch round pans and then lightly flour them. Preheat oven to 300°. Cream the butter and sugar together until well combined, then beat in the eggs one at a time until batter is light and fluffy. Add the vanilla. Combine the measured flour with soda, salt, and spices, then sift together three times.

Add this flour mixture alternately to the butter and egg mixture with the applesauce, beginning and ending with the flour. Stir in the raisins and nuts. Spoon batter into prepared pans, then bake for 45 minutes to 1 hour. Remove from oven and place on racks to cool for 5 to 10 minutes, then remove from pans and complete cooling on racks.

Make the icing: Melt the butter, then add the cream and brown sugar. Stir over moderate heat until mixture begins to simmer, then cook without stirring to the soft ball stage (238° to 240° on a candy thermometer). Cool to room temperature without stirring. Add the vanilla and then beat until it is of spreading consistency. If icing becomes too thick, thin it with a tiny bit of cream; if not thick enough, use it anyway because it will gradually thicken on the cake.

Assemble: Put half the icing between the two cake layers, then spread the rest of it on the top and sides. If desired, garnish the top with toasted walnut halves. When the icing is firm, wrap the cake in plastic, then wrap it again in foil. Let the cake stand at room temperature at least 24 hours.

A BASIC YELLOW CAKE

Makes 2 or 3 9-inch layers

- ½ pound butter (2 sticks), room temperature
- 2 cups sugar
- 4 eggs, room temperature (or warmed in their shells in hot water)
- 1 ½ teaspoons vanilla
- 3 cups cake flour (sift before measuring)
- 3 teaspoons baking powder
- ¾ teaspoon salt
- 1 cup milk, room temperature

WHEN NO ONE IS LOOKING
Bake these cakes 1 day ahead; wrap and refrigerate.

FROZEN POWER
Freeze these layers unwrapped until firm, then double-wrap or seal in plastic bags.

Preheat oven to 350°. Grease and flour 2 or 3 9-inch layer cake pans (depending on desired thickness), or line them with nonstick parchment paper. Beat the butter until creamy, then beat in the sugar until light and fluffy. Beat in one egg at a time, then add the vanilla. After measuring the flour, sift it together with the baking powder and salt 2 or 3 times—or place the dry ingredients in a bowl and mix thoroughly with a whisk. Add these dry ingredients to the butter and egg mixture alternately with the milk, starting with the flour mixture and ending with it. Do not overbeat.

Divide batter into prepared pans and bake for 20 to 30 minutes. If baked in 3 pans, they will be ready sooner. Cool briefly on racks, then remove from pans and finish cooking on racks.

SPICY LAVENDER AND OLD LACE CAKE

Makes 12 to 16 servings

¼ pound butter (1 stick), room temperature
1 cup sugar
2 eggs, room temperature
½ cup molasses
2 cups cake flour (sift before measuring)
1 teaspoon cinnamon
½ teaspoon nutmeg
¼ teaspoon cloves
½ teaspoon salt
1 teaspoon baking soda
1 cup sour milk (or add 1 teaspoon vinegar to 1 cup of milk)
1 teaspoon vanilla

for the sea foam icing:
¾ cup brown sugar (pack to measure)
¼ cup light corn syrup
2 tablespoons water
¼ teaspoon salt
¼ teaspoon cream of tartar
1 teaspoon vanilla
2 egg whites

WHEN NO ONE IS LOOKING
Bake this cake and fill it 1 day ahead. Refrigerate overnight, but serve it at room temperature.

FROZEN POWER
Freeze the cake layers, but without the icing. Ice the cake after defrosting.

Prepare the cake layers: Preheat oven to 350°. Grease and flour two 9-inch layer cake pans (or line them with nonstick parchment paper). Cream butter and sugar together until light and fluffy, then beat in the eggs. Add the molasses and combine thoroughly. Sift the measured flour, spices, baking soda, and salt together and add them to the butter and egg mixture alternately with the sour milk. Stir in the vanilla. Divide the batter in the prepared pans and bake for about 35 minutes. Remove from oven and cool for 5 minutes, then remove cakes from pans and finish cooling on racks.

Make the sea foam icing: Combine all icing ingredients in the top of a double boiler or in a stainless steel bowl placed over simmering water. Beat with a whisk or rotary beater until frosting holds its shape—5 to 7 minutes. Remove from heat and spread the icing between layers and on top and sides of the cake.

ALMOND CAKE

Makes 8 to 10 servings

- 5 ½ to 6 ounces butter, room temperature
- ¾ cup sugar
- 3 eggs, room temperature
- ½ cup blanched almonds, lightly toasted, then ground
- ½ cup sifted flour (sift before measuring)
- ¼ teaspoon salt
- ½ teaspoon baking powder
- ¼ cup kirsch

WHEN NO ONE IS LOOKING
Bake this cake 1 day ahead; cover and refrigerate but serve at room temperature.

FROZEN POWER
Yes, freeze this cake. First, freeze it unwrapped, and when firm, double-wrap and return to the freezer.

Grease and lightly flour an 8-inch springform pan. Preheat oven to 350°. Cream the butter and sugar together. Beat in the eggs one at a time. Sift together (or mix well) the measured flour, salt, and baking powder, then add to the batter with the kirsch. Add ground almonds and stir only to combine. Spoon or pour into prepared pan and bake for 30 to 35 minutes. Remove and cool for 5 minutes, then remove from the pan and cool on a rack.

ALMOND CAKE WITH ALMOND PASTE

Makes 6 to 10 servings

8 ounces of almond paste
½ cup sugar
¼ pound butter (1 stick), room temperature
3 eggs (room temperature)
¼ teaspoons salt
2 ½ tablespoons flour
3 tablespoons kirsch

WHEN NO ONE IS LOOKING
Bake this cake 1 or 2 days ahead; keep covered and refrigerated, but serve it at room temperature.

FROZEN POWER
Freeze the cake first; when firm, wrap in double foil or seal in a plastic bag and return to the freezer.

Line an 8-inch layer cake pan with nonstick parchment paper or grease and flour the pan. Preheat oven to 325°.

Dice almond paste and place it in a large bowl. Beat with an electric mixer to break it up, then gradually beat in the sugar until all lumps have disappeared. Beat in the butter and continue to beat until smooth, then add the eggs one at a time and beat well. Add the salt, flour, and kirsch and stir until combined.

Spoon the mixture into the prepared pan and bake for 45 minutes. Reduce oven to 300° and bake 15 to 20 minutes longer. The top should be brown and the sides of the cake should have pulled away from the sides of the pan. Remove and cool briefly on a rack. Cut around sides, then turn upside down and remove the paper. Finish cooling right side up on a rack.

SUPER DELUXE POUND CAKE

Makes 12 to 16 servings

- ¾ pound butter (3 sticks), room temperature
- 2 ¼ cups sugar
- 8 eggs, room temperature
- grated rind of 1 lemon
- 2 tablespoons lemon juice
- 2 ½ teaspoons vanilla
- 2 ¼ cups sifted flour (sift before measuring)
- ¼ teaspoon baking soda
- ½ teaspoon baking powder
- ¼ teaspoon salt
- 1 ½ teaspoons cream of tartar

WHEN NO ONE IS LOOKING
Bake this cake 2 to 3 days ahead; double-wrap it in foil and leave at room temperature.

FROZEN POWER
Yes, do freeze this cake. Double-wrap in foil. To serve, defrost the cake overnight in its wrapping at room temperature.

Preheat oven to 325°. Grease and flour a large bundt pan. Cream butter with 1 ¼ cups of the sugar until light and fluffy. Separate the eggs and beat the yolks into the butter-sugar mixture, reserving the whites for later. Sift the measured flour with the baking soda and baking powder twice, then add to yolk mixture, mixing only until combined. *Do not overmix.* Add the lemon rind, lemon juice, and vanilla. Place the egg whites in another large bowl and add the salt and cream of tartar. Beat until frothy, then gradually beat in the remaining 1 cup of sugar—mixture should be stiff but not dry. Fold the egg white mixture into the egg yolk mixture, then pour into the prepared pan. Bake for 1 ¼ to 1 ½ hours, or until cake shrinks slightly from pan sides. Turn off heat and leave cake in the oven for 10 minutes, then remove and place on a rack for 5 minutes. Invert cake and remove from pan; finish cooling on cake rack.

LEMON CAKE WITH LEMON ICING

Makes 8 to 12 servings

½ pound butter (2 sticks), room temperature
2 cups sugar
3 eggs, room temperature
3 cups cake flour, sift before measuring (10 ½ ounces)
½ teaspoon baking soda
½ teaspoon salt
1 cup buttermilk or sour milk
grated rind of 2 lemons
2 tablespoons lemon juice

for lemon icing:
1 pound powdered sugar
¼ pound butter (1 stick), soft
grated rind of 1 lemon
¼ cup (or more) lemon juice

WHEN NO ONE IS LOOKING
Bake this 2 or 3 days ahead; double-wrap in foil and refrigerate, but bring to room temperature before serving.

FROZEN POWER
Double-wrap in foil and freeze. To serve, defrost overnight at room temperature (in the foil wrapping).

Make the cake: Preheat oven to 325°. Grease and flour either a large, 4-quart bundt pan or 2 pans each about 1 ½ quart size. Cream butter and sugar together until light and fluffy, then beat in the eggs. Add the lemon rind and lemon juice. Sift dry ingredients together and add them to the butter-egg mixture alternately with the buttermilk or sour milk. Spoon batter into pan or pans and bake for about 1 hour and 10 minutes (for the large pan), and less for two smaller ones. Test with a wooden pick inserted in center; it should come out dry. Remove from oven and cool for 5 to 10 minutes, then invert on a rack and frost with the lemon icing.

Make the icing: Make the icing while the cake is baking. Cream butter and powdered sugar together, then add the lemon rind and slowly beat in lemon juice until desired spreading consistency.

CINNAMON-ALMOND CAKE WITH CHOCOLATE ICING

Makes 10 to 16 servings

- 7 egg whites (room temperature)
- 1 ¼ cups sugar
- ¼ teaspoon salt
- 2 teaspoons cinnamon
- ½ pound blanched almonds, toasted, then finely chopped
- "Ganache" (p. 283)

WHEN NO ONE IS LOOKING
Bake this cake 1 or 2 days ahead; keep it wrapped and refrigerated but serve at room temperature.

FROZEN POWER
Yes, freeze this cake unwrapped for about 1 hour, or until icing is firm, then double-wrap it in foil and return to the freezer. Serve at room temperature.

Preheat oven to 350°. Grease and flour a pan about 9 x 13 inches (or line with nonstick parchment paper). Beat egg whites until barely stiff. Mix sugar, salt, and cinnamon together, then gradually beat into the whites. Fold in the finely chopped almonds and spread mixture in the prepared pan. Bake for 20 to 25 minutes. Remove from oven and place on a rack for 5 minutes, then invert on waxed paper (or parchment paper) to finish cooling. When cool, divide cake into thirds horizontally, and use these as the layers. Fill and frost the layers with the ganache.

HAPPINESS GÂTEAU

Makes 10 to 12 servings

for meringue nut layers:
8 egg whites
¼ teaspoon salt
¼ teaspoon cream of tartar
1 ½ cups sugar
1 ½ cups blanched almonds, toasted, then ground
1 cup filberts (hazelnuts), toasted, then skins rubbed off and ground

for the fillings:
1 quart "Buttercream" (p. 394)
¼ cup "Praline Paste" (p. 395)
1 ½ teaspoons vanilla
9 ounces semisweet chocolate

WHEN NO ONE IS LOOKING
This gâteau lends itself beautifully to cooking when no one is looking. Prepare the meringue layers, chocolate wafers, buttercream, and praline paste 1 to 3 days ahead; keep them covered and refrigerated. Or assemble the entire gâteau several days ahead; cover with plastic wrap and keep refrigerated.

FROZEN POWER
Each part of this gâteau freezes well. Or, assemble the entire gâteau, double-wrap and freeze. To serve, defrost overnight in the refrigerator.

Make the meringue-nut layers: Preheat oven to 275°. Mix ground nuts with 1 cup of the sugar. Beat egg whites, cream of tartar, and salt until whites begin to stiffen, then gradually beat in remaining ½ cup sugar. Fold in the nut mixture. Line two large baking pans (cookie sheets with sides) with nonstick parchment paper. Draw two rectangles on each (for a total of four) that are 4 x 12 inches. Spread each rectangle with this meringue mixture and bake about 35 to 40 minutes—until crusty on top but still a little pliable. Remove, invert, and remove paper. Cool.

Make the chocolate wafers: Melt 6 ounces of the semisweet chocolate. Cut out 2- or 2 ½-inch circles of waxed paper and place them on a large, flat cookie tin. Spread the circles thinly with the chocolate and chill. When hardened remove them from the paper, but keep wafers chilled until ready to use.

Prepare three fillings:

1. Whip the vanilla into 1 cup of the buttercream.

2. Whip the ¼ cup praline paste into another cup of buttercream.

3. Melt the remaining 3 ounces of semisweet chocolate and cool it to room temperature. Whip this into the remaining 2 cups of buttercream.

Assemble: Place one meringue-nut layer on a serving dish and spread with the vanilla buttercream. Top with second layer and spread this with the praline buttercream Top with the third meringue layer and spread with half the chocolate buttercream. Place fourth layer on top, then frost top and sides of the gâteau with the remaining chocolate buttercream.

Press the chocolate wafers around the sides, and, if desired, on the top. Cover gâteau with plastic wrap and keep refrigerated until time to serve.

A BEAU GÂTEAU

Makes 12 to 16 servings

3 9-inch genoise layers (p. 285 or p. 287)
2 cups "Favorite Pastry Cream," make a double recipe (p. 393)
seedless raspberry jam

for the kirsch syrup:
½ cup sugar
½ cup water
⅓ cup kirsch

for the macaroon mixture:
4 ounces almond paste
½ cup sugar
2 to 2 ½ egg whites

WHEN NO ONE IS LOOKING
Prepare the pastry cream, and the genoise layers 1 day before; keep them covered and refrigerated. Prepare the macaroon mixture, cover and refrigerate but bring to room temperature several hours before using. Assemble the whole gâteau in the morning and keep chilled until time to serve.

FROZEN POWER
Freeze the genoise layers as directed in that recipe. You can freeze the macaroon mixture too, but be sure to bring it to room temperature before using.

Prepare the syrup: Place sugar and water in a saucepan and stir until sugar has dissolved. Remove from heat and add the kirsch. Set aside.

Prepare the macaroon mixture: Beat the almond paste with the sugar to remove lumps, then very gradually beat in the egg whites until the mixture is a little softer than you would use for almond macaroons.

Assemble: Preheat oven to 400°. Place one layer of genoise on an ovenproof plate or platter. Brush with ⅓ of the kirsch syrup. Spread with about ¼ of the pastry cream. Place second layer on top and brush it with ⅓ of the syrup and top with ¼ of the pastry cream. Top with the third layer and brush with remaining syrup. Then use all the remaining pastry cream to cover the entire cake.

Place macaroon mixture in a pastry bag with a no. 2 round tube, then decorate the top by piping strips 1 inch apart in a lattice pattern. Place small rosettes around the outer edge. Bake in the upper part of the oven for 15 to 20 minutes. If top does not brown, place it under a broiler unit for 1 or 2 minutes.

Remove from oven and cool for 10 to 15 minutes. Fill the open spaces within the lattice top with raspberry jam, using a spoon or a small pastry bag. Chill for several hours, and serve.

MACAROON CAKE SPECTACULAR

Makes 12 to 16 servings

- 2 10-inch genoise cake layers (p. 285 or p. 287)
- 1 ½ cups strawberry jam
- 3 dozen "Almond Macaroons" (p. 317, or purchase them)
- ½ cup sherry
- 1 ½ cups heavy whipping cream
- "Ganache" (p. 283), softened to spreading consistency
- ¼ cup chopped pistachios (optional)

WHEN NO ONE IS LOOKING
Prepare the entire cake 1 day ahead; cover and keep refrigerated.

FROZEN POWER
Freeze some of the cake's elements, such as the almond macaroons and the genoise layers, or freeze the entire assembled cake.

Whip the cream and keep chilled. Cut genoise cake layers in half horizontally, making a total of four layers. Place 1 layer on a cake dish and cover with some strawberry jam. Dip 1 dozen of the macaroons in sherry and place them on the jam. Cover this with ⅓ of the whipped cream. Place a second layer of cake on top and repeat entire process. Place third cake layer on top and again repeat process. Place fourth layer on top and sprinkle with a little sherry. Chill for 1 hour, then cover top and sides with the ganache, and if desired, sprinkle with chopped pistachios.

CONTEMPORARY FRUIT CAKE

Makes a large cake or several smaller ones

- 2 cups dark seedless raisins
- 1 ½ cups candied cherries (left whole)
- 1 ½ cups sliced dates
- 1 pound butter, room temperature
- 2 cups sugar
- 7 eggs, room temperature
- 2 teaspoons vanilla
- 3 ½ cups sifted flour (sift before measuring)
- 1 teaspoon salt
- 1 teaspoon baking powder
- ½ teaspoon cream of tartar

WHEN NO ONE IS LOOKING
Bake this cake 1 or 2 weeks ahead, keep wrapped in double foil and refrigerate, but serve at room temperature.

FROZEN POWER
Double-wrap and freeze the cake. Defrost overnight at room temperature.

Preheat oven to 300°. Grease and flour a large bundt pan (3 ½ to 4 quart size). Soak raisins in hot water, then drain and dry on paper towels. Combine raisins, sliced dates, and cherries in a large bowl. Cover with 1 ½ cups of the measured flour.

Cream butter with the sugar until fluffy. Beat in the eggs one at a time. Add vanilla. Continue to beat until very light and fluffy. Combine the remaining measured flour, salt, baking powder, and cream of tartar and sift together twice. Add this to the butter mixture, then add the floured fruit mixture and stir until all is thoroughly combined. Spoon batter into the prepared pan and bake about 2 hours. Remove from oven, cool a few minutes, then invert cake and finish cooling it on a rack.

FILBERT TORTE WITH A RASPBERRY GLAZE

Makes 12 to 16 servings

½ pound filberts (hazelnuts)
6 eggs (yolks and whites separated)
1 cup sugar
⅛ teaspoon salt
¼ cup fine dry bread crumbs
¼ teaspoon baking powder
grated rind of 1 orange
¼ cup orange juice
¾ cup seedless raspberry jam melted with 1 tablespoon of water
sweetened whipped cream (optional)

WHEN NO ONE IS LOOKING
Bake this cake and glaze it 1 day ahead; keep covered and leave at room temperature.

FROZEN POWER
Freeze this cake unwrapped for 1 hour, then double-wrap and return to freezer. Defrost at room temperature in its wrapping.

Toast the filberts in a 325° oven for 10 to 15 minutes, then rub off as much of the brown skins as possible. Finely chop the filberts in a food processor (but *not* to a paste!), then place in a bowl and mix with the bread crumbs, salt, and baking powder. Set aside.

Preheat oven to 325°. Grease and flour a 10-inch springform pan and line the bottom with nonstick parchment. Beat egg yolks with ½ cup of the sugar until pale yellow and thick, then beat in the orange rind and orange juice. Fold in the nut mixture. In a separate bowl beat egg whites until they begin to stiffen, then gradually beat in the remaining ½ cup of sugar. Fold beaten whites into the nut mixture. Pour or spoon into prepared pan and bake for 45 minutes or longer, until cake tests done. Remove from oven and invert on a rack. When cold, remove from the springform pan. Glaze with the raspberry jam and, if desired, serve with whipped cream

COOKIES, CONFECTIONS, AND PASTRIES

COCONUT PHYLLO STICKS

Makes 6 dozen or more

12 to 18 phyllo pastry sheets
2 cups sugar
2 ½ cups sweetened, flaked coconut
¾ pound butter, melted

WHEN NO ONE IS LOOKING
Bake these 5 to 7 days ahead. Layer them between sheets of wax paper in containers that can be sealed; store at room temperature or in the refrigerator.

FROZEN POWER
By all means, freeze these. Place them between layers of waxed paper in containers that can be tightly sealed (or tightly wrapped in foil). Defrost them at room temperature in their sealed containers.

Mix the sugar and coconut together in a bowl. Butter a sheet of phyllo and fold in half across its length to make a rectangle. Turn the folded side toward you. Brush with butter and sprinkle with 2 tablespoons of the coconut mixture, leaving about ¾ inch of top edge free of the mixture. Roll up into a firm roll, starting from the folded side. Cut into 6 equal pieces and place them on a buttered baking pan. Repeat with the other phyllo sheets, using more pans as needed. Brush tops with melted butter. Bake in a preheated 350° oven for 10 to 15 minutes, until golden brown and crisp. Cool, then store in containers that can be tightly sealed. Serve as a dessert cookie with fruit or custard desserts.

ALMOND FLORENTINES

Makes 2 to 3 dozen

- ½ pound (2 sticks) butter
- 1 cup sugar
- ⅓ cup honey
- ⅔ cup flour
- ⅓ cup heavy whipping cream
- 4 cups sliced, blanched almonds, lightly toasted
- 8 ounces semisweet chocolate

WHEN NO ONE IS LOOKING
Bake and frost these with the chocolate 1 or 2 days ahead; keep refrigerated.

FROZEN POWER
Yes, freeze these cookies; if kept tightly sealed they should keep well for 1 month or longer. Serve them directly out of the freezer.

Preheat oven to 350°. Combine the butter, sugar, honey, flour, and cream in a large saucepan and bring to a boil over moderate heat, stirring until smooth. Cook 1 or 2 minutes, stirring constantly. Remove from heat and stir in the almonds. Spoon tablespoons of this mixture on nonstick cookie sheets, leaving at least 2 inches between each. Using wet hands, press tops down gently. Bake 8 minutes or longer—until a rich brown. Remove and when somewhat cooled, use a large flat spatula to remove cookies to nonstick parchment paper to completely cool.

Melt the chocolate and spread on the bottom sides of the cooled cookies. Let them stand until chocolate sets, or hurry the process by putting them in the refrigerator briefly. Store between sheets of waxed paper in containers with tight-fitting lids.

CARAMELIZED ALMOND SLICES

Makes about 2 dozen

- ½ recipe of "Pâte Sucrée" (p. 354)
- 1 cup slivered almonds, lightly toasted
- ¾ cup sugar
- ¼ cup honey
- ¼ cup heavy cream
- ⅛ pound butter (½ stick)

WHEN NO ONE IS LOOKING
Bake these up to 5 days ahead. Store them in airtight containers between layers of nonstick parchment paper.

FROZEN POWER
These freeze beautifully; pack them between layers of nonstick parchment paper and store in airtight containers.

You will need a rectangular 7 x 11-inch tart pan, preferably nonstick, with a loose bottom.

Roll out the pâte sucrée into a rectangle 1 inch larger than the pan, and then fit it into the tart pan. Prick well with a fork, then chill at least 20 minutes. Preheat oven to 375°. Line pastry with foil and weight it down with beans or metal pie weights. Bake for 12 to 15 minutes—until pastry is golden brown. Remove from oven and remove foil and beans. Set pastry aside.

Make the filling: Combine sugar, honey, cream, and butter in a saucepan and bring to a boil, stirring constantly. Reduce heat to moderate and add the slivered almonds. Cook, stirring occasionally, until mixture reaches 240° on a candy thermometer, or until a drop forms a soft ball in cold water. Remove from heat, cool half a minute, then pour into the prebaked pastry shell.

Bake the almond slices: Bake filled shell in the preheated 375° oven for 15 minutes; reduce heat to 350° and bake another 8 to 10 minutes, or until filling has turned a deep caramel color. Watch the almonds; if they begin to clump in the tart, spread them around with the back of a spoon.

Remove and cool briefly on a rack, then lift out the whole almond-filled pastry and place on greased foil. Cool completely, then cut into tiny slices or bars.

DOUBLE-THE-CHOCOLATE-CHIPS COOKIES

Makes about 6 to 8 dozen

- ½ pound butter (2 sticks), room temperature
- ¾ cup brown sugar (pack to measure)
- ¾ cup white sugar
- 2 eggs, room temperature
- 2 ¼ cups flour
- 1 teaspoon salt
- 1 teaspoon baking soda
- 2 teaspoons vanilla
- 1 ½ cups toasted walnuts, coarsely chopped
- 4 cups (24 ounces) semisweet chocolate chips

WHEN NO ONE IS LOOKING
Bake these up to 1 week ahead. Store them at room temperature in containers with tight-fitting covers, or to keep them longer and fresher, store them in the refrigerator.

FROZEN POWER
Yes, indeed; freeze these cookies.

Cream butter until soft, then beat in the brown and white sugars until light and fluffy. Beat in the eggs and then add the vanilla. Combine the flour, salt, and baking soda together, then add it to the butter mixture. Add walnuts and combine well, then stir in the chocolate chips.

Preheat oven to 375°. Drop batter by spoonfuls on nonstick pans or on baking pans lined with nonstick parchment paper. Bake for 8 to 10 minutes, but check to make sure the oven is not too hot. Cookies should be well browned, but not burned.

CANDIED GINGER COOKIES

Makes 6 to 10 dozen

- 1 ½ cups candied ginger, pack to measure
- ½ pound butter (2 sticks), room temperature
- 1 cup dark brown sugar, pack to measure
- 1 cup white sugar
- ½ teaspoon baking powder
- ½ teaspoon baking soda
- 1 teaspoon salt
- 2 teaspoons vanilla
- 1 egg
- 2 ¾ cups flour (11 ounces)

WHEN NO ONE IS LOOKING
Bake these 3 to 4 days ahead and store them between sheets of waxed paper in containers with tight-fitting covers. They may either be kept at room temperature or refrigerated.

FROZEN POWER
Cool, then freeze the cookies in tins or plastic containers with tight-fitting covers.

Place candied ginger with ½ cup of the white sugar in a food processor. Process until ginger is finely chopped, but not mashed. Combine butter with the remaining white sugar and all the brown sugar in a large bowl and beat, preferably with an electric mixer, until light and creamy. Add the vanilla and the egg and mix well. Combine the baking powder, baking soda, and salt with the flour and sift together or mix well with a whisk. Add this flour mixture and the chopped ginger mixture and mix again. Form this dough into four logs about 1 ½ inches round. Wrap each in plastic and chill overnight (or at least for several hours).

Preheat oven to 350°. Remove cookie logs and slice thinly, keeping unsliced logs refrigerated. Place slices on nonstick baking sheets with space in between because they will spread. Bake for 10 to 12 minutes, or until browned.

COCONUT TUILES

Makes 4 dozen or more

2 eggs
⅓ cup sugar
3 tablespoons melted butter
1 ⅓ cups sweetened flaked coconut (about 3 ½ ounces)

WHEN NO ONE IS LOOKING
Bake these up to 4 or 5 days ahead, but keep them between layers of waxed paper or parchment paper in tins that can be tightly sealed. Store them at room temperature or in the refrigerator.

FROZEN POWER
Freeze these by arranging the cookies between layers of waxed paper in tins or plastic cartons that can be tightly sealed.

Beat sugar and eggs together until well combined. Stir in the melted butter and coconut. Let mixture stand for 30 minutes, then stir again. Preheat oven to 325°. Drop batter by small spoonfuls on nonstick pans or pans lined with nonstick baking parchment. Bake for about 10 minutes or until centers are light golden and edges are somewhat darker. Remove and let stand briefly, then place each tuile on the rounded sides of drinking glasses to curve them like roof tiles, or simply remove them from the baking pans and leave them flat.

SESAME SEED TUILES

Makes 4 dozen or more

4 egg whites
¼ teaspoon salt
¾ cup sugar
¼ pound butter (1 stick), melted and cooled
¼ cup flour
2 cups sesame seeds, lightly toasted

WHEN NO ONE IS LOOKING
Pack these cookies between layers of waxed paper and store in tins or plastic containers that have tight-fitting lids. They will keep up to 1 week at room temperature.

FROZEN POWER
Freeze these for months! Pack the cookies as directed above, then store them in the freezer.

Beat egg whites with salt and sugar until slightly thickened. Add butter and beat again. Combine flour and toasted sesame seeds and add to the whites. Stir well. Preheat oven to 350°. Drop batter by teaspoonfuls (or larger if you like) on baking pans lined with nonstick parchment paper. Bake for about 10 minutes, or until well browned. Remove, then roll them up or leave them flat. Cool, then pack between layers of waxed paper in airtight tins (or large plastic containers with tight-fitting lids).

CORNFLAKE MACAROONS

Makes several dozen

- 3 egg whites
- ½ teaspoon salt
- 1 ½ cups sugar
- 1 teaspoon vanilla
- 3 ½ to 4 cups cornflakes
- 1 to 1 ½ cups sweetened coconut flakes or shreds

WHEN NO ONE IS LOOKING
Bake these several days ahead, then pack them in containers with tight-fitting lids (and in layers between sheets of waxed paper) and store at room temperature or in the refrigerator

FROZEN POWER
Most cookies thrive in the freezer, as do these. Pack them as described in the paragraph above, then freeze.

Beat egg whites with the salt until slightly stiff, then gradually beat in the sugar and vanilla. Fold in the cornflakes and coconut. Preheat oven to 350°. Drop batter by teaspoonfuls on baking pans lined with nonstick parchment paper and bake for 15 to 20 minutes. Remove and cool.

PECAN BALLS

Makes several dozen

½ pound butter (2 sticks), room temperature
½ cup sugar
2 teaspoons vanilla
2 cups flour (9 ounces)
2 cups pecans, toasted lightly, then ground
powdered sugar, sifted

WHEN NO ONE IS LOOKING
Bake these up to 1 week ahead; store them in the refrigerator between layers of waxed paper in containers with tight-fitting lids. Serve cold.

FROZEN POWER
Freeze the pecan balls in tins or plastic cartons with tight-fitting lids. They are delicious served straight out of the freezer!

Cream butter and sugar together until well mixed and fluffy. Add the vanilla, then stir in the flour and mix briefly. Add ground pecans. Preheat oven to 300°. Shape dough into small balls about the size of a walnut. Place them on nonstick baking pans or on nonstick parchment-lined pans and bake for 25 to 30 minutes. Remove from oven, then roll pecan balls in the powdered sugar.

CINNAMON-WALNUT BARS IN THE GREEK STYLE

Makes 3 dozen or more

3 ⅓ ounces butter (⅔ cup), room temperature
⅔ cup sugar
3 egg yolks
¾ cup farina
¼ teaspoon salt
1 ½ teaspoons cinnamon
1 ½ cups finely chopped walnuts, lightly toasted
3 egg whites

for the syrup:
⅓ cup sugar
3 tablespoons water
½ teaspoon vanilla

WHEN NO ONE IS LOOKING
Bake these 1 or 2 days ahead; layer them between sheets of plastic wrap or waxed paper and keep sealed in tins or plastic containers with tight-fitting lids; store in the refrigerator. Serve at room temperature.

FROZEN POWER
Freeze these after they have cooled. Pack them as directed above.

Prepare the syrup: Bring sugar, water, and vanilla to a boil in a saucepan, stirring to dissolve the sugar; then set aside.

Cream butter with ½ cup of the sugar until thoroughly mixed. (Set aside remaining sugar to use when beating the egg whites.) Beat in the egg yolks. Mix together the farina, salt, and cinnamon, then add to the butter mixture. Stir in the chopped walnuts. Beat whites until frothy, then gradually beat in the remaining sugar—beat until stiff but *not* dry! Fold into the nut mixture. Preheat oven to 375°. Grease a pan about 9 x 14 inches and sprinkle it with flour—shaking out the excess. Spoon or pour batter into prepared pan, then bake for 20 minutes.

Remove from oven and spoon the prepared syrup evenly over the entire cake. Return to oven for 15 minutes or until firm to the touch. Remove from oven, cool on a rack, then cut into squares or diamonds.

REASONABLE COOKIES

Makes 6 dozen or more

- ¾ pound butter (3 sticks), room temperature
- 1 cup sugar
- 1 cup brown sugar (pack to measure)
- 2 eggs
- 1 teaspoon vanilla
- 2 cups flour (9 ounces)
- ½ teaspoon baking soda
- ½ teaspoon salt
- ½ teaspoon baking powder
- 1 cup quick-cooking oats
- 3 cups cornflakes
- 1 cup sweetened coconut flakes
- ½ to ¾ cup chopped walnuts, lightly toasted

WHEN NO ONE IS LOOKING
Bake these several days ahead, then store them at room temperature in containers with tight-fitting lids.

FROZEN POWER
Put these on your list of easy-to-make goodies that freeze well.

Cream butter and sugars together. Beat in eggs and vanilla. Combine flour, soda, salt, and baking powder, then stir into the butter mixture. Add remaining ingredients. Heat oven to 350°. Drop batter by spoonful on nonstick pans or pans lined with nonstick parchment paper. Bake for 10 to 15 minutes.

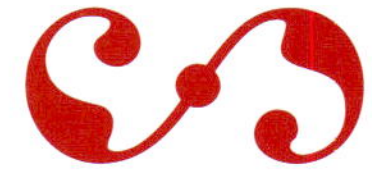

GLORY-OF-FRANCE ALMOND COOKIES FILLED WITH CHOCOLATE

Makes 4 dozen or more

- ¾ cup blanched almonds, toasted then ground
- ½ cup filberts, toasted, skins rubbed off, then ground
- ¼ cup sugar
- 4 egg whites
- ⅛ teaspoon cream of tartar
- ⅛ teaspoon salt
- ½ cup additional sugar
- "Ganache" (p. 283)

WHEN NO ONE IS LOOKING
Bake these cookies 1 or 2 days ahead and store them between layers of waxed paper in tightly sealed plastic cartons or tins with tight lids. Fill shortly before serving.

FROZEN POWER
Freeze these cookies unfilled and stored in tightly sealed plastic cartons or in tins with tight-fitting lids. Defrost, then fill with the ganache and serve.

Mix ground almonds and filberts with the ¼ cup sugar and set aside. Beat egg whites, cream of tartar, and salt until barely stiff, then gradually beat in the ½ cup sugar—beat only until shiny peaks are achieved. Fold into the nut mixture.

Using a pastry bag with a no. 6 round tube, press out cookies on a nonstick baking pan (or on nonstick parchment-lined pans)—making them about 1 inch in diameter. Preheat oven to 300°. Bake for 10 to 15 minutes, or until crusty on top but still slightly soft. Remove from oven, then using a spatula, remove cookies to cool.

Place 2 cookies together with the ganache and then serve them as soon as possible to avoid softening the cookies too much. They are also delicious served without ganache!

SPICE-FRUIT BAR COOKIES

Makes about 3 dozen

¼ pound butter (1 stick), room temperature
1 ¼ cups brown sugar (pack to measure)
1 egg
½ cup honey
2 cups flour (9 ounces)
1 teaspoon baking powder
¼ teaspoon baking soda
1 teaspoon salt
1 teaspoon cinnamon
½ teaspoon nutmeg
¼ teaspoon cloves
¾ cup sliced candied cherries
¾ cup sliced dates
1 cup walnuts, toasted and chopped

for the glaze:
1 cup powdered sugar, sifted
1 teaspoon vanilla
water

WHEN NO ONE IS LOOKING
Bake these several days ahead, but do not frost. Cut into bars and store between layers of waxed paper in airtight tins or plastic cartons, and refrigerate.

FROZEN POWER
Freeze these bars after they have cooled. If they are glazed, be prepared to see the glaze crack after they have been frozen; it's better to freeze them without the glaze.

Cream butter and sugar together until fluffy. Add the egg and honey and mix well. Combine all dry ingredients and mix them together thoroughly. Sprinkle half of the dry ingredients on the fruit and coat well. Add remaining half of dry ingredients to the batter and stir until blended; then do the same with the coated fruit mixture and the chopped walnuts.

Preheat oven to 350°. Grease and flour a 9 x 13-inch pan and spread batter in it. Bake for about 25 to 30 minutes. Cool in the pan on a cake rack.

Prepare the glaze: Add vanilla to the powdered sugar with a spoonful of water, adding more water as needed to achieve a glaze of spreading consistancy. Frost the cookies, then cut into bars.

ALMOND MACAROONS

Makes about 2 dozen

8 ounces almond paste
1 cup sugar
3 egg whites

WHEN NO ONE IS LOOKING
Bake these 1 week ahead. Pack them between layers of waxed paper and store in tins or plastic cartons with tight-fitting lids.

FROZEN POWER
Freeze the macaroons for delicious eating later and for the preparation of special desserts.

Cut almond paste into small cubes, then beat with the sugar until crumbly. Beat in the egg whites very gradually, slowly adding the whites until mixture is smooth. Place mixture in a pastry bag with a no. 6 round tube and drop on baking pans lined with nonstick parchment—make each macaroon about ¾ inch in diameter. Preheat oven to 325°. Bake for 20 to 30 minutes. Remove from oven, cool briefly, then remove with a spatula.

CHOCOLATE FILBERT SPICE BISCOTTI

Makes several dozen

- ¼ pound filberts (hazelnuts), toasted, then skins rubbed off
- ¼ pound butter (1 stick), room temperature
- ¾ cup sugar
- 2 eggs
- ¼ pound semisweet chocolate, melted and cooled to room temperature
- 2 cups flour (9 ounces)
- 2 teaspoons baking powder
- ¼ teaspoon salt
- 1 teaspoon cinnamon
- ¼ teaspoon each of nutmeg, cloves, and mace

WHEN NO ONE IS LOOKING
Bake these cookies 1 week ahead; keep them packed in containers with tight-fitting lids, layered between sheets of waxed paper.

FROZEN POWER
Freeze these delicious chocolate slices packed between layers of waxed paper in plastic cartons or tins that have tight-fitting lids.

Chop filberts in a food processor, but do not pulverize. Cream butter and sugar, then beat in the eggs. Add melted chocolate and chopped filberts and stir well. Combine flour, baking powder, salt, and spices, then mix them together thoroughly. Add dry ingredients to the creamed mixture and stir only until combined. Chill for 30 minutes or longer. Preheat oven to 350°. Divide dough in half and form each portion into a roll 1 or 1½ inches wide. Place the rolls on a nonstick baking pan (or one lined with nonstick parchment) and bake for 25 minutes. Remove from oven, cool briefly, then cut rolls crosswise into slices ½ to ¾ inch thick. Place slices cut sides down on the baking pan (or pans) and return to oven. Bake for 20 to 30 minutes, gradually reducing oven to 225° until biscotti are crisp. Cool, then remove from the pans.

APRICOT BARS

Makes 2 dozen or more

for the pastry base:
1 cup flour (5 ounces)
¼ cup powdered sugar
¼ teaspoon salt
¼ pound (1 stick) cold butter, sliced
1 egg, beaten with 1 teaspoon cold water

for the filling:
1 ¼ cups dried apricots (5 ounces)
zest of 1 lemon
1 ¼ cups sugar
2 eggs
¼ cup lemon juice
⅛ teaspoon salt

WHEN NO ONE IS LOOKING
Bake these bars several days ahead, but store them between layers of waxed paper in airtight tins or plastic cartons and keep refrigerated. Bring to room temperature before serving.

FROZEN POWER
Freeze these bars by placing them between layers of waxed paper inside tins or plastic cartons with tight-fitting lids.

Soak dried apricots in hot water. Make the pastry base while they are soaking. Place flour, powdered sugar, and salt in a food processor and process for 2 seconds. Add sliced butter and pulse, turning on and off, only until butter is distributed and cut into tiny bits. Add egg-water mixture and process 1 or 2 seconds, then remove pastry to a floured board and form into a flat disk. Wrap in plastic and chill about 30 minutes. Roll out and fit into a 9-inch square pan. Preheat oven to 350°. Bake pastry for 20 minutes, then set aside.

Make the filling: Drain the soaked apricots, then place apricots in a food processor and add the lemon zest and sugar. Process until apricots are finely chopped. Add eggs, lemon juice, and salt, then pulse, turning on and off, only until mixed. Do not purée. Spoon mixture on top of prebaked crust and return to the oven for 30 minutes or until well browned. Cool, then cut into small squares.

FLAT (NOT CURLED) TUILES

Makes several dozen

- 4 large egg whites
- ¼ teaspoon salt
- 1 cup sugar
- ¼ pound butter (1 stick), melted, then cooled to room temperature
- 3 cups sliced, blanched almonds, lightly toasted
- ½ cup sifted flour (2 ¼ ounces)
- 2 teaspoons vanilla

WHEN NO ONE IS LOOKING
Do not hesitate to bake these 1 week ahead and store them between layers of waxed paper in airtight containers; store either at room temperature or in the refrigerator.

FROZEN POWER
Freeze these between layers of waxed paper in airtight containers.

Beat egg whites with salt and sugar only until barely thickened. Add melted butter and beat again. Combine almonds and flour, then add and stir. Add vanilla. Preheat oven to 350°. Drop batter by rounded teaspoonfuls on baking pans lined with nonstick parchment paper. Bake cookies until well browned—about 10 minutes. Remove with the aid of a spatula and cool on nonstick parchment paper.

VERY THIN AND VERY CRISP SUGAR COOKIES

Makes at least 12 dozen

¾ pound butter (3 sticks), soft
3 cups sugar
2 eggs
grated rind of 2 lemons
2 teaspoons vanilla
6 cups flour (27 ounces)
1 teaspoon baking powder
¾ teaspoon salt
¾ cup milk

WHEN NO ONE IS LOOKING
Bake these 1 week ahead and keep them stored between layers of waxed paper in airtight containers. They keep well at room temperature, but longer if refrigerated.

FROZEN POWER
Perfect for freezing, if they last that long. Pack them as described above.

Cream butter and sugar together until light and fluffy. Beat in the eggs, lemon rind, and vanilla. Sift together—or mix together—the dry ingredients, then add them to the butter-egg mixture alternately with the milk. Do not beat; merely stir together until well blended. Chill for at least several hours or overnight.

Preheat oven to 300°. Divide dough into 16 or more portions and keep them in the refrigerator. Roll out only 1 at a time because it is important to use a very small amount of dough in order to roll out as thin as possible. Cut into desired shapes and place on nonstick baking pans. Bake for 10 to 15 minutes, or until delicately browned. Remove from pan and cool on waxed paper.

ALMOND BREAD (MANDELBROT)

Makes several dozen

- ¼ pound butter (1 stick), room temperature
- 2 ½ cups sugar
- 3 teaspoons vanilla
- 6 eggs
- 6 ¼ cups flour (28 ounces)
- 1 ½ teaspoons salt
- 3 teaspoons baking powder
- 2 cups chopped almonds, lightly toasted

WHEN NO ONE IS LOOKING
Bake these up to 1 week ahead. Store them between layers of waxed paper in plastic cartons or tins that have tight-fitting lids. They can be kept at room temperature.

FROZEN POWER
Freeze these almond cookies between layers of waxed paper in tins or plastic cartons with tight-fitting lids.

Cream butter and sugar together until light and fluffy. Beat in vanilla and eggs. Combine the flour, salt, and baking powder and mix together thoroughly. Gradually stir the dry ingredients into the butter mixture, then add the toasted almonds. Chill at least 30 minutes or overnight.

Preheat oven to 350°. Divide dough into 4 parts, and form each into a long roll about 1 ½ inches wide. Place the rolls on nonstick baking pans (or nonstick parchment-lined pans) and bake for 25 to 30 minutes. Remove from oven and cool for 5 minutes. Slice rolls into 1 or 1 ½ inch slices. Place them cut sides down on the baking pans and return to the oven for about 30 minutes, gradually reducing oven heat. Bake until lightly toasted and dry.

JANET'S MACADAMIA NUT TOFFEE

- ½ pound butter
- 1 ½ cups sugar
- 1 tablespoon light corn syrup
- ¼ cup water
- 1 cup unsalted, toasted macadamia nuts, cut in quarters or halves
- ¾ cup unsalted, toasted macadamia nuts, chopped (double this amount if you want chocolate on both sides)
- 9 ounces semisweet chocolate (double this amount if you want chocolate on both sides)

WHEN NO ONE IS LOOKING
Prepare this toffee weeks ahead, but be sure to keep it in a tightly covered container in the refrigerator. If possible, serve at room temperature.

FROZEN POWER
Yes, freeze this delicious confection; then remove as little or as much as you like.

Butter a 9 x 13-inch jelly roll pan. Combine butter, sugar, syrup, and water in a heavy pan. Cook over medium heat at a low, rolling boil, stirring occasionally. Use a pastry brush dipped into cold water (or a fork wrapped in paper towel and dipped in cold water) to remove any crystallized sugar on the sides of the pan. Cook to the hard crack stage—300° on a candy thermometer—then mix in the 1 cup of cut macadamia nuts and quickly pour into the buttered pan. Cool completely.

When cold and firm, turn toffee block over onto a sheet of nonstick parchment paper. Wipe off excess butter. Melt 9 ounces of chocolate and spread on the toffee, then press in the chopped nuts. Let it harden. To hasten the process, refrigerate briefly. If double chocolate coating is desired, turn toffee block over and cover with more chocolate and more chopped nuts. Let chocolate harden. Break or cut into pieces. Store in a tightly-covered container, layered between sheets of waxed paper, plastic, or foil.

CHOCOLATE BUTTERFLIES

1⁄6 bar paraffin (1⁄2 ounce)
12 ounces semisweet chocolate, finely chopped

WHEN NO ONE IS LOOKING
Make these up to 2 weeks ahead and keep refrigerated in airtight tins.

FROZEN POWER
Freeze these for up to several months, stored in airtight tins.

Cut pieces of waxed paper into 2 x 3-inch rectangles. Fold each rectangle in half crosswise, forming a 1 1⁄2 x 2-inch rectangle. Open them and place them on a lightly greased pan (to hold the paper in place). Lightly draw the outline of a butterfly on each—with wings and antennae. Place paraffin in the top of a double boiler to melt; remove and cool but let it remain liquid. Add the chopped chocolate and stir until the chocolate has melted. Cool to room temperature.

Spoon melted chocolate into a parchment cone or a pastry bag with a no. 3 tip and pipe it in a stream to form butterflies, guided by your drawings. Remove papers from greased pan or pans using a large spatula and transfer them to the chambers of an empty egg cartons so that the chocolate butterflies on their papers are bent along a center fold. The wings should appear to be in a semi-open position. Refrigerate until chocolate has hardened, then remove papers and carefully store the butterflies in airtight tins. Keep refrigerated until ready to use.

CHOCOLATE ROLLS AND CURLS

You will need two rectangular pans with flat bottoms—each about 11 x 17 inches

12 ounces semisweet chocolate

WHEN NO ONE IS LOOKING
Prepare these up to 2 weeks ahead, but keep them in tightly sealed containers or in zip-lock bags and refrigerate.

FROZEN POWER
Ideal for the freezer if you can spare the space. Be sure to keep them carefully packed in a crush-proof container.

Melt the chocolate over barely simmering water or in a microwave oven. Spread the chocolate on the bottoms of 2 pans, each 11 x 17 inches, and refrigerate. After it has cooled briefly, use a ruler and a knife and mark off sections about 3 ¾ x 5 ¾ inches (which will give 9 sections to each pan). Chill again, then bring pans out of refrigerator and let them stand briefly to warm up slightly. Use a metal pastry scraper or heavy spatula and roll up the sections from the 3 ¾-inch sides. Move the scraper by pushing it gently from side to side into rolls. You may have to wait a few minutes until chocolate is soft enough to roll but not mushy. If it is too hard it will break, but if it is too soft it will collapse. If it becomes too soft, refrigerate again, etc., until you have finished. Not all the rolls will be perfect, but that is fine; use the ones that have not rolled as chocolate shavings.

CARAMELIZED ALMONDS

⅓ cup sugar
2 tablespoons water
¼ teaspoon lemon juice
2 cups sliced unblanched almonds

WHEN NO ONE IS LOOKING
Prepare these almonds up to 1 week ahead, but keep them in an airtight tin.

FROZEN POWER
Freeze these prepared almonds for several months, stored in an airtight tin.

Line a heavy baking pan with nonstick parchment paper. Combine sugar, water, and lemon juice in a saucepan and cook over moderate heat, stirring constantly, until sugar dissolves. Then, stop stirring, raise the heat and bring syrup to a boil for 1 minute. Stop.

Preheat oven to 325°. Place almonds in a bowl and gently combine the syrup and almonds using a rubber spatula. Do *not* overmix. Spread into the lined pan in a single layer. Bake in the preheated oven for approximately 15 minutes or until almonds are golden brown and sugar has caramelized. Cool, then store caramelized almonds in an airtight tin.

CARMELIZED PECANS, ALMONDS, AND POPCORN

2 cups pecan halves
1 ⅓ cups blanched almonds
8 cups popped popcorn
1 ⅓ cups sugar
½ pound butter (2 sticks)
½ cup light corn syrup
1 ½ teaspoons vanilla

WHEN NO ONE IS LOOKING
Prepare this confection many weeks in advance, but you must store it in containers with tight-fitting lids.

Toast the nuts in a preheated 325° oven. Watch that they do not burn. Mix the toasted nuts with the popcorn and spread in a large well-buttered baking pan. Bring the sugar, butter, and syrup to a boil in a saucepan over moderate heat, stirring constantly, until mixture boils. Then continue cooking and stir occasionally until it is a light caramel (about 250° on a candy thermometer). Remove from the heat and add the vanilla. Pour over the popcorn-nut mixture and stir. Preheat oven to 350° and bake about 30 minutes, until popcorn and nuts are glazed to a rich brown. Remove from oven and turn onto lightly buttered foil. Cool completely, then store in airtight tins or jars.

CANDIED ORANGE OR LEMON PEELS

Makes 1 pint or more

- 6 large oranges *or* 8 large lemons
- 2 cups sugar
- 1 cup water

WHEN NO ONE IS LOOKING
Prepared candied peels weeks ahead. Keep them refrigerated in glass jars with tight-fitting covers.

FROZEN POWER
Freeze candied peels; they should keep well for at least 6 months.

Squeeze oranges (or lemons) and use the juice to drink or for another purpose. Put the remaining fruit in a saucepan and cover with water. Boil 10 minutes, then drain. Repeat by covering fruit with fresh water and boiling again for 5 to 10 minutes. Drain, cool, and remove pulp. Cut rinds into strips and measure 2 cups. Set aside.

Combine the sugar and 1 cup water and stir over low heat until sugar dissolves. Boil this syrup for 5 minutes, then add peel strips and cook covered over moderate heat, stirring occasionally, for 30 to 45 minutes—until peel looks transparent. Remove from heat and cool to room temperature. Let it stand (covered) overnight. Bring to a gentle boil the next day, then place peel and syrup in glass jars with tight-fitting covers and refrigerate.

BATHSHEBAS

Makes 3 to 4 dozen

1 pound powdered sugar
¼ pound (1 stick) soft butter
⅓ cup bourbon whiskey
¾ cup pecans, toasted, then chopped
additional sifted powdered sugar

for dipping:
⅙ bar paraffin (½ ounce)
1 ounce unsweetened chocolate
11 ounces semisweet chocolate, chopped

WHEN NO ONE IS LOOKING
These will keep for several weeks in the refrigerator, stored in airtight tins.

FROZEN POWER
Freeze these in airtight tins, and they will keep for months.

Cream the 1 pound of powdered sugar with the butter, using an electric beater. Gradually beat in the bourbon. Stir in the pecans and chill for several hours. Form the mixture into small balls, using the additional sifted powdered sugar on your hands. Place them on wax paper-lined pans. Chill thoroughly.

Make the dipping: Melt the paraffin in the top of a double boiler. Remove from heat and cool briefly, then add the chocolate and stir until completely melted. Dip the chilled Bathshebas in the chocolate and place them on wax paper-lined pans. Chill again. Pack them in foil-lined, airtight tins and keep refrigerated.

BAKLAVA, MY VERSION

Makes about 24 pieces

1 ½ pounds phyllo sheets
3 ½ cups blanched almonds, toasted, then ground
2 ½ cups walnuts, toasted, then coarsely chopped
2 cups honey
1 cup sugar
1 cup water
grated rind of 2 oranges
1 ½ teaspoons cinnamon
1 ½ pounds melted butter

WHEN NO ONE IS LOOKING
Bake the baklava several days ahead. Keep tightly covered and refrigerated. Serve chilled or at room temperature.

FROZEN POWER
Freeze the baklava. Defrost completely, then serve cold or at room temperature.

Prepare the syrup: Mix the nuts together and set aside. Combine the honey, sugar, water, grated orange rind, and cinnamon in a saucepan and stir until it comes to a boil. Reduce heat and simmer for 5 minutes. Set aside.

Brush a 12 x 17 x 2-inch baking pan with melted butter. Place one phyllo sheet in the pan and brush with melted butter. Continue to add phyllo sheets brushing each with melted butter until you have placed 14 phyllo sheets in the pan. Sprinkle with ¼ of the nuts. Cover with 4 more phyllo sheets, each brushed with butter. Next another ¼ of the nuts and then 4 more phyllo sheets brushed with butter. Again ¼ of the nuts and 4 more phyllo sheets brushed with butter. Now the final ¼ of the nuts. Top with 8 to 12 phyllo sheets, each brushed with butter. Using a sharp knife, score the pastry into rectangles or diamonds. Preheat oven to 400°. Bake for five minutes, then reduce heat to 325° and bake for 30 minutes. Reduce heat again, now to 300° and bake approximately 30 to 35 minutes, until well browned but not burned.

Remove from oven and cool for 20 minutes. Cut scored pieces through. Pour the honey syrup (warm but not hot) over the baklava. Leave at room temperature for several hours before serving. Serve at room temperature or chilled.

INDIVIDUAL CHEESE STRUDELS

Makes about 24

- 12 to 13 ounces (about ¾ pound) farmer cheese
- 10 ounces cream cheese
- 1 cup sugar
- pinch of salt
- 3 egg yolks
- ½ cup raisins, rinsed in hot water, then drained
- ⅓ cup cognac or California brandy
- grated rind of 1 lemon
- 24 sheets of phyllo pastry (about 1 ½ pounds)
- 1 pound butter, melted
- sweetened whipped cream (optional)

WHEN NO ONE IS LOOKING
Prepare the cheese mixture 1 day ahead; keep covered and refrigerated. Or assemble the strudels 1 day ahead; keep covered and refrigerated. If they are cold they will take 5 to 10 minutes longer to bake.

FROZEN POWER
These freeze beautifully; they are best if frozen before baking. Defrost them for only 30 minutes and bake 10 to 15 minutes longer than directed above. Watch them because they should be well baked, but not burned.

Note: For friends abroad who cannot find farmer cheese or cream cheese, try the following: 340 grams of ricotta, well drained for at least 1 hour; 125 grams of very mild goat cheese (not aged!); or 125 grams mascarpone cheese

Prepare cheese mixture: Soak raisins in the cognac or brandy for at least 1 hour. Cream the cheeses together, then beat in the sugar, salt, egg yolks, and lemon rind. Stir in the raisins with the cognac or brandy that remains after soaking. Cover and refrigerate—best if done a day before, but the mixture must be chilled at least 2 hours.

Assemble: For each strudel, brush 1 sheet of phyllo with melted butter and fold it in half lengthwise. Put a heaping tablespoon of the chilled cheese mixture along the short end of the phyllo and inside about 1 inch from all the edges. Fold over that 1 inch of phyllo all around, then roll up the sheet to enclose the filling. Place strudel seam side down on a lightly greased baking pan—or if freezing—place in a pan that you plan to freeze. Continue to make additional strudels in the same way.

Bake: Preheat oven to 375°. Brush the strudels with melted butter and bake for about 25 minutes. Watch carefully that they do not burn. If bottoms look too brown, place another baking sheet under them, and reduce oven heat a little. Serve warm (not hot) sprinkled with powdered sugar and, if desired, with sweetened whipped cream.

INDIVIDUAL PHYLLO APPLE STRUDELS

Makes about 24

- 8 large tart apples, peeled, cored, and thinly sliced
- 2 ½ cups sugar
- ¼ cup water
- pinch of salt
- 3 teaspoons cinnamon
- 3 tablespoons lemon juice
- 2 cups raisins, soaked in hot water, then drained
- 1 ¼ cups toasted pine nuts (optional)
- 24 to 30 sheets of phyllo (1 ½ to 2 pounds phyllo)
- 1 to 1 ½ pounds butter, melted
- vanilla ice cream (optional)

WHEN NO ONE IS LOOKING
Prepare the apple mixture 1 or 2 days ahead and keep it chilled. Or assemble the strudels 1 day ahead; keep covered and refrigerated. If they are cold they will take 5 to 10 minutes longer to bake.

FROZEN POWER
These freeze wonderfully. Freeze them before baking. Arrange them in foil pans that you can double-wrap. To serve, defrost about 30 minutes, then bake as directed above, but 10 to 15 minutes longer.

Prepare filling: Place apples, sugar, water, salt, cinnamon, and lemon juice in a heavy saucepan and bring to a boil over moderate heat. Cover and cook until apples are almost tender. Add raisins, uncover pan, and continue cooking and occasionally stirring, for 5 minutes more or longer, until apples are tender and syrup has reduced and thickened. Stir in pine nuts, if desired, and set aside to cool.

Assemble: For each strudel, brush one sheet of phyllo with melted butter and fold it in half lengthwise. Spread one heaping tablespoon of apple filling at a short end of the phyllo and within 1 inch from the edges. Fold over the 1 inch of phyllo all around, then roll up the sheet to enclose the filling. Place strudel seam side down on a lightly greased baking pan—or if freezing—place in a pan or pans that you plan to freeze. Repeat until all strudels have been made.

Bake: Preheat oven to 375°. Brush strudels with melted butter and bake for 20 minutes. Reduce heat to 350° and continue to bake for 10 to 15 minutes, or until golden brown. Watch that they do not burn. If browning too quickly, reduce oven heat and place another baking sheet under them. Serve warm sprinkled with powdered sugar, and if desired, with scoops of vanilla ice cream.

PHYLLO BASKETS

Makes 24 mini-baskets or 12 small- to medium-size baskets

Phyllo pastry sheets
Melted butter (preferably clarified)

WHEN NO ONE IS LOOKING
Bake these 1 or 2 days ahead and store in tightly sealed plastic bags at room temperature.

FROZEN POWER
By all means, freeze these. Keep them in tightly sealed containers or plastic bags. To use, simply lift them out and fill; they do not need to be reheated.

For mini-baskets: Brush one sheet of phyllo with melted butter, then place a second sheet on top and brush it with butter. Top them with two more sheets brushing each with butter so that you have a total of four sheets. Cut into 24 squares (now four phyllo sheets thick) as shown in the diagram. Brush mini-muffin tins with melted butter and push the squares into the tins. Preheat oven to 325° and bake the phyllo squares 10 to 15 minutes—until brown and crisp. See diagram below at left.

For small- to medium-size baskets: Brush one sheet of phyllo with melted butter, top with a second sheet and brush it with butter. Repeat with two more so that you have a total of four sheets. Divide into 12 squares, as shown in the diagram. Brush regular-size muffin tins with melted butter and push the squares into the tins. Preheat oven to 325° and bake 10 to 15 minutes or until brown and crisp. See diagram below at right.

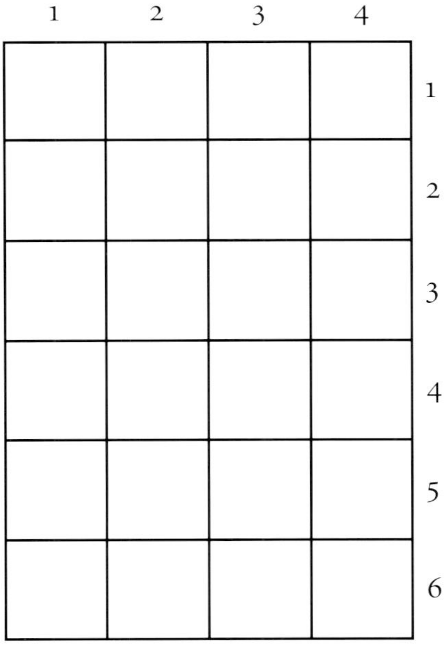

1 2 3 4
1
2
3
4
5
6

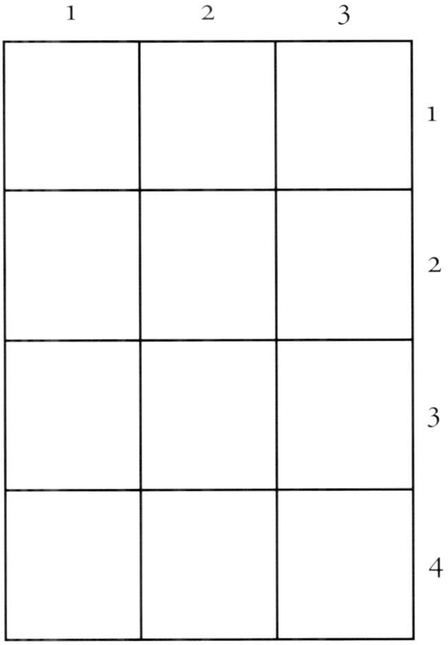

1 2 3
1
2
3
4

ROLLED PUDDING LIKE MOTHER USED TO MAKE

Makes 8 to 10 servings

for the noodle dough:
2 eggs
1 tablespoon oil
¼ teaspoon salt
2 tablespoons water
1 ½ cups flour

for the filling:
4 medium-size tart apples, peeled and thinly sliced
1 cup dark raisins, soaked in hot water, then drained
6 ounces butter (1 ½ sticks), melted
3 teaspoons cinnamon
1 cup dark Karo syrup

WHEN NO ONE IS LOOKING
Bake this pudding 1 day ahead. Cool, then wrap in plastic or foil and refrigerate. Bring to room temperature and reheat in a preheated 350° oven for 15 or 20 minutes. Serve hot, warm, or cold.

FROZEN POWER
Bake, cool, then double-wrap this pudding and freeze. To serve, defrost completely, then reheat in a 325° oven.

Prepare noodle dough: Mix the eggs, oil, salt, and water together, then stir in the flour. Turn out on a floured board and knead thoroughly until smooth and spongy. Place in a bowl and cover or wrap in plastic; let it rest at least half an hour or longer at room temperature.

Assemble and bake: Preheat oven to 350°. Spread ¼ cup of the melted butter in a 9 x 9-inch Pyrex casserole. Roll out noodle dough as thin as possible. It should be a circle about 24 inches in diameter. Cover with ½ cup of the melted butter, then with the apples, raisins, and cinnamon. Pour the Karo syrup over them as evenly as possible. Roll up like a jelly roll and with the aid of spatulas transfer to the butter-lined pan and arrange in a coil shape. Bake about l hour, basting with the juices once or twice, then reduce oven to 275° and bake about ½ hour or longer. Serve hot, warm, or cold.

WALNUT BARQUETTES WITH COFFEE ICING

Makes 24 or more, depending on the size of the barquette molds

"Pâte Brisée" (p. 355)

for the walnut filling:
½ cup (¼ pound) soft butter
⅔ cup sugar
2 eggs
1 teaspoon vanilla
2 cups walnuts, lightly toasted, then finely chopped
⅛ teaspoon salt

for the coffee icing:
1 pound powdered sugar, sifted
2 tablespoons melted butter
6 teaspoons powdered coffee
⅓ cup boiling water

for garnish:
toasted walnut halves

WHEN NO ONE IS LOOKING
Prepare the pastry 1 or 2 days ahead; keep wrapped and refrigerated. And make the coffee icing 1 day ahead too. Bring icing to room temperature before using and stir it well.

FROZEN POWER
Freeze the baked walnut barquettes without the coffee icing. Defrost the barquettes, reheat them for a few minutes in a 325° oven; then ice them. Freeze the icing separately; defrost, warm it slightly, and stir gently.

Make the walnut filling: Cream butter and sugar, then beat in the eggs and vanilla. Stir in the salt and walnuts. Set aside.

Make the barquettes: Line small barquette (boat-shaped) molds with pastry. Fill each ¾ full with the walnut mixture. Preheat oven to 425°. Bake walnut barquettes for 12 to 15 minutes. Remove and cool on racks.

Make the icing: Dissolve powdered coffee in the boiling water. Place sugar in a large bowl. Beat in the butter, and beat in dissolved coffee gradually—until it reaches spreading consistency.

Finish: Frost the top of each walnut barquette with coffee icing and garnish each with a toasted walnut half.

HOT BANANA PASTRIES WITH KIRSCH CREAM

puff pastry (homemade, p. 356, or purchased)
ripe but firm bananas, thinly sliced (need ½ banana per person)
sugar
kirsch (to taste)
heavy cream

WHEN NO ONE IS LOOKING
Prepare the pastry rounds 1 day ahead; stack them between layers of plastic wrap or waxed paper, then cover and refrigerate. Bake them the next morning, cool, cover, and leave at room temperature.

FROZEN POWER
Freeze the pastry rounds unbaked; stack them between parchment or waxed paper.

Whip the cream, then sweeten and flavor it with kirsch. Cover and keep refrigerated.

Roll puff pastry very thin. Cut into circles 5 inches in diameter and place them on baking pans lined with nonstick parchment paper. Chill. Preheat oven to 425°. Bake pastry for 15 minutes, then reduce oven to 350° and continue baking until well browned (but not burned). Set aside.

Shortly before serving gently reheat pastry rounds in a preheated 300° oven for 5 to 10 minutes. Do not overheat or overbake.

Turn on your broiling unit. Cover each pastry round with overlapping slices of banana—be generous and cover every part of the pastry. Sprinkle bananas with sugar. Place under the broiling unit and be sure to *watch.* Grill only long enough to melt and partly caramelize the sugar. Remove from oven and quickly place them on dessert plates. Sprinkle each with half a teaspoon of kirsch. Pass the flavored whipped cream separately.

RUGELACH

Makes 32

for the pastry:
½ pound butter (2 sticks), room temperature
½ pound cream cheese, room temperature
1 egg
1 teaspoon vanilla
2 ¾ cups flour (12 ounces)
½ cup sugar
½ teaspoon salt

for the filling:
2 cups apricot jam
1 ¼ cups walnuts, toasted, then chopped
½ cup sugar
1 teaspoon cinnamon

for egg glaze:
1 egg beaten slightly with 1 tablespoon water

WHEN NO ONE IS LOOKING
Bake these 1 or 2 days ahead; keep them refrigerated in airtight containers. Before serving, freshen them briefly (3 to 5 minutes) in a preheated 350° oven.

FROZEN POWER
Freeze these between layers of waxed paper or plastic wrap in airtight containers. To serve, defrost them and freshen them for 3 to 5 minutes in a preheated 350° oven.

Prepare the pastry: Beat butter and cream cheese together until well combined. Beat in the egg and vanilla. In a separate bowl mix flour, sugar, and salt. Stir into the butter mixture, but do not beat. Turn out on a floured board and knead gently only to smooth the dough. Do *not* overwork. Divide into two pieces, form each into a disk, wrap in plastic and chill at least 2 hours or overnight.

Make the filling: If apricot jam has large lumps, put it through a sieve or whirl in a food processor. Set aside. Combine the other filling ingredients in a separate bowl.

Assemble and bake: Preheat oven to 350°. Roll 1 pastry disk into a 15-inch round. Spread half the jam over the pastry and sprinkle with half the walnut mixture. Cut into 16 wedges, and starting at the wide end, roll up each, ending with the pointed edge. Repeat the whole process with the other pastry disk. Arrange the rugelach with pointed edges down on nonstick pans or on pans lined with nonstick parchment paper. Brush each with the egg glaze. Bake for 30 to 35 minutes, or until browned and crisp. If rugelach seem to brown too quickly, gradually reduce oven temperature or place another pan beneath them. Cool on racks, then store in airtight containers between layers of waxed paper or plastic wrap.

MAPLE SUGAR PIE

Makes about 6 servings

- 9 ½-inch pastry shell, "Pâte Brisée" (p. 355)
- 1 cup granulated 100% maple sugar (8 ounces)
- ¼ cup flour
- 1 ½ cups heavy cream
- whipped cream or vanilla ice cream (optional)

WHEN NO ONE IS LOOKING
Bake the pastry shell 1 day ahead; wrap in foil or plastic and refrigerate. Mix the filling in the morning, then bake it later.

FROZEN POWER
Remember that pastry shells freeze well—baked or unbaked.

Bake the pastry shell, then set aside. Leave the baked shell in the pan.

Sift maple sugar and flour together in a bowl so that they are thoroughly combined. Stir in the cream and whisk until mixture is smooth.

Preheat oven to 350°. Place tin with the baked shell on a cookie sheet. Pour mixture into the pastry shell and bake about 40 minutes or until filling is set. Remove from oven and place on a rack to cool somewhat so that it is warm. Serve warm or at room temperature. If desired, accompany with whipped cream or vanilla ice cream.

PUMPKIN PIE

Makes about 6 servings

This requires a pie dish 10 ½ or 11 inches in diameter and 1 inch deep

½ recipe for "Pâte Brisée" (p. 355)

for the filling:
3 eggs
1 cup heavy cream
½ cup milk
¾ cup dark brown sugar, packed to measure
¼ cup sugar
¼ teaspoon salt
1 ½ teaspoons cinnamon
¼ teaspoon cloves
½ teaspoon nutmeg
½ teaspoon ginger
1 (15- or 16-ounce) can of pumpkin

for the topping:
sweetened, vanilla-flavored whipped cream

WHEN NO ONE IS LOOKING
Bake the pastry shell 1 day ahead. Wrap in plastic or foil and refrigerate. Bring to room temperature, then proceed as directed.

FROZEN POWER
Freeze the pastry shell either baked or unbaked. Wrap in plastic or foil and freeze. Defrost, then proceed as directed.

Prepare pie shell: Roll pastry into a circle somewhat larger than the baking pan or dish. Fit it in carefully. Chill for 15 minutes. Line pastry with foil and weight it down with beans or metal pie weights. Preheat oven to 425°. Bake shell for 12 minutes. Remove from oven and remove foil and beans. Reduce heat to 350° and bake 10 to 15 minutes longer, until a golden color.

Prepare filling and bake: Preheat oven to 425°. Beat eggs slightly, then whisk in remaining ingredients until smooth. Pour mixture into the prebaked shell and bake for 10 minutes. Reduce heat to 325° and bake approximately 50 to 60 minutes, until custard is firm. Remove and cool on a rack. Serve at room temperature and offer sweetened vanilla-flavored whipped cream.

RICH LEMON PIE

Makes about 6 servings

prebaked 10-inch pastry shell, "Pâte Brisée," p. 355, or "Pâte Sucrée," p. 354

for the filling:
4 tablespoons flour
3 tablespoons cornstarch
¼ teaspoon salt
1 cup sugar
2 cups milk
5 egg yolks
grated rind of 1 or 2 lemons
juice of 2 medium-size lemons
⅛ pound (½ stick) melted butter

for the meringue:
5 egg whites
10 tablespoons sugar

WHEN NO ONE IS LOOKING
Bake the pastry shell 1 or 2 days ahead, but keep it in an airtight plastic bag or wrapped in foil. Store at room temperature or in the refrigerator. Prepare the lemon filling 1 day ahead; keep covered and refrigerated. Finish the meringue the day you plan to serve the pie.

FROZEN POWER
Freeze the prebaked pastry shell.

Make the filling: Mix the flour, cornstarch, salt, and sugar together until well combined. Stir in the milk, then place in a heavy saucepan and cook over moderate heat, stirring constantly, until mixture begins to boil. Remove from heat. Beat egg yolks in a separate bowl, then beat the milk mixture into them and combine thoroughly. Return to the saucepan and add the lemon juice, lemon rind, and butter, then cook over low heat, stirring constantly, until very thick. Remove from heat, cool, then chill.

Make the meringue and bake: Beat egg whites until barely stiff, then gradually beat in the 10 tablespoons sugar and continue beating until stiff and glossy. Preheat oven to 425°. Spoon chilled lemon filling into prebaked crust. Top with the meringue, then bake for about 5 minutes. Cool the pie on a rack, then chill. Serve chilled.

BILLY BOY'S CHERRY PIE

Makes about 6 servings

- pastry for a 10-inch pie, "Pâte Brisée" (p. 355)
- 2 cans red tart cherries—drain and reserve the juice; you will need 3 to 3 ½ cups of drained cherries
- 5 tablespoons cornstarch
- 1 tablespoon lemon juice
- 1 ½ cups sugar (or to taste)

WHEN NO ONE IS LOOKING
Bake this pie 1 day ahead, but underbake it slightly. After it has cooled, wrap in foil and refrigerate. Reheat until hot and completely baked.

FROZEN POWER
Freeze this pie, but underbake it slightly. Defrost, then reheat and complete the baking before serving.

Mix sugar and cornstarch together in a saucepan, then stir in the reserved cherry juice. Add lemon juice, then cook, stirring constantly, until mixture comes to a boil. Remove from heat and add the cherries. Set aside to cool. Roll out a bottom crust and line the pan. Pour in the cherry mixture. Cover with a top crust and seal the edges. Cut a design in the top crust. Preheat oven to 425°. Bake the pie on the lower level of the oven for 20 minutes; reduce heat to 400° and bake 15 minutes or longer—until pastry is browned and the filling is bubbling.

APPLE PIE

Makes about 6 servings

"Pâte Brisée" (p. 355)
6 large green apples (need 7 cups sliced apples)
1 ¼ cups sugar (or to taste)
3 tablespoons flour
¼ teaspoon salt
½ teaspoon nutmeg
1 teaspoon cinnamon
2 teaspoons lemon juice

WHEN NO ONE IS LOOKING
Bake this apple pie 1 day ahead but underbake it slightly. Cool the pie, then wrap in plastic or foil and refrigerate. Reheat in a 375° oven until hot and juices are bubbling. Serve hot or warm.

FROZEN POWER
Freeze this pie after baking, but underbake it slightly. To serve, defrost the pie then reheat and finish the baking in a 375° oven.

Core, peel, and thinly slice the apples. In a separate bowl mix sugar, flour, salt, and spices together. Roll out half the pastry and line a 10-inch Pyrex pie pan. Combine sliced apples with the sugar mixture, add lemon juice and toss well. Preheat oven to 425°. Spoon apple mixture into pastry-lined pan. Roll out other half of the pastry and cover the apples. Press the upper and lower crusts together, using cold water in between to seal. Prick top crust or cut a design. Place pie on the lower level of the oven and bake for 50 to 60 minutes—until juices begin to bubble. If pastry browns too quickly, reduce oven temperature slightly.

BANANA CREAM PIE IN A COCONUT CRUST

Makes about 6 servings

for the crust:
2 cups sweetened flake coconut
⅓ cup melted butter

for the filling:
3 tablespoons flour
3 tablespoons cornstarch
¼ teaspoon salt
½ cup sugar
1 cup milk
1 ½ cups light cream
2 tablespoons butter
5 egg yolks
2 teaspoons vanilla
2 large bananas
whipped cream for garnish (optional)

WHEN NO ONE IS LOOKING
Bake the crust and prepare the custard 1 day ahead; keep each separately covered and refrigerated. Assemble pie before serving.

FROZEN POWER
Freeze the coconut crust after baking. Cool it, then wrap carefully in foil.

Make the coconut crust: Combine coconut and butter in a bowl and mix. Press mixture into a generously buttered 10-inch pie pan. Preheat oven to 300°. Bake for about 30 minutes or longer—until well toasted. Remove from oven and cool.

Make the filling: Combine flour, cornstarch, salt, and sugar in a heavy saucepan and mix thoroughly. Stir in the milk and cream. Cook over moderate heat, stirring constantly, until thick, then add the butter and stir again. Beat egg yolks in a separate bowl, then gradually beat the hot mixture into them. Return to the saucepan and cook again, stirring constantly, until very thick. Remove from heat and add vanilla. Cool over ice, stirring occasionally. Chill.

Finish: Slice bananas and place some on the crust. Add some custard, then more bananas, and top with remaining custard. Garnish, if desired, with whipped cream and chill until time to serve.

COCONUT CREAM PIE

Makes about 6 servings

one 10-inch prebaked pie shell, "Pâte Brisée," p. 355
2 to 2 ½ cups sweetened coconut flakes

for the filling:
¾ cup sugar
3 tablespoons cornstarch
3 tablespoons flour
¼ teaspoon salt
2 ½ cups milk
¼ cup butter, melted
5 egg yolks
1 teaspoon vanilla

for the meringue:
5 egg whites
⅛ teaspoon cream of tartar
¼ teaspoon salt
10 tablespoons sugar

WHEN NO ONE IS LOOKING
Prepare the custard 1 day ahead; keep covered and chilled. Prepare the toasted coconut 3 days ahead; store in a airtight container.

FROZEN POWER
Freeze the toasted coconut in an airtight container; it will keep well for several months. Freeze the pastry shell baked or unbaked.

Preheat oven to 350°. Spread flaked coconut on a large baking pan and toast in the oven for 10 minutes. Reduce oven to 300° and continue to toast—stirring occasionally—until coconut flakes are golden brown. Remove from oven and cool.

Make the filling: Mix sugar, cornstarch, flour, and salt in a heavy saucepan, then stir in the milk and butter. Cook over moderate heat, stirring constantly, until mixture comes to a boil. Remove from heat. Beat egg yolks in a separate bowl, then beat the milk mixture into them. Return to the saucepan and cook over moderate heat, stirring constantly, until mixture has thickened. Remove from heat and cool over ice, stirring occasionally. Add vanilla and 1 cup of the toasted coconut, then cover and chill.

Make the meringue: Preheat oven to 350°. Beat egg whites with the salt and cream of tartar until barely stiff, then gradually beat in the 10 tablespoons of sugar, and continue beating until stiff and glossy but not dry.

Assemble and bake: Fill pastry shell with chilled custard. Spread meringue in peaks over the custard and sprinkle with remaining coconut. Bake in the preheated 350° oven until meringue has browned—15 to 20 minutes. Remove, cool on a rack, then chill. Serve cold.

OPEN FACE, FRESH PEACH PIE

- "Cream Cheese-Butter Pastry," ½ recipe (p. 354)
- 1 cup brown sugar (pack to measure)
- ¼ cup sugar
- ¼ teaspoon salt
- 1 teaspoon nutmeg
- ½ cup flour
- ⅛ pound butter (½ stick), room temperature
- 6 or 7 fresh peaches, peeled, then cut into eighths

WHEN NO ONE IS LOOKING
Bake this 1 day ahead. Cool, wrap, and refrigerate. Reheat before serving. Serve hot or warm or cold.

FROZEN POWER
Bake, cool, then wrap and freeze this pie. Defrost, then reheat before serving.

Line a 10-inch pie dish with the pastry and chill. Combine the two kinds of sugar, salt, nutmeg, and flour and mix thoroughly. Place about ¾ cup of this mixture in the bottom of the chilled pastry shell. Cover with the sliced peaches. Mix butter with the remaining sugar-flour mixture and sprinkle on top of the peaches. Preheat oven to 400°. Bake pie 40 to 50 minutes.

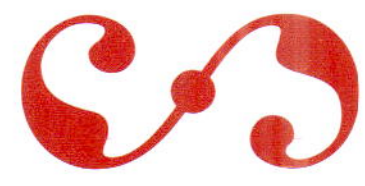

CARAMELIZED ALMOND TART

Makes about 6 servings

"Pâte Sucrée" (p. 354)

for the filling:
1 cup sugar
1 cup heavy whipping cream
pinch of salt
⅛ teaspoon almond extract
2 tablespoons kirsch
1 ⅓ cups sliced, blanched almonds, lightly toasted

WHEN NO ONE IS LOOKING
Bake this 1 day ahead; cool, cover, and leave at room temperature. Or, bake this tart 2 days ahead; cover and refrigerate. Bring to room temperature before serving, or reheat it briefly in a 350° oven.

FROZEN POWER
Freeze this almond tart after baking and cooling. To serve, defrost, then freshen in a 350° oven for 5 to 10 minutes.

Roll out pastry and fit into a 9- or 9 ½-inch tart pan with a loose bottom. Chill at least 30 minutes or freeze for 15 minutes. Preheat oven to 425°. Line pastry with foil and fill with metal pie weights or dried beans. Bake for 10 minutes. Remove from oven and remove foil and beans. Reduce oven heat to 350° and return pastry shell to oven for 10 to 15 minutes—until golden brown.

Make the filling: Heat cream with the sugar and salt, then stir until it comes to a boil. Reduce heat and let it boil gently over moderate heat until it begins to thicken slightly. Remove from heat, then add kirsch, almond extract, and almonds. Stir well. Preheat oven to 350°. Fill the baked pastry shell with the almond mixture and bake approximately 45 minutes, or until top is browned and mixture has caramelized. (If mixture begins to boil over, place the tart pan on heavy duty foil.) When the almond tart is done, remove it from the oven and cool only 1 minute, then using cotton gloves or hot pad holders, remove tart from the pan rim and if possible, remove from the bottom of the pan too. You must do this while the tart is hot so that caramel on the tin does not harden and stick. Cool tart on nonstick parchment paper.

BLUE PLUM TART

Makes about 6 servings

- "Pâté Brisée," ½ recipe (p. 355)
- 1 tablespoon sugar
- ½ cup graham cracker crumbs
- 1 pound blue plums, pitted and halved
- ⅓ cup sugar
- 3 tablespoons powdered sugar
- ¼ to ½ teaspoon cinnamon

WHEN NO ONE IS LOOKING
Bake this tart 1 day ahead, but underbake slightly and do not add the powdered sugar-cinnamon mix. Cool, then wrap and refrigerate. Before serving, bring to room temperature, finish baking, and then add sugar-cinnamon mix.

FROZEN POWER
Underbake this tart slightly, but do not add the powdered sugar-cinnamon. Cool, wrap and freeze it. To serve, defrost, finish baking, and then add sugar-cinnamon mix.

Line an 8-inch loose-bottom tart pan with the pastry. Sprinkle with the 1 tablespoon of sugar and the graham cracker crumbs. Arrange halved plums, cut sides up, on top of the crumbs and sprinkle with the ⅓ cup sugar. Preheat oven to 450°. Bake the tart for 20 minutes. Reduce heat to 350° and bake 20 to 30 minutes more, or until plums are glazed and juices have begun to bubble. (If pastry darkens too quickly, cover top of tart loosely with foil.) Remove from oven and cool on a rack for 15 minutes. Combine the powdered sugar with the cinnamon, then sprinkle over the plums. Serve warm or at room temperature.

APPLE, RAISIN, AND PINE NUT TARTLETS

Makes 24 or more medium-size tartlets

double recipe of "Pâte Brisée" (p. 355)
9 large green apples, peeled and thinly sliced (9 cups)
1 ¾ cups sugar
4 ½ tablespoons flour
¾ teaspoon salt
¼ teaspoon nutmeg
1 ½ teaspoons cinnamon
5 tablespoons butter
1 tablespoon lemon juice
½ cup raisins, rinsed in hot water, then drained
¾ cup toasted pine nuts

WHEN NO ONE IS LOOKING
Bake these tartlets 1 day ahead. Cover and keep refrigerated. Reheat them briefly.

FROZEN POWER
These are ideal freezer goodies. Defrost, then reheat briefly in a 350° oven.

Combine apples, sugar, flour, salt, spices, butter, lemon juice, and raisins and place in a large skillet or large pot. Cook over moderate heat, stirring, until apples are almost but not quite cooked. Remove from heat and stir in pine nuts. Set aside.

Line medium-size tart pans (or muffin pans) with the pâté brisée. (If possible use nonstick pans). Spoon in the apple filling. Decorate the top of each with a few pastry strips crisscrossed. Preheat oven to 425°. Bake the tartlets about 20 to 25 minutes or until pastry is well browned and apples are cooked. Do not overbake.

Remove from oven and using kitchen mitts or pot holders, carefully remove baked tartlets from the pans, then place them right sides up on greased racks. This must be done while the pastry is still hot because any sugared juice that weeps over will stick as it cools and make it impossible to loosen. Loosen pastry from edges of pans with a small sharp knife before trying to remove.

CONGRESS TARTS

Makes about 24

"Pâte Brisée" (p. 355)
raspberry jam

for the filling:
¼ pound butter (1 stick), room temperature
½ cup plus 2 tablespoons sugar
2 eggs
1 ¼ cups blanched almonds, ground
1 ½ teaspoons almond extract

WHEN NO ONE IS LOOKING
Bake these tarts 1 or 2 days ahead. Store them in containers that have tight-fitting tops and refrigerate. Bring to room temperature and refresh them for 3 to 5 minutes in a preheated 350° oven.

FROZEN POWER
Freeze these tarts after baking. Cool, then store them between layers of waxed paper in airtight tins. To serve, defrost, then refresh them for 3 to 5 minutes in a preheated 350° oven.

Make the filling: Cream butter and sugar together until light and fluffy, then beat in the eggs. Stir in the almonds and almond extract.

Make the tarts: Roll out pastry to ⅛-inch thickness and cut circles about 3 inches in diameter. Line shallow pastry-shell pans with the circles. Place ½ teaspoon raspberry jam in the bottom of each, then cover each with a small spoonful of the filling. Decorate tops with two crisscrossed strips of pastry (use pastry leftover from rolling). Preheat oven to 425°. Bake the tarts for about 15 minutes. Remove from oven and carefully remove tarts from pans; cool them on racks.

PARADISAICAL OPEN-FACE APPLE TARTS

Makes 4

1 pound puff pastry (homemade, p. 356, or purchased)
4 or 5 tart, flavorful apples
12 tablespoons melted butter (1 ½ sticks)
8 tablespoons sugar
vanilla ice cream (optional)

WHEN NO ONE IS LOOKING
Freeze the unbaked pastry circles stacked with waxed paper in between, then wrap in foil. Or, assemble the tarts but only do the first baking; cool, then add the second round of butter and sugar but do *not* bake. Cover and refrigerate them. Finish the final baking just before serving.

FROZEN POWER
Unbaked puff pastry circles freeze well. Stack them as described above and wrap in foil. Use them directly from the freezer. Even more spectacular, you can take these pastries through the first baking, cover them with their second butter and sugar topping, cool, then wrap each tart individually in foil and freeze. To serve, unwrap the tarts and defrost about 30 minutes; then finish the final baking, which may take a little longer because they will be partly frozen.

Roll pastry out very thin (about 1⁄16 inch thick). Cut into 8-inch circles—use a plate or a cardboard circle as a template. Place circles on baking pans (with sides) and chill thoroughly or freeze. Peel, quarter, seed, and slice apples as thin as possible, then arrange them on the pastry circles, overlapping them to form a flower design. Use the simple and inexpensive Feemster slicer, described on p. 17. Sprinkle each tart with 2 tablespoons of the butter and 1 tablespoon of the sugar.

Preheat oven to 425°. Bake for 20 minutes. Remove from oven and this time sprinkle each with 1 tablespoon of butter and 1 tablespoon sugar, then bake tarts an additional 10 to 15 minutes. Serve hot on individual plates. If desired, offer vanilla ice cream on the side.

FRENCH LEMON TART

Makes about 6 servings

"Pâte Brisée" (p. 355) or
"Pâte Sucrée" (p. 354)
4 eggs
1 cup sugar
grated rind of 3 lemons
⅔ cup lemon juice
⅛ teaspoon salt
3 tablespoons soft butter

WHEN NO ONE IS LOOKING
Bake the pastry shell 1 day ahead; wrap and refrigerate. Prepare the lemon filling 1 day ahead as well; keep covered and refrigerated.

FROZEN POWER
Freeze the pastry shell.

Roll out pastry and fit into a loose-bottomed 10-inch tart pan. Line with foil and weight with metal pie weights or dried beans. Preheat oven to 400°. Bake shell for 10 minutes. Remove from oven and remove foil and beans. Reduce heat to 350° and bake 10 to 15 minutes more. Cool, then remove shell from tin and place on a cookie sheet.

Combine eggs, sugar, grated lemon rind, lemon juice, and salt in a saucepan (not aluminum) and whisk over moderate heat until thick. Remove from heat, add butter, then stir. Cool to lukewarm. Spoon filling into prebaked shell and bake in the lower part of a preheated 350° oven for 10 minutes. Remove from oven. Increase oven to 425° and return tart to upper part of oven for 5 minutes. Remove and cool on a rack. Chill and serve cold or at room temperature.

PECAN TARTS

Makes 12 large 4 ½-inch tarts or 16 smaller ones

triple recipe of "Pâte Brisée" (p. 355)

for the filling:
6 cups pecan halves, lightly toasted
6 eggs
1 pound dark brown sugar
1 ¼ cups dark corn syrup
¼ teaspoon salt
¼ pound (1 stick) butter, melted
2 teaspoons vanilla
whipped cream or banana ice cream (optional)

WHEN NO ONE IS LOOKING
Bake the tarts 1 day ahead; cool, then wrap each in foil and refrigerate. Before serving, heat briefly in a preheated 350° oven.

FROZEN POWER
Bake, cool, then double-wrap in foil. To serve, defrost completely, then heat briefly in a preheated 350° oven.

Line tart pans with pastry; chill. Preheat oven to 425°. Generously cover the bottom of each pastry-lined pan with pecan halves. Combine eggs, sugar, syrup, salt, butter, and vanilla and beat well—until sugar has almost dissolved. Spoon filling over pecans—until pans are ⅔ to ¾ full. Bake for 10 minutes. Reduce heat to 325° and bake 20 to 25 minutes longer. Remove from oven and cool only 1 minute. Filling tends to boil over and thus pastry will stick; for that reason they must be removed while they are hot. Use a small knife and pot holders (to protect your hands), and remove tarts from pans. Place them on greased foil on top of racks to cool. Serve warm or at room temperature. If desired, accompany with whipped cream or "Banana Ice Cream," p. 386.

MACADAMIA NUT TARTS

Makes about 24 4-inch tarts

triple recipe of "Pâte Brisée" (p. 355)

for the filling:
- 8 cups of unsalted macadamia nuts
- 6 eggs
- 1 ¼ cups corn syrup (half light and half dark)
- 1 pound dark brown sugar
- ¼ pound (1 stick) butter, melted
- 2 teaspoons vanilla
- ⅓ cup hazelnut liqueur, such as Frangelico

WHEN NO ONE IS LOOKING
Bake the tarts 1 day ahead; cool, then wrap each in foil and refrigerate. Before serving, heat briefly in a preheated 350° oven.

FROZEN POWER
Bake, cool, then double-wrap each in foil. To serve, defrost completely, then heat briefly in a preheated 350° oven before serving.

Preheat oven to 325°. Toast macadamia nuts by placing them on a baking pan in the preheated oven for 10 to 15 minutes. Watch that they only get a light brown; do not burn or let them turn dark. Set aside.

Line tart pans (nonstick, if possible) with pastry and chill. Preheat oven to 400°. Combine remaining ingredients in a bowl and beat until sugar has almost dissolved. Cover bottoms of lined pans with toasted macadamias and spoon filling over the nuts until pans are ⅔ to ¾ full. Bake on the lower level of the oven for 10 minutes. Reduce heat to 325° and bake 20 to 25 minutes longer. Remove from oven and cool only 1 minute. Filling tends to boil over and thus pastry will stick; for that reason they must be removed while they are hot. Use a small knife and pot holders (to protect your hands) and remove tarts from pans. Place them on greased foil on top of racks to cool. Serve warm or at room temperature.

CREAM CHEESE-BUTTER PASTRY

½ pound butter (2 sticks)
8 ounces cream cheese
2 cups flour (9 ounces)
¼ teaspoon salt

WHEN NO ONE IS LOOKING
Prepare this pastry up to 3 days ahead; keep well wrapped and refrigerated.

FROZEN POWER
By all means, freeze this pastry.

Cream butter and cheese until combined. Add the flour and salt, blending it with a fork or pastry blender or with your fingers, then gradually forming it into a ball. Divide into desired portions, flatten, wrap, and chill—at least 1 hour or longer.

PÂTE SUCRÉE (SWEET PASTRY)

Enough for two 10-inch pie shells

10 ounces flour (about 2 ¼ cups spooned lightly into metal measuring cups, then leveled with a sharp-edge knife)
½ teaspoon salt
⅓ cup sugar plus 1 tablespoon
½ pound cold butter (2 sticks)
2 eggs (cold)
1 to 3 teaspoons cold water

WHEN NO ONE IS LOOKING
Prepare this pastry up to 2 days ahead; keep double wrapped and refrigerated.

FROZEN POWER
This pastry freezes well. Double-wrap for long storage—first in plastic, then in foil.

Combine flour, salt, and sugar in a food processor. Pulse for 1 or 2 seconds. Slice the butter and add it to the work bowl, then pulse at 1-second intervals until the mixture resembles coarsely ground cornmeal. Remove to a large mixing bowl. Beat eggs and 1 teaspoon of cold water together, then add to the flour-butter mixture and combine with a fork or knife until dough begins to form a mass—adding additional water if needed. Turn dough out on a lightly floured surface, divide it in half and form into two flat disks. Wrap in plastic and refrigerate at least 1 hour before using.

PÂTE BRISÉE (RICH PIE PASTRY)

Enough for a 2-crust 9-inch pie or 1 10-inch shell

- 10 ounces flour (about 2 ¼ cups spooned lightly into metal measuring cups, then leveled with a sharp-edged knife)
- ¼ to ½ teaspoon salt
- ½ pound butter (2 sticks)
- 4 to 6 tablespoons cold water

WHEN NO ONE IS LOOKING
Prepare this pastry up to 2 days ahead; keep it wrapped and refrigerated.

FROZEN POWER
By all means, freeze this pastry. Double-wrap for long storage.

Mix flour and salt together, then cut in the butter. This can be done in a food processor, but finish it by hand. Add 4 tablespoons of the water and cut in with a dinner knife until dry ingredients are absorbed, adding more water as needed. Do *not* overwork the pastry. Turn out on a lightly floured board and knead gently and very briefly, then form into two disks. Wrap and chill at least 1 hour before using.

PUFF PASTRY

Makes 3 ½ pounds

for the butter paste:
1 ¼ pounds butter (5 sticks), cool but not cold
4 ounces cake flour (1 ¼ cups—sifted before measuring)

for flour paste:
1 pound flour (4 ½ cups—sifted before measuring)
1 teaspoon salt
1 ½ cups ice water

WHEN NO ONE IS LOOKING
Prepare the puff pastry 1 or 2 days ahead. Double-wrap the pastry and keep it refrigerated.

FROZEN POWER
Although frozen puff pastry is available in markets now, homemade is much more delicious, and it freezes well. Divide it into the size portions you will probably want; double-wrap them, and then freeze. Defrost puff pastry overnight in the refrigerator.

Make the butter paste: Mix butter and cake flour together in a bowl using a wooden spoon, or in a mixer with a paddle. Spread in a 9 x 9-inch pan, then cover and chill 15 minutes.

Make the flour paste: Mix the flour and salt together in a bowl, then add the ice water and stir until combined; do *not* beat or overmix. Cover and chill for 15 minutes.

To roll and fold the pastry:

Special tip! Do not hesitate to use a generous amount of flour when rolling the pastry. Do not worry about the excess. Merely use a pastry brush to brush off excess flour when you are folding the dough.

STEP 1: (*See diagram*) Roll out the flour paste into a 12 x 18-inch rectangle and mark it in thirds. Place half of the butter paste in the center portion. Fold one third of the dough over this butter paste, then top with the remaining butter paste. Fold remaining third of the dough over and press down. Wrap in plastic or waxed paper and chill 30 minutes.

STEP 2: (*See diagram*) Place dough on a floured board with the open edges facing you. Roll into a rectangle about 18 x 30 inches. Fold ends to the middle. Brush off excess flour, then fold double—like a book—and press gently but firmly.

STEP 3: Turn dough around so that open edges face you again. Repeat step 2. Now wrap in plastic or waxed paper and chill again for 30 to 45 minutes.

STEP 4: Repeat step 2, but do not chill.

STEP 5: Repeat step 2, and wrap again and chill several hours or overnight.

To summarize: You first roll and fold the pastry in thirds, then you roll and fold it in fourths four times.

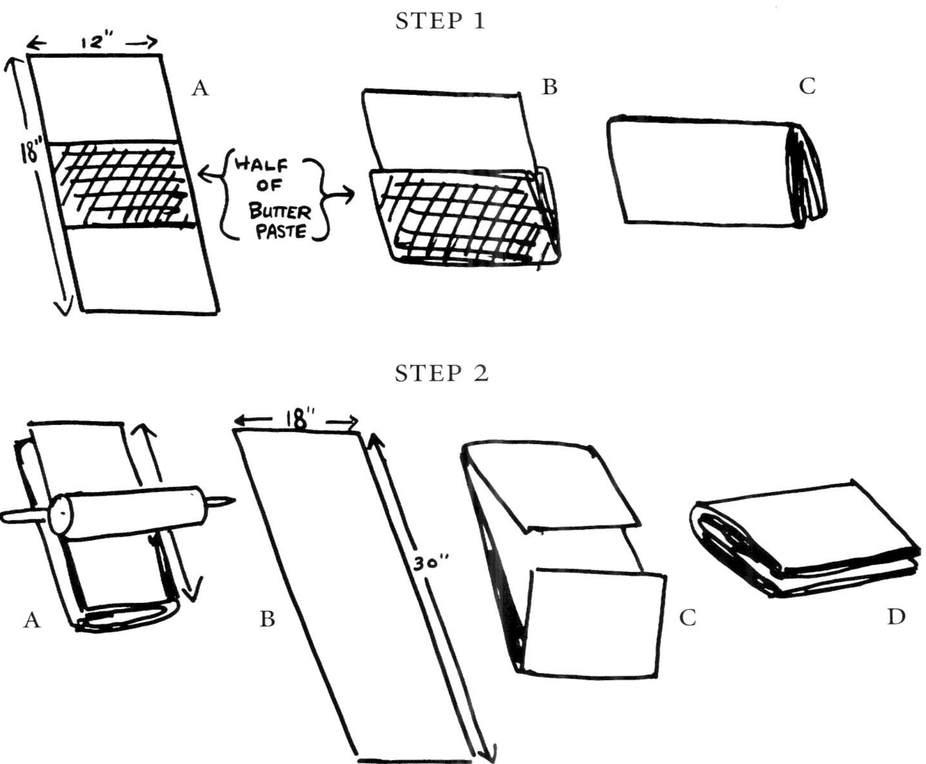

DESSERTS

OLD-FASHIONED STRAWBERRY SHORTCAKES

Makes 6 servings

2 cups sifted flour (9 ounces)
¾ teaspoon salt
4 teaspoons baking powder
3 tablespoons sugar
½ cup plus 2 tablespoons vegetable shortening
¾ cup milk
fresh strawberries, about 2 pints
1 cup heavy whipping cream
sugar
1 teaspoon vanilla
soft butter (optional)

WHEN NO ONE IS LOOKING
Prepare (but do not bake) the shortcakes in the morning; cover them with plastic wrap and refrigerate until shortly before serving. Prepare the berries and whipped cream in the morning as well, and keep them refrigerated. Whisk the cream several hours before serving.

FROZEN POWER
Although the shortcakes are best eaten immediately after baking, you can freeze baked leftovers and then heat and eat them as breakfast biscuits.

Clean and quarter the strawberries, then sweeten to taste. Whip the cream, sweeten, and add the vanilla. Keep berries and cream refrigerated until time to serve.

Prepare shortcakes: Mix dry ingredients together with a whisk (or sift together 3 times). Cut in the shortening with a pastry blender or with two knives. Add milk and stir only until blended. Knead on a floured board 2 or 3 times, but do *not* overwork or the shortcakes will be tough. Pat dough to a ¾-inch thickness and cut into disks 3 inches in diameter. Place on a greased pan and keep chilled until time to bake. Preheat oven to 450° and bake for 12 to 15 minutes just before serving so they will be very hot. Split them and, if desired, spread with soft butter. Cover each half with the prepared strawberries and top with flavored whipped cream.

CHOCOLATE CHEESECAKE

Makes about 20 servings

for the crust:
1 ½ cups graham cracker crumbs
¼ cup sugar
6 tablespoons melted butter

for the cheesecake:
40 ounces cream cheese (must be room temperature)
2 cups sugar
¼ cup flour
3 egg yolks
5 whole eggs
¼ teaspoon salt
1 cup sour cream
12 ounces semisweet chocolate, melted
3 tablespoons dark rum

For the optional whipped cream garnish:
2 cups heavy whipping cream
¼ cup sugar (or to taste)
¼ cup cognac

WHEN NO ONE IS LOOKING
Prepare this 1 day ahead without the whipped cream garnish; cover and refrigerate.

FROZEN POWER
After the cheesecake is completely cooled, wrap well, then freeze (without the whipped cream garnish). If possible, defrost slowly in the refrigerator; this will take 36 to 48 hours.

Combine ingredients for the crumb crust in a bowl, then press this mixture on the sides and bottom of a 10-inch springform pan. Chill at least 15 minutes. Preheat oven to 475°. Beat cream cheese in an electric mixer at medium speed until smooth, then gradually beat in the sugar. Add the flour and then the remaining cheesecake ingredients; beat only until smooth and blended. Do *not* overbeat. Pour into the prepared pan and bake for 10 minutes. Reduce heat to 300° and bake an additional 45 to 50 minutes. Turn off oven heat, but leave cheesecake in the oven for another 30 minutes. Remove and cool on a cake rack, then remove sides of pan; wrap and refrigerate.

Prepare the optional whipped cream garnish: Whip cream until almost stiff, then beat in sugar and cognac. Decorate top of cheesecake with this or serve separately and let guests help themselves.

WARM CHOCOLATE MARVELS

Makes 10

¼ pound (1 stick) plus 1 tablespoon butter
9 ounces semisweet chocolate, chopped
3 tablespoons Dutch processed cocoa powder
pinch of salt
4 egg whites
¼ cup (scant) meringue powder (available through baking supply catalogs)
⅓ cup sugar
1 teaspoon vanilla

for the garnish:
whipped cream, flavored with sugar and vanilla
chocolate sauce (p. 376 or 379)

WHEN NO ONE IS LOOKING
Prepare the chocolate mixture up to 2 hours ahead of baking; fill the cups and refrigerate them until time to bake.

FROZEN POWER
Yes, freeze these fabulous marvels. Fill the cups, then freeze them. Once they are solid, double-wrap the cups and keep them up to 2 weeks. When almost ready to serve, defrost them for only 15 minutes, then bake them in a preheated 400° oven for 12 to 14 minutes.

Preheat oven to 400°. Butter small foil baking cups—the kind available in supermarkets that hold a ½-cup quantity—and then sprinkle with sugar. Place them on a large baking sheet.

Melt the ¼ pound plus 1 tablespoon butter in a heavy saucepan over medium heat, then remove from the heat and add the chopped chocolate, cocoa powder, and salt. Stir until all the chocolate has melted. Set aside.

Whip the egg whites in a large bowl with an electric mixer on medium speed until foamy. Meanwhile, combine the meringue powder and sugar. Increase the mixer speed and add the meringue-sugar mixture a tablespoon at a time, continuing to whip until the whites form stiff but not dry peaks. Fold the chocolate mixture into the meringue, but do not overmix.

Spoon the mixture into the prepared foil baking cups, filling them ¾ full. Bake in the preheated oven for 8 to 10 minutes. Do not overbake; the centers should remain very moist. Remove the chocolate marvels from the oven and immediately invert them onto individual dessert plates (warm, if possible). Cover each with some warm chocolate sauce and serve with flavored whipped cream.

PROFITEROLES

Makes about 24 to 30

for the cream puff paste:
1 cup water (or ½ cup water and ½ cup milk)
¼ pound butter (1 stick)
½ teaspoon salt
1 teaspoon sugar
1 cup flour (5 ounces)
5 eggs (1 cup of eggs)
ice cream: vanilla (p. 381), chocolate (p. 382), or coffee (p. 387)
hot chocolate sauce (p. 376 or 379)

WHEN NO ONE IS LOOKING
Bake the puffs 1 day ahead; store them in sealable plastic bags in the refrigerator. Make the chocolate sauce up to 3 days ahead; keep covered and refrigerated. Refresh puffs in a preheated 350° oven for 1 or 2 minutes.

FROZEN POWER
Freeze the puffs after they have cooled. To serve, defrost them briefly, then refresh them for a few minutes in a preheated 350° oven. To simplify serving the profiteroles, scoop the ice cream into tiny balls 1 or 2 days ahead but keep them well covered and frozen. Do not hesitate to freeze chocolate sauce; defrost, then reheat gently and stir before using.

Heat water (or water and milk) with the butter, salt, and sugar. Stir with a wooden spoon, and as soon as the mixture comes to a boil, remove from the heat and add the flour all at once. Return to moderate heat and stir constantly until mixture no longer sticks to sides of pan. Remove from heat, and add eggs one at a time; beat well after each addition. You may not need all of the last egg, but use as much egg as possible. The goal is to achieve a smooth mixture—shiny and flexible, yet thick enough to keep it from running.

Preheat oven to 425°. Place mixture in a pastry bag with a no. 6 plain round tube, and pipe out 1-inch rounds on nonstick pans (or on pans lined with nonstick parchment paper). Bake for 10 minutes. Reduce oven to 350° and bake an additional 20 minutes. Remove from oven, and using a tiny, pointed knife make a tiny slash in each. Return to oven, turn off the heat, and leave them in the oven another 5 minutes or so. Remove and cool puffs on a rack.

Cut puffs into halves, place small scoops of ice cream on the bottoms and cover with the tops. Serve with the hot chocolate sauce.

CHEESECAKE WITH A PECAN-CARAMEL CRUST AND A CARAMEL TOPPING

Makes 12 to 16 servings

1 cup "Caramel Filling" (p. 366)
toasted pecan halves for garnishing

for the caramel pecan crust:
2 cups pecans, toasted in a 325° oven for about 10 minutes
⅔ cup brown sugar (pack to measure)
¼ cup flour
½ teaspoon cinnamon
⅛ pound (½ stick) butter, sliced

for the cheesecake:
2 pounds cream cheese (must be room temperature)
⅛ teaspoon salt
1 cup sugar
4 eggs (room temperature)
1 ½ tablespoons lemon juice
2 teaspoons vanilla

WHEN NO ONE IS LOOKING
Prepare this cheesecake 1 day ahead but do not add the toasted pecans. Cover and refrigerate. Remove from the refrigerator 1 or 2 hours before serving and add the toasted pecans.

FROZEN POWER
Freeze this cheesecake after it has cooled but without the caramel and pecan decoration. Double-wrap in foil. Defrost at room temperature or in the refrigerator for 36 to 48 hours. Remove from refrigerator 2 hours before serving, then cover with the caramel and garnish with toasted pecans.

Make the caramel pecan crust: Preheat oven to 325°. Place pecans, brown sugar, flour, cinnamon, and butter in a food processor and process until nuts are crushed and butter incorporated. Press the crumb mixture on the bottom and up about 2 inches on the sides of a 10-inch springform pan and bake 15 minutes. Remove from oven. If sides have slipped down, press them up with the back of a spoon. Cool.

Make the cheesecake filling: Preheat oven to 350°. Be sure cream cheese is at room temperature, then place it in an electric mixer with the salt and beat until smooth. When smooth gradually beat in the sugar on low speed, intermittently scraping down the sides of the bowl to remove any lumps. Using low or moderate speed, beat in the eggs, lemon juice, and vanilla. Do not overbeat—mix only long enough to incorporate the ingredients. (Beating too vigorously will cause the cheesecake to rise too much and crack.)

Wrap the bottom and exterior sides (2 inches up) of the springform pan with foil. Pour or spoon mixture into the crust. Bake 10 minutes at 350°, then reduce heat to 325° and bake about 45 to 60 minutes longer. The top should be lightly browned and firm to the touch. Remove from oven and cool on a rack, but do not remove the sides of the pan. When it has cooled, cover and chill.

Finish: Spoon caramel filling on the top of the cheesecake, then remove sides of the springform pan. Decorate with toasted pecan halves. Serve cold or at room temperature.

CARAMEL FILLING FOR TARTLETS AND OTHER THINGS

Makes about 2 cups

2 cups sugar
¼ cup hot water
1 cup heavy whipping cream
¼ pound (1 stick) unsalted butter, sliced
toasted walnuts (optional)

WHEN NO ONE IS LOOKING
Prepare this caramel filling several weeks ahead; keep it tightly covered and refrigerated.

FROZEN POWER
Freeze the caramel (it will keep at least 1 year). Store it in airtight containers.

Place sugar in a heavy skillet and melt it, shaking or stirring all the while, until caramelized; but be sure not to burn it, or it will become bitter. Begin this process on high heat, then reduce it to moderate or low. When sugar is caramelized, remove from the heat, then add the water—*watch out because it may sputter and spatter.* Return to low heat and stir until mixture becomes smooth. This can take 10 to 15 minutes.

Add half of the cream to the sugar mixture and stir over moderate or low heat until it begins to simmer. At this stage, if desired, you can strain the mixture through a sieve to remove any remaining tiny lumps and then return it to a clean saucepan. Add remaining cream and the sliced butter and cook again, stirring occasionally, until this mixture reaches the jelly stage. This will take 10 to 20 minutes. You can test it by dropping a little on a plate—it should be jelly-like. Remove from the heat and cool to room temperature. Pour into a jar or plastic container that can be sealed, then refrigerate until ready to use. If the caramel is too difficult to spoon after chilling, heat it a little in a microwave oven.

Serve this caramel in small pastry or phyllo tartlets, and if desired, top with toasted walnuts. You can also use it as the topping for the "Cheesecake with a Pecan-Caramel Crust" (p. 364).

TRIFLE

Makes 12 servings

- 5 eggs
- 3 cups milk
- ⅛ teaspoon salt
- ½ cup sugar
- 1 teaspoon vanilla
- 3 dozen ladyfingers (purchased will do)
- apricot jam
- raspberry jam
- ½ cup sherry
- 1 cup toasted almonds
- ½ cup crushed macaroons (homemade, p. 317, or purchased)
- 1 ½ cups heavy cream, whipped
- candied cherries and angelica (for garnish)

WHEN NO ONE IS LOOKING
Prepare this 1 day ahead, but do *not* add the whipped cream until a few hours before serving.

FROZEN POWER
Keep ladyfingers, almonds, and almond macaroons handy in your freezer.

Heat the milk with the salt and sugar in a heavy saucepan over moderate heat, stirring until sugar has dissolved. Beat the eggs in a separate bowl, then gradually pour the milk mixture over the eggs, stirring while pouring. Return all to the saucepan and cook, stirring constantly, until the resultant custard coats the spoon. Remove from heat and place saucepan over ice water and cool, stirring occasionally. Add the vanilla. Cover and chill until needed.

Split ladyfingers and spread some with apricot jam and others with raspberry jam. Press halves together. Place a layer of these filled ladyfingers in a large glass serving bowl. Sprinkle with sherry and spoon on some custard mixture. Sprinkle with some of the macaroon crumbs and with some toasted almonds. Repeat this whole procedure until ingredients are used up; reserve some almonds for garnishing. Cover and chill several hours.

Before serving, cover the top of the trifle with the whipped cream and garnish with toasted almonds, bits of candied cherries, and tiny slices of angelica. Cover and keep refrigerated until time to serve.

ENCHANTMENT PEACHES FLAMED AT TABLE

Makes 12 servings

This may yield too much for some households; if so, divide the recipe in half.

vanilla ice cream, 12 small servings (homemade, p. 381, or purchased)

for the tray or trays:
½ pound butter (2 sticks), sliced
2 ⅔ cups dark brown sugar (pack to measure)
⅔ cup heavy cream
3 teaspoons ground nutmeg
12 peach halves (fresh or canned)
½ cup cognac or brandy
2 tablespoons 151 proof rum—as a magic torch (p. 20)

WHEN NO ONE IS LOOKING
Arrange everything in the morning—ice cream dished up waiting in the freezer and remaining ingredients on a tray or trays (peaches covered).

FROZEN POWER
Keep vanilla ice cream available for this fabulous recipe.

Scoop the ice cream, then arrange the scoops in large, individual bowls and place them in the freezer; or store the scoops on a tray in the freezer until time to complete the dessert.

When ready to prepare dessert bring a large chafing dish and remaining ingredients to the dining table or a side table. Proceed slowly and calmly; guests enjoy the spectacle. Melt butter in the blazer of the chafing dish. Let it sizzle, then add the sugar, cream, and nutmeg. Stir and cook until syrup begins to thicken slightly. Add the peach halves and continue to cook, spooning sauce over the peaches. After peaches are heated and sauce is bubbling, add the cognac or brandy. Finally add the 151 proof rum and ignite the sauce (*carefully*) and spoon it over the peaches.

After peaches and sauce are finished, bring the bowls of ice cream into the dining room; add a peach half to each bowl along with plenty of sauce.

CHOCOLATE MERINGUE GÂTEAU

Makes 12 or more servings

for the chocolate meringue layers:
2 cups powdered sugar
⅔ cup unsweetened powdered cocoa
10 egg whites
1 ⅓ cups granulated sugar
½ teaspoon salt
¼ teaspoon cream of tartar

for chocolate mousse filling:
10 ounces semisweet chocolate, finely chopped or grated
½ pound butter (2 sticks)
6 egg yolks
8 egg whites
½ cup sugar

WHEN NO ONE IS LOOKING
Bake the meringues 1 or 2 days ahead. Wrap them in foil or store in sealable plastic bags in the refrigerator or at room temperature. Prepare the chocolate mousse 1 day ahead; keep covered and refrigerated. Assemble the gâteau in the morning, cover and keep chilled.

FROZEN POWER
Freeze the meringues and the mousse separately. The meringues defrost in a few minutes, but the mousse requires several hours (or overnight in the refrigerator). Complete the assembly several hours before serving, then keep in the refrigerator.

Make meringues: Line 3 baking pans with baking parchment, then on each draw an outline oval (8 x 14 inches) or a circle (10 ½ to 11 inches in diameter). Preheat oven to 300°.

Sift powdered sugar and cocoa together and set aside. Beat whites with salt and cream of tartar until they begin to stiffen, then gradually beat in the granulated sugar until stiff. Remove beater, then quickly fold in the cocoa-powdered sugar mixture. Place the mixture in a pastry bag with a ½-inch nozzle (no. 7) and pipe out ovals (or circles) following the outlines on the papers and fill them in so that the meringues are ¼ to ½ inch thick. Line a fourth pan with parchment and using remaining mixture and a pastry bag with a nozzle only ⅛-inch thick (no. 2) pipe out strips on the parchment—as many as you can. Bake meringues for about an hour, gradually reducing oven heat to 275°; the strips will be ready sooner—in 20 to 30 minutes. Remove and cool.

Make the chocolate mousse filling: Melt the chocolate and butter together over lowest heat, stirring until well combined. Beat egg yolks in a separate bowl, then beat in the melted chocolate-butter mixture. Set aside to cool. Beat egg whites until they begin to stiffen, then gradually beat in the sugar. Fold mixtures together, then cover and chill until ready to use.

Assemble the gâteau: Fill and stack the large meringues with chocolate mousse, leaving enough mousse to frost the gâteau. Cut meringue strips into 1-inch pieces and top the gâteau with them. Keep lightly covered and refrigerated until time to serve.

SUGARED LEAVES WITH A SURPRISE

Makes about 12 servings

1 to 1½ pounds puff pastry (homemade, p. 356, or purchased)
1 pound powdered sugar, sifted
1 quart or more of vanilla ice cream (homemade, p. 381, or purchased)
fresh raspberries

for the raspberry sauce:
2 (10-ounce) packages frozen raspberries
⅓ cup sugar

WHEN NO ONE IS LOOKING
Prepare the raspberry sauce 3 days ahead; cover and refrigerate. Bake the sugared leaves up to 2 days ahead and refrigerate in tightly sealed plastic bags.

FROZEN POWER
Bake and freeze the sugared leaves in tightly sealed bags. Freeze the raspberry sauce too. Prepare the ice cream discs 2 days ahead and freeze them on trays, keeping them covered with plastic or foil. The vanilla ice cream can be made far in advance.

Divide the puff pastry into two pieces. Roll out each piece into a long, very thin rectangle, about 14 x 18 inches. Brush very lightly with a little water, then roll up each rectangle tightly from the short end, into a jelly-roll shape. Wrap rolls in plastic, then in foil, and refrigerate several hours or overnight.

Preheat oven to 400°. Cut 3 or 4 slices, each ¼ inch thick, from one of the rolls, then return the roll to refrigerator. It is important to keep the rolls chilled. Place a generous amount of sifted powdered sugar (do *not* use granulated sugar) on a pastry board and roll each slice into a thin disc, 7 to 8 inches in diameter; they will shrink when baked. Place these discs (they will become your sugared leaves) on nonstick baking pans (or pans lined with nonstick parchment paper) and bake until they are golden brown and caramelized. Watch that they do not burn. Remove baked sugared leaves from the pans and cool on parchment paper or waxed paper. Repeat this process with the remaining rolls. When cool, package the sugared leaves in plastic bags that can be tightly sealed.

Make the raspberry sauce: Defrost the frozen raspberries and combine them with the sugar in a saucepan. Stir and bring to a boil. Lower heat and simmer for 1 or 2 minutes. Remove from heat, cool, then purée in a food processor and sieve to remove the seeds. Cover and refrigerate.

Ready the ice cream: Scoop ice cream using a medium-size scoop, then flatten these round scoops into flat discs by pressing down on them with a flat-bottom water glass. Keep the ice cream discs frozen until time to serve.

Assemble and serve: Place one sugared leaf-disc on each individual dessert plate, then top it with an ice cream disc and a few fresh raspberries. Cover with a second sugared leaf-disc and press down gently. Pour raspberry sauce around the assembled desserts and scatter with more fresh raspberries.

HALLELUJAH CRÊPE SUZETTE TORTE

Makes 12 to 16 servings

for the crêpes:
12 eggs
4 cups milk (plus some extra)
3 cups flour
½ teaspoon salt
½ pound (2 sticks) melted butter

for the suzette filling:
1½ cups sugar
grated rind of 1 orange
grated rind of 1 lemon
2 cups orange juice
juice of half a lemon
2 tablespoons cornstarch dissolved in ¼ cup cold water
½ pound (2 sticks) butter
¼ cup orange liqueur (Grand Marnier or Cointreau)

for the suzette sauce:
grated rind of 2 oranges
2 cups orange juice
1½ cups sugar
½ pound butter (2 sticks)
⅔ cup orange liqueur (Grand Marnier or Cointreau)

WHEN NO ONE IS LOOKING
Prepare this whole glorious torte 1 day ahead; keep wrapped in foil and refrigerated. Prepare the suzette sauce 1 day ahead too; cover and refrigerate. Remove torte from the refrigerator 5 hours before the final heating. Heat suzette sauce gently.

FROZEN POWER
Freeze this dessert and it becomes a fabulous asset. Double-wrap it in foil, and also freeze the suzette sauce. To serve, defrost the torte completely (overnight at room temperature), then proceed as directed.

Prepare the crêpe batter: Beat the eggs, then add the flour and milk alternately to the eggs. Add salt and melted butter, and let the batter stand at least 1 hour (or overnight in the refrigerator).

Prepare the suzette filling: Place the dissolved cornstarch, sugar, grated rinds, orange and lemon juice in a saucepan and stir over moderate heat until mixture comes to a boil. Reduce heat and simmer 5 minutes. Stir in the butter, and after it has melted, remove from heat and add the orange liqueur. Set aside.

Prepare the suzette sauce: Place the grated rind, orange juice, and sugar in a saucepan and stir until mixture comes to a boil. Simmer 4 or 5 minutes, then add the butter and stir until melted. Remove from heat and add the orange liqueur. Set aside.

Cook crêpes and assemble the torte: Check the batter to see that it is the consistency of heavy cream. Heat a nonstick 9-inch skillet, and if desired, add a teaspoon of butter. Use ¼ to ⅓ cup of batter per crêpe. Try it out. Pour the batter into the skillet, trying to achieve a very thin crêpe. If crêpes seem too thick, add more milk to the batter. Continue to cook the crêpes, and as each is cooked, stack it on a ovenproof round dish or platter with a tablespoon of the suzette filling between each crêpe. You will end up with a tall cakelike dessert. Cover it and the dish itself with heavy-duty foil and set aside until ready to heat and serve.

To serve: Preheat oven to 350°. Place the foil-wrapped torte in the oven and heat for at least 30 minutes, or if cool, much longer. It must be piping hot! Bring the torte to the table and also bring the suzette sauce, which you have reheated. Cut the torte in wedges and serve with a spoonful of the heated suzette sauce.

Note! If desired, flambé this torte at the table. Pour an ounce of Cognac over it—or much easier, use the magic torch (p. 20)—151 proof rum—and ignite. Take care to let the flames burn out, then add sauce and serve.

BANANA OR STRAWBERRY BONANZA WITH RUM-EGGNOG SAUCE

Makes about 16 servings

for the genoise cake:
4 eggs (warmed in their shells in hot water)
1 cup sugar
1 cup cake flour
1 teaspoon baking powder
¼ teaspoon salt
3 tablespoons melted butter, cooled to room temperature

for the rum-eggnog sauce:
3 egg yolks
1 cup powdered sugar (packed to measure)
1 cup heavy whipping cream
⅓ cup light or medium rum
drop of yellow food coloring (optional)

for the filling and frosting:
1½ quarts of heavy whipping cream
½ cup sugar
3 teaspoons vanilla
1 tablespoon powdered gelatin
¼ cup cold water
8 to 10 bananas or 6 cups of fresh strawberries

WHEN NO ONE IS LOOKING
Bake the genoise cake 1 day ahead; keep it covered and refrigerated. Prepare the rum-eggnog sauce 1 day ahead and keep it covered and refrigerated. Completely assemble this creation in the morning; cover it with plastic wrap, and keep it refrigerated until time to serve.

FROZEN POWER
Freeze the baked genoise.

Prepare the genoise: Grease an oblong pan (11 x 17 x 1 inches), then line with parchment paper (or waxed paper), and grease and flour the paper. Preheat oven to 350°. Sift the flour, baking powder, and salt together, then leave in the sifter. Beat the eggs with an electric mixer until light and thick, then gradually beat in the sugar, continuing to beat until the mixture is light lemon color and thick. Sift the flour mixture over the egg-sugar mixture and gradually fold it in with a few strokes. Fold in the butter with a few strokes; do *not* overmix! Pour into the pan and bake for 15 to 20 minutes. Remove from oven and cool a few minutes, then turn upside down, remove paper, and turn right side up to finish cooling.

Prepare rum-eggnog sauce: Combine egg yolks with the sugar in a saucepan and whisk over moderate heat until very hot but not boiling. Remove from heat and stir in the rum. Chill over ice or in the refrigerator. Whip the cream and fold it into the egg mixture. If desired, add the drop of yellow food coloring. Cover and chill until time to serve.

Prepare the filling and frosting: Soak the gelatin in cold water in a Pyrex cup or small bowl for 5 minutes, then place the cup or bowl in simmering water and dissolve the gelatin. Whip the cream until it begins to stiffen, then beat in the vanilla and sugar, but do *not* overbeat. Add the melted gelatin all at once and beat cream simultaneously. This amount of gelatin will give the whipped cream stability but will not make it taste jelled.

Assemble: Slice the bananas (or strawberries) and keep covered. Cut the genoise into three equal lengthwise sections. Place one on a long board or platter and cover it with some of the sliced bananas (or strawberries) and with some of the prepared whipped cream filling. Repeat this layering with the second portion of genoise. Repeat once more with the third layer, but then cover both top and sides with the whipped cream frosting. Chill for several hours.

Serve: Cut the dessert in slices and surround each serving with some of the rum-eggnog sauce.

CHOCOLATE ROLL WITH CHOCOLATE RUM SAUCE

Makes 8 to 10 servings

5 eggs, separated
1 cup powdered sugar
¼ cup granulated sugar
¼ cup cocoa powder
2 tablespoons flour
1 quart of ice cream:
coffee (p. 387),
vanilla (p. 381),
or chocolate (p. 382)

for the chocolate rum sauce:
¾ pound semisweet chocolate
½ cup strong coffee
3 tablespoons butter
2 or 3 tablespoons rum

WHEN NO ONE IS LOOKING
Prepare the chocolate rum sauce 3 or 4 days ahead; keep covered and refrigerated.

FROZEN POWER
This is frozen power indeed! Freeze this chocolate roll baked, filled, and even sliced, but keep it well covered in the freezer. Freeze the chocolate sauce as well.

Prepare the chocolate rum sauce: Melt the chocolate in the coffee over lowest heat, stirring constantly. Remove from heat, then stir in the butter and rum. Serve hot or cold.

Prepare the chocolate roll: Preheat oven to 350°. Grease an 11 x 17-inch baking pan and line it with waxed paper or parchment paper. Then grease and flour the paper. Sift sugars, cocoa, and flour together. Beat egg yolks until very light and very thick, then gradually add the sugar-cocoa mixture and beat until smooth and thick. In a separate bowl beat egg whites until stiff, but only to the point where they form a soft peak. Fold into the egg yolk mixture, then pour into the prepared pan. Bake for 15 to 20 minutes. Do not overbake.

Turn cake out on a damp towel. Remove paper and cut off crisp edges. Lift towel to help the cake into a roll. Let the roll cool, then place it on waxed paper or parchment paper that has first been sprinkled with powdered sugar. Leave it rolled up until time to fill.

Assemble: Carefully open up the cake roll. Cover with a layer of ice cream about 1 inch thick. Roll up and place the roll in a freezer at least for a short time. To serve, cut into diagonal slices ¾ inch thick and serve with the chocolate rum sauce.

PRALINE SOUFFLÉ

Makes 4 servings

- ⅛ pound butter
- ¼ cup flour
- pinch of salt
- 1 ¼ cups milk (warmed)
- 4 egg yolks
- 3 tablespoons Frangelico liqueur
- 1 cup "Praline Paste" (p. 395)
- ⅓ cup sugar
- 6 egg whites
- "Praline Ice Cream" (p. 386)

WHEN NO ONE IS LOOKING
Prepare the soufflé base in the morning; cover and leave at room temperature. Finish shortly before serving. Prepare the praline paste and praline ice cream ahead of time as directed in those recipes.

Grease a 1 ½-quart soufflé dish, then wrap a greased waxed-paper collar and tie it around the outside of the top of the dish.

Melt butter in a saucepan, stir in flour and salt, then add the milk and cook over moderate heat, stirring constantly until mixture comes to a boil. Beat egg yolks in a separate bowl and whisk in the milk mixture. Return all to the saucepan, then heat and whisk until hot. Remove from heat, stir in the liqueur and ⅓ of the cup of praline paste. Pour into a large bowl, cover and set aside.

Preheat oven to 375°. Beat egg whites until beginning to stiffen, then gradually beat in the ⅓ cup of sugar. Beat until mixture forms soft peaks. Do *not* overbeat. Fold beaten whites into the praline mixture and spoon one-half of this mixture into the prepared dish. Sprinkle with ⅓ of the cup of praline paste. Add the remaining soufflé mixture and top with remaining praline paste. Bake at once for 35 minutes. Serve at once and,

DEPENDABLE CHOCOLATE SOUFFLÉ

Makes 4 servings

2 ounces unsweetened chocolate
⅛ pound butter (½ stick)
¼ cup flour
pinch of salt
1 ¼ cups milk (warmed)
5 egg yolks
1 teaspoon vanilla
1 tablespoon cognac
6 egg whites
⅔ cup sugar

to accompany the soufflé:
sweetened whipped cream
hot chocolate sauce (p. 376 or 379)

WHEN NO ONE IS LOOKING
Prepare the chocolate base in the morning; cover with plastic and leave at room temperature. Ready the soufflé dish and collar. About 1 hour before serving preheat the oven; then, beat egg whites with the sugar and fold them into the base. Bake and serve.

Grease a 1 ½-quart soufflé dish, then wrap a greased waxed-paper collar around the outside of the top of the dish and tie it on.

Melt chocolate in a microwave oven or over simmering water, then set aside. Melt butter in a saucepan and stir in the flour and salt. Add the milk and stir constantly until mixture comes to a boil. In a separate bowl beat egg yolks, then "temper" them by adding and whisking in the hot milk mixture. Return all to the saucepan, add the melted chocolate and whisk together over moderate heat until mixture is very hot but *not* boiling. Add vanilla and cognac. Remove and pour into a large bowl. Cover with plastic and leave at room temperature.

Preheat oven to 375°. Shortly before baking, beat egg whites until barely stiff, then gradually beat in the sugar and beat until soft peaks are formed. Do not overbeat. Fold this into the chocolate mixture and pour into the prepared soufflé dish. Bake for 40 to 45 minutes. Serve at once with sweetened whipped cream and chocolate sauce.

CHOCOLATE SOUFFLÉ WITH WHITES ONLY

Makes 4 servings

4 ounces semisweet chocolate
2 tablespoons water
6 tablespoons sugar
8 egg whites
pinch of salt

for sweetened whipped cream:
½ cup heavy whipping cream
1 tablespoons sugar
1 teaspoon vanilla

for chocolate sauce:
4 ounces semisweet chocolate
½ cup heavy cream
1 teaspoon vanilla

WHEN NO ONE IS LOOKING
Prepare the chocolate sauce 1 to 3 days ahead; keep covered and refrigerated. Heat gently before serving. Prepare the soufflé base in the morning; cover and leave at room temperature, then finish while guests are eating the main course or a salad served after the main course.

FROZEN POWER
Freeze the chocolate sauce and have it handy for this dessert and for many others.

Prepare the chocolate sauce: Combine chocolate and cream in a saucepan and heat over lowest heat, stirring until chocolate has melted. Remove from heat and stir in the vanilla.

Prepare the whipped cream: Whip the cream with the sugar and vanilla; then cover and refrigerate.

Prepare the soufflé: Grease four individual soufflé dishes. Preheat oven to 375°. Melt chocolate with the water over lowest heat, stirring constantly (or melt in a microwave oven). Stir in 2 tablespoons of the sugar and place this chocolate mixture in a large bowl. Beat egg whites with the salt until barely stiff, then gradually beat in remaining sugar, beating until mixture forms soft peaks; do *not* overbeat. Fold into the chocolate mixture, then spoon into the prepared dishes. Bake for 15 minutes, then reduce heat to 350° and bake an additional 10 minutes. Serve at once and pass the whipped cream and the chocolate sauce.

PINEAPPLE ROMANOFF

Makes 6 servings

1 fresh ripe pineapple, peeled, cored, and diced
½ cup sugar (or to taste)
⅓ cup Grand Marnier liqueur
grated rind of 1 orange
1 cup heavy whipping cream
3 tablespoons sugar
2 additional tablespoons Grand Marnier liqueur

WHEN NO ONE IS LOOKING
Prepare the pineapple mixture 1 day ahead; cover and keep refrigerated. Prepare the whipped cream mixture in the morning; keep covered and refrigerated. Combine shortly before serving.

Combine diced pineapple with the ½ cup sugar and ⅓ cup Grand Marnier. Stir until sugar has dissolved. Cover and set aside. Whip cream with the 3 tablespoons sugar, then fold in the grated orange rind and the 2 tablespoons Grand Marnier. Cover and chill. Shortly before serving, combine the two mixtures, then serve in dessert glasses or bowls.

CRÈME CARAMEL

Makes 5 or 6 servings

¾ cup sugar
5 tablespoons hot water
2 whole eggs
2 egg yolks
⅓ cup sugar
2 cups half and half (or half milk and half heavy cream)
1 teaspoon vanilla

WHEN NO ONE IS LOOKING
These are best if prepared 1 day ahead; cool and cover, then chill overnight.

Prepare the caramel: Heat the ¾ cup sugar in a heavy skillet and cook over moderate heat, stirring constantly, until sugar melts and turns a caramel color. Remove from heat and add the hot water. (Watch out! The mixture may splatter.) Return to low heat and continue stirring until the syrup simmers and everything has again dissolved. Pour this caramel into 5 or 6 baking molds or cups or small French soufflé dishes. Turn the molds or crocks so the sides get a caramel coating as well as the bottoms. Set aside.

Prepare the custard: Beat whole eggs and egg yolks together in a bowl. Heat the half and half (or milk and cream) with the sugar and stir to dissolve the sugar. Add this to the eggs and stir, then add the vanilla.

Assemble and bake: Preheat oven to 325°. Pour the custard into the caramel-lined cups and place these in a shallow baking pan. Pour about ½ inch of hot water into that baking pan, then bake for 40 to 60 minutes. Custard is done when knife inserted in center comes out clean. Chill for at least half a day or preferably overnight. Cut around sides of cups, then turn each upside down on individual dessert plates.

MY BEST VANILLA ICE CREAM

Makes 1 quart

¾ cup sugar (scant)
pinch of salt
1 cup milk
4 egg yolks
2 cups heavy whipping cream
3 or 4 teaspoon vanilla

WHEN NO ONE IS LOOKING
Prepare the ice cream mixture 1 day ahead; cover and keep chilled. Freeze the mixture the next day in an ice cream machine.

FROZEN POWER
Of course ice cream freezes! But how long will it retain its flavor? That depends on your freezer and how often you must open it; see p. 12 for general freezing information and instructions.

Combine sugar, salt, and milk in a saucepan and stir over moderate heat until sugar has dissolved and mixture is hot. Beat egg yolks in a separate bowl, then pour the milk mixture over the yolks, whisking as you pour. Return to saucepan and stir constantly over low or moderate heat until custard coats a spoon. Remove from heat, then stir in whipping cream and vanilla. Cover and chill thoroughly, then freeze in an ice cream machine.

DARK RICH CHOCOLATE ICE CREAM

Makes 1 quart

6 ounces semisweet chocolate
¾ cup sugar (scant)
1 cup milk
pinch of salt
4 egg yolks
2 teaspoons vanilla
2 cups heavy whipping cream

WHEN NO ONE IS LOOKING
Prepare the chocolate mixture 1 day ahead; keep covered and refrigerated.

FROZEN POWER
If you have a freezer that holds a very cold temperature, this ice cream will keep its fine flavor for 1 to 2 weeks. See p. 12 for general freezing information and instructions.

Melt chocolate in a double boiler over simmering water or in a microwave oven. Stir well. Combine sugar, milk, and salt in a saucepan and stir over moderate heat until sugar has dissolved. Combine milk mixture with melted chocolate and return to saucepan. Whisk together over low heat until smooth.

Beat egg yolks in a bowl, then whisk in the chocolate mixture. Return to saucepan and cook over low heat, stirring constantly, until hot and thickened. Remove from heat. Add vanilla and cream and whisk together. Cover and chill thoroughly. Freeze in an ice cream machine, then store in an airtight container in the freezer.

COCONUT ICE CREAM DELUXE

Makes 1 quart

- 1 cup milk
- ¼ cup sugar
- ⅛ teaspoon salt
- 1 pound frozen fresh grated coconut (found in Thai markets)
- 1 ½ cups sweetened coconut cream, such as Coco Lopez
- 4 egg yolks
- 2 cups heavy whipping cream
- 1 ½ teaspoons vanilla
- packaged sweetened coconut flakes

WHEN NO ONE IS LOOKING
Prepare the toasted coconut flakes 1 or 2 days ahead. Store in an airtight container.

FROZEN POWER
Freeze this ice cream; see p. 12 for general freezing information and instructions. Freeze the toasted coconut flakes, and use them straight out of the freezer.

Make the toasted coconut flakes: Preheat oven to 350°. Spread coconut flakes in a large baking pan and toast in the oven for 10 minutes. Reduce oven to 300° and continue to toast—stirring occasionally—until coconut flakes are golden brown. Remove from oven and cool.

Make the ice cream: Defrost the frozen grated coconut. Heat milk, sugar, salt and the defrosted coconut. Bring to a boil, then reduce heat, cover and simmer very gently for 20 minutes. Remove from heat and let this mixture stand at room temperature for about 1 hour. Strain, pressing down firmly on the grated coconut. Discard the grated coconut. Beat egg yolks in a bowl, then beat in the strained milk mixture. Return to a heavy saucepan and stir constantly over moderate heat until mixture is hot and has begun to thicken. Remove from heat, then stir in the sweetened coconut cream, the heavy whipping cream, and vanilla. Cover and chill thoroughly. Freeze in an ice cream machine. Serve scoops of the ice cream topped with the toasted coconut flakes.

CARAMEL ICE CREAM

Makes about 1 quart

¾ cup sugar
1 cup hot milk
2 cups heavy whipping cream
pinch salt
4 egg yolks
2 teaspoons vanilla

WHEN NO ONE IS LOOKING
Prepare the dissolved caramel mixture 1 day ahead; cover and keep refrigerated. Bring to room temperature and reheat gently; then complete the custard. Chill, then freeze in an ice cream machine.

FROZEN POWER
This will keep well for a month or longer if your freezer is not opened frequently. See p. 12 for general freezing information and instructions.

Caramelize the sugar in a heavy skillet. It should be a dark caramel color, but watch carefully so it does not burn. Remove from heat and add the hot milk, salt, and ½ cup cream. Return to the stove and stir it on moderate heat until caramel has dissolved; be patient, this take time. Beat egg yolks, then pour hot caramel mixture over the yolks, beating all the while. Return to saucepan and stir constantly over low heat until custard coats a spoon. Remove from heat and combine with remaining cream and vanilla. Chill thoroughly, then freeze in an ice cream machine.

GINGER ICE CREAM

Makes a generous quart

- ½ cup sugar
- pinch of salt
- 1 cup milk
- 4 egg yolks
- 2 cups heavy whipping cream
- 1 cup chopped ginger preserved in syrup (6 to 8 ounces)
- 2 tablespoons ginger syrup (from jar of preserved ginger)

WHEN NO ONE IS LOOKING
Prepare the ice cream mixture 1 day ahead; keep covered and refrigerated. Add the chopped ginger after it has frozen.

FROZEN POWER
See p. 12 for general freezing information and instructions.

Combine sugar, salt, and milk in a saucepan and stir over moderate heat until sugar has dissolved and mixture is hot. Beat egg yolks in a separate bowl, then pour milk mixture over the yolks, whisking as you pour. Return to saucepan and stir constantly over low or moderate heat until custard coats a spoon. Remove from heat, then stir in the cream and the syrup. Chill thoroughly, then freeze in an ice cream machine. Stir in the chopped ginger and freeze in an airtight container.

BANANA ICE CREAM

Makes about 1 ¼ quarts

- 3 large ripe bananas
- 1 ½ tablespoons lemon juice
- ¾ to 1 cup sugar (to taste)
- 2 cups heavy whipping cream (or half milk)
- 3 teaspoons "fruit fresh"—a dry powder that keeps fruit from turning brown (optional)
- 2 teaspoons vanilla

WHEN NO ONE IS LOOKING
Prepare the ice cream mixture in the morning, then freeze it later.

FROZEN POWER
See p. 12 for general freezing information and instructions.

Purée the bananas, then combine them with the remaining ingredients. Stir until sugar has dissolved. Cover and chill for several hours, then freeze in an ice cream freezer.

PRALINE ICE CREAM UNPARALLELED

Makes 1 quart

- ½ cup sugar (scant)
- pinch of salt
- 1 cup milk
- 4 egg yolks
- 2 cups heavy whipping cream
- 1 teaspoon vanilla
- 1 cup "Praline Paste" (p. 395)

WHEN NO ONE IS LOOKING
Prepare the ice cream mixture 1 day ahead or in the morning, then freeze and add the praline paste.

FROZEN POWER
See p. 12 for general freezing information and instructions.

Combine sugar, salt, and milk in a saucepan and stir over moderate heat until sugar has dissolved and mixture is hot. Beat egg yolks in a separate bowl, then pour milk mixture over the yolks, whisking as you pour. Return to saucepan and stir constantly over low or moderate heat until custard coats a spoon. Remove from heat, then stir in whipping cream and vanilla. Cover and chill thoroughly. Freeze in an ice cream machine, then stir in the praline paste and store in an airtight container in the freezer.

COFFEE ICE CREAM

Makes 1 ½ quarts

- 1 ¼ cups sugar
- 5 level tablespoons powdered coffee
- 1 cup milk
- pinch of salt
- 3 cups heavy whipping cream

WHEN NO ONE IS LOOKING
Prepare the ice cream mixture 1 day ahead (or in the morning); keep covered and refrigerated.

FROZEN POWER
The quality of frozen food of any kind depends on the quality of your freezer and how often you must open it. See p. 12 for general information about freezing.

Combine sugar, coffee, milk, and salt in a saucepan and stir over moderate heat until sugar has dissolved. Remove from heat and add the cream. Cover and chill thoroughly, then freeze in an ice cream machine.

FROZEN EGGNOG WITH FRUIT AND PECANS

Makes 2 quarts

½ cup sugar
pinch of salt
1 cup milk
4 egg yolks
2 cups heavy whipping cream
2 teaspoons vanilla
1 cup halved candied cherries
½ cup raisins, soaked in hot water, then drained
1 cup toasted pecans, cut in halves or quarters
½ cup fine quality rum

WHEN NO ONE IS LOOKING
Prepare the eggnogg mixture 1 day ahead; cover and keep refrigerated. Soak the cherries and raisins in the rum 1 day ahead; cover and leave at room temperature.

FROZEN POWER
See p. 12 for general freezing information and instructions.

Soak cherries and raisins in the rum for several hours or overnight.

Prepare the eggnog mix: Combine sugar, salt, and milk in a saucepan and stir over moderate heat until sugar has dissolved and mixture is hot. Beat egg yolks in a separate bowl, then pour milk mixture over the yolks, whisking as you pour. Return to saucepan and stir constantly over low or moderate heat until custard coats a spoon. Remove from heat, then stir in whipping cream and vanilla. Cover and chill thoroughly.

Finish: Drain the fruit, but save the rum. Add the rum to the chilled eggnog mix. Freeze the prepared eggnog mix in an ice cream machine, and when frozen stir in the cherries, raisins, and toasted pecan pieces.

FROZEN AMBER-COFFEE FANTASY

Makes about 8 servings

1 quart "Coffee Ice Cream" (p. 387)
1 cup pecans
2 tablespoons butter

for the amber sauce:
1 cup brown sugar (pack to measure)
½ cup light corn syrup
½ cup heavy cream
⅛ pound butter (½ stick)
1 teaspoon vanilla

WHEN NO ONE IS LOOKING
Prepare the amber sauce 2 or 3 days ahead; keep covered and refrigerated.

FROZEN POWER
A delicious dessert ready to be served from freezer to table. Keep well wrapped. See p. 12 for general information about freezing.

Prepare the amber sauce: Combine all ingredients except the vanilla and cook over low heat, stirring constantly for 4 to 5 minutes. Remove from heat, add vanilla, then cool to room temperature.

Prepare the pecans: Sauté the pecans in the 2 tablespoons butter until lightly browned, then remove from heat and cool to room temperature.

Assemble: Use small dessert dishes or demitasse cups. Place a few pecans in the bottom of each dish, then add a spoonful or so of the amber sauce. Next add a small scoop of coffee ice cream. Top with more sauce and a few more pecans. Cover with foil or plastic wrap and keep frozen until time to serve.

CHOCOLATE ICE CREAM TRUFFLES

Makes 6 servings

1 quart "Chocolate Ice Cream" (p. 382)
12 candied cherries
½ pound semisweet chocolate

WHEN NO ONE IS LOOKING
You *must* do this when no one is looking—at least several hours ahead of serving.

FROZEN POWER
Keep each of these frozen (separately, making sure to double-wrap each). They make a delicious and elegant dessert. To gild the lily, pass a bowl of whipped cream, and watch how many guests will gladly indulge.

Chop the chocolate into coarse pieces—about the size of small peas—and set aside. Form the ice cream into 6 balls, with 2 candied cherries in the center of each. Freeze these until solid, then roll in the chopped chocolate and return to freezer until time to serve.

ORANGE SORBET

grated rind of 1 orange
3 cups fresh orange juice
2 teaspoons unflavored gelatin soaked in ¼ cup cold water
1 cup sugar

WHEN NO ONE IS LOOKING
Prepare orange mixture 1 day ahead; keep covered and refrigerated.

FROZEN POWER
Keep this for up to 1 or 2 months. The length of time will depend on your freezer and how often it is opened.

Combine sugar with 1 cup of the orange juice and stir over moderate heat until sugar has dissolved. Add soaked gelatin and stir until gelatin has dissolved. Remove from heat and add the orange rind and the remaining orange juice. Chill for several hours, then freeze in an ice cream machine.

LEMON SORBET

Makes about 1 ¼ quarts

2 cups water
1 ½ cups sugar
2 teaspoons unflavored gelatin
¼ cup cold water
grated rind of 2 lemons
1 cup lemon juice

WHEN NO ONE IS LOOKING
Prepare the lemon mixture 1 day ahead; cover and keep refrigerated.

FROZEN POWER
See p. 12 for general freezing information and instructions.

Combine the 2 cups water with the sugar and cook over moderate heat, stirring until sugar has dissolved. Soak gelatin in the cold water for

5 minutes, then add to the hot sugar mixture and stir until dissolved. Remove from heat and add lemon rind and lemon juice. Cover and chill, then freeze in an ice cream machine.

PEAR SORBET

Makes about 1 quart

- 4 medium to large ripe pears, peeled, diced, and puréed (need 2 cups)
- 1 teaspoon unflavored gelatin
- ¼ cup cold water
- 1 cup sugar (or to taste)
- ¾ cup water
- ¼ cup lemon juice
- 3 tablespoons pear eau-de-vie (optional)

WHEN NO ONE IS LOOKING
Prepare this 1 day ahead, but add 1 or 2 teaspoons of a powder called "fruit fresh" to prevent the mixture from turning brown (or you can substitute a little more lemon juice).

FROZEN POWER
See p. 12 for general freezing information and instructions.

Soak gelatin in the ¼ cup cold water for 5 minutes. Combine sugar and the ¾ cup water in a saucepan and cook over low heat, stirring, until sugar has dissolved. Remove from heat and immediately stir in the soaked gelatin. Add pear purée, lemon juice and, if desired, the eau-de-vie. Chill thoroughly, then freeze in an ice cream machine.

RASPBERRY SORBET

Makes about 1 quart

- 1 ¼ teaspoons unflavored gelatin
- ¼ cup cold water
- ½ cup sugar (or to taste)
- ⅓ cup water
- 2 (10-ounce) packages frozen raspberries, defrosted, puréed and strained to remove seeds
- 3 tablespoons Framboise (raspberry) liqueur or eau-de-vie

WHEN NO ONE IS LOOKING
Prepare the sorbet mixture 1 day ahead; keep covered and refrigerated.

FROZEN POWER
See p. 12 for general freezing information and instructions.

Soak gelatin in the cold water for 5 minutes. Combine sugar and the ⅓ cup water in a saucepan and stir over moderate heat only until the sugar has dissolved, then remove from heat and stir in the soaked gelatin. Add the gelatin mixture to the raspberry purée. Add Framboise, stir, then chill. Freeze in an ice cream machine.

FAVORITE PASTRY CREAM

Makes about 2 cups

- ½ cup sugar
- ¼ cup flour
- ⅛ teaspoon salt
- 1 ½ cups milk
- 4 egg yolks
- 1 teaspoon vanilla

WHEN NO ONE IS LOOKING
Make this 1 day ahead; keep covered and refrigerated.

Sift sugar, flour, and salt together and place in a heavy saucepan (not aluminum). Add the milk and whisk until smooth. Cook over moderate heat, stirring constantly, until mixture comes to a boil. Remove from heat.

Beat egg yolks in a separate bowl, then whisk in the hot milk mixture. Return to saucepan and cook over moderate or low heat, again stirring constantly, until mixture has thickened. Immediately remove from heat and stir in the vanilla. Cool over ice and water. Place in a bowl, cover and refrigerate.

BUTTERCREAM

Makes 2 quarts

2 cups sugar (1 pound)
¾ cup water
⅛ teaspoon cream of tartar
⅛ teaspoon salt
8 egg whites
1 pound and 6 ounces of butter (half unsalted and half salted), cool but not cold

WHEN NO ONE IS LOOKING
Prepare this several days ahead; keep covered and refrigerated. Bring to room temperature before adding flavorings and whisk with a wire whisk. If it looks "curdled," just whisk 1 teaspoon of boiling water into the mixture and it will "catch" again.

FROZEN POWER
Yes, happily this kind of buttercream freezes well. Defrost overnight in the refrigerator, then bring to room temperature and follow directions under "When No One Is Looking."

Place sugar, water, cream of tartar, and salt in a heavy saucepan and stir over low heat until sugar has dissolved. Bring slowly to a boil, then cook *without stirring* until mixture reaches the soft ball stage (when a few drops of syrup in cold water form a soft ball). While the syrup is cooking remove any sugar crystals that form around the sides of the pan with the aid of wet paper towels wrapped tightly around a fork.

While syrup is cooking, ready your egg whites in a bowl that you can use with an electric mixer. As soon as syrup has reached the soft ball stage remove syrup from heat and *immediately* beat egg whites until stiff but not dry and add the hot syrup to them slowly, beating constantly, until all syrup has been added. Continue beating until this meringue has cooled to room temperature. Gradually beat in the butter. Flavor as desired.

Note: You will notice as you beat in the butter that the mixture will look peculiar, but keep going until the moment when the two "catch" and you see the beautiful buttercream texture achieved.

PRALINE PASTE

Makes about 3 to 4 cups

- 2 cups sugar
- 1 cup blanched almonds (whole or slivered)
- 1 cup filberts (hazelnuts), toasted, then skins rubbed off

WHEN NO ONE IS LOOKING
Prepare this up to 1 month ahead and keep refrigerated in a tightly sealed jar.

FROZEN POWER
Store this in a tightly sealed jar in the freezer for up to 1 year!

Grease a large metal pan and set it aside. Place sugar in a heavy skillet. Melt sugar slowly to a caramel over moderate heat, stirring occasionally. Add nuts and stir over lowest heat until nuts are completely coated with caramel. Pour at once into the greased pan. Place on a rack to cool and harden.

Break the caramelized nuts into smallish pieces. Place them in a food processor and chop them to desired consistency.

INDEX

ALSO BY RUTH MELLINKOFF

COOKBOOKS

1959 *The Something Special Cookbook*
Los Angeles: Ward Ritchie Press (Rev. ed. 1971).

1968 *The Uncommon Cookbook*
Los Angeles: Ward Ritchie Press.

1974 *The Just Delicious Cookbook*
Los Angeles: Ward Ritchie Press.

1980 *The Easy, Easier, Easiest Cookbook*
New York: Warner Books.

1984 *The Invisible Cook*
Los Angeles: Pangloss Press.

SCHOLARLY BOOKS

1970 *The Horned Moses in Medieval Art and Thought*
Berkeley: University of California Press.

1981 *The Mark of Cain*
Berkeley: University of California Press.

1988 *The Devil at Isenheim: Reflections of Popular Belief in Grünewald's Isenheim Altarpiece*
Berkeley: University of California Press.

1993 *Outcasts: Signs of Otherness in Northern European Art of the Late Middle Ages*
Berkeley: University of California Press.

1999 *Antisemitic Hate Signs in Hebrew Illuminated Manuscripts Made in Germany*
Jerusalem: Center for Jewish Art, Hebrew University of Jerusalem.